A history of

anglo-latin literature

597-1066

A history of

Anglo-Latin literature

597-1066

volume 1: 597-740

By W. F. Bolton

Princeton, New Jersey
Princeton University Press
1967

Printed in the United States of America
by Princeton University Press, Princeton, New Jersey

preface

THIS BOOK is intended to provide students of Old English with a guide to the Latin literature which existed alongside the vernacular, and I hope it will be of use to others as well. It takes the period and area of Anglo-Saxon domination as its chronological and geographical limits. It includes the forms associated with individual (although sometimes anonymous) writers, the histories, biographies, letters, poetry, treatises, and some liturgy, but not the institutional or official forms, the laws, charters, glossaries, concilia, or penitentials.

Its models were the already available histories of Old English literature, particularly Kemp Malone's contribution to *A Literary History of England* (ed. A. C. Baugh, N. Y. 1947), and the standard surveys of patristic and medieval Latin writings, especially Max Manitius' *Geschichte der lateinischen Literatur des Mittelalters* (3 vols., Munich 1911-1931). But Malone's chapter on Anglo-Latin is brief, and Manitius' second volume, which includes the end of the Anglo-Saxon period, is now forty years old. Besides, it is in German, lacks a national focus, and overlooks some Anglo-Latin.

As a literary history, the book describes the primary materials and brings together a listing of the secondary. Apart from the distinction between the "individual" and "official" genres, I have exercised no selection in the primary materials: I hope to have included them all, emphasizing the most important ones, but not suppressing the less important. The reader who approaches the book as a continuous account of pre-Conquest English latinity may find irksome the inclusion of a fragmentary letter by an anonymous celibate, but the reader who requires a work of reference may not be entirely disappointed. Both will find a book which seeks chiefly to assemble, rather than to advance, information and opinion about its subject.

[v]

The bibliographies, the listing of the secondary materials, have occupied a large part of my attention in writing the book. To make them available without further delay, the work has been divided so that the first part could be published while the second was in progress. They are full—more so than any others I know—but not complete. No enumerative bibliographer ever had enough wisdom or industry to be sure he had missed nothing. I have made limitations in addition to the ones I could not avoid. Where there is a sound modern edition, I have not always attempted to list all the earlier ones. I have included little published before the nineteenth century. I have tried to find all the informative books and articles, leaving the reader to estimate the accuracy and originality of the information, but I have excluded reference works and some purely hortatory *oeuvres d'édification*. Where a work deals at length with more than two of my subjects, I have listed it only once—in the General Bibliography—rather than separately under each subject. In most cases I have given little space to medieval lives of my authors; textual studies of the *Tripartite Life of St. Patrick*, for example, have not found a place. In the Introduction, I have made no entries for works which appeared prior to the publication of the article or book which initiated the modern study of the subject; such are rarely of use to anyone but a historian of scholarship, and they are invariably mentioned in the major works that followed them. In the cases of Pelagius, Patrick, and Columban, I have economized by restricting my bibliographies to works not already listed in one of three recent and readily accessible books; without this device, the lists would have grown by some 500 items.

Apart from these limitations, voluntary and involuntary, the bibliographies aim at completeness, and are an important part of the book's role as guide to the literature. I have read all the items I could obtain; those I could not,

I have marked with an asterisk. I have avoided footnotes, preserving instead relevant information in the text, omitting altogether what I took to be irrelevant.

For general surveys of medieval Latin, the reader should consult Karl Strecker, *Introduction to Medieval Latin* (trans. and rev. Robert B. Palmer, Berlin 1957), especially pp. 90-105. The same excellent book lists instruments like dictionaries and grammars, as well as (pp. 118-120 *et passim*) most of the periodicals by means of which the bibliographies in this book may be continued, and it provides a grounding in the linguistic characteristics of medieval latinity. I have added to the General Bibliography a few items, especially dictionaries, that have appeared since 1957, but an introductory bibliography to the study of medieval Latin will list little that is more accessible than Strecker's work, and little that is not in it; readers who wish to set about the study of medieval Latin cannot do without Strecker.

Some explanation of the texts quoted, and of the translations appended, is in order. The texts have been drawn from the best modern editions, but some works have received more recent and more careful attention than others, so the versions printed here are not all equally reliable. It would, on the other hand, have been impossible for me to prepare new editions from the MSS for this book. The editions I have employed are also uneven in editorial practice: the same word may appear as *iuuencae, juvencæ, iuvencae,* and so forth. I have on request attempted a normalization of these spellings to the standard of the *Latin Dictionary* of C. T. Lewis and C. Short (Oxford, many editions), an accessible and authoritative work which forms the basis or model of many others. Some of the forms arrived at this way would have looked strange to a medieval author, but medieval practice was by no means uniform itself (see, for example, the discussion in M.L.W. Laistner's edition of Bede's *Exp.*, Cambridge, Mass. 1939, xli-xlv). Scriptural references are to the Vulgate Latin or Douay-Rheims English version.

I have also on request supplied translations of the passages quoted, except where the quotation (usually brief) illustrates an untranslatable feature of the original, such as the morphology, or where the quotation is a title. The translations offered considerable difficulty. Some passages are obscure in themselves, and some words appear to have taken on specialized meanings in medieval Latin which even the latest dictionaries do not clarify. Sometimes, particularly in passages from older editions, there appeared to be something positively wrong with the text, but I have done what I could without emendation. The greatest problem, however, lay in finding the right idiom. Bede's command of Latin sentence structure was very strong. To observe his patterns of hypotaxis when translating his prose is to reveal something about how he wrote, but it is also to compose very awkward English: can awkward English be a faithful translation of polished Latin, particularly when literary values are under consideration? Yet to translate more freely than this is to confront oneself with innumerable alternatives, any one of which will in some measure misrepresent the original. Many of the passages have, as far as I know, been translated for the first time in this book; but in consulting earlier translations where they existed, I have most often been dissatisfied with those that were the freest. I offer my own versions with much diffidence, aware that they cannot take the place of the originals, hopeful merely that they will be better than nothing for those who have recourse to this book but cannot read Latin.

I have now to thank all those (individuals *and* institutions) who gave me aid in writing this book: the Research Board of the University of Reading for a Research Fellowship and later repeated research grants; the Department of English at the University of California (Berkeley), for two research grants; the Librarians and their colleagues at the University of Reading, the University of California (Berkeley), the British Museum, and the Bodleian Library, Oxford; my pupil, friend, and research assistant at Berkeley, Dr. Anne M. Saxon; my colleagues at Berkeley, especially Professor C. W. Jones; my colleagues at Reading, especially Professor D. J. Gordon, Dr. Jean I. Young, Mrs. J. F. Mitchell, and Dr. B. R. Morris, and the staff and students of the Medieval Latin Special Subject; my typists, Mrs. J. Chennells and Miss C. Norriss; my proofreader and indexer, Miss J. M. Field; and my wife. To them I owe whatever this book achieves; I am responsible for its shortcomings. The thousand items in the bibliographies betoken my thousand thanks to latinists and medievalists past and present, most of all to Max Manitius: *diligentia a diligere dicta.*

W.F.B.

November 1965

contents

CONTENTS

ABBReViATiONS

The more obvious abbreviations, such as Proc., Soc., Bull., etc. (for Proceedings, Society, Bulletin), are omitted.

AB   *Analecta Bollandiana*
AHR   *American Historical Review*
ALMA   *Archivum latinitatis medii aevi* (*Bulletin Du Cange*)
Apoc.   *Explanatio apocalypsis*, auctore Beda
Arch. Ael.   *Archaeologia aeliana*
Arch. Cant.   *Archaeologia cantiana*
Archiv   *Archiv f. d. Studium d. neueren Sprachen und Literaturen*
CC   *Corpus christianorum*
CCCC   Corpus Christi College Cambridge
CP   *Classical Philology*
CPL   *Clavis patrum latinorum*, eds. E. Dekkers and A. Gaar (editio altera) Brugge 1961
CQ   *Classical Quarterly*
CQR   *Church Quarterly Review*
CR   *Classical Review*
CSEL   *Corpus scriptorum ecclesiasticorum latinorum*
d.   das, der, des, dem, den, die
DTL   *De temporibus liber*, auctore Beda
DTR   *De temporum ratione*, auctore Beda
EHR   *English Historical Review*
EphL   *Ephemerides liturgicae*
Exp.   *Actuum apostolorum expositio*, auctore Beda
f.   for, für
Gött. Abh.   *Abhandlungen d. Göttinger Gesellschaft d. Wissenschaften*
Gött. Nachrichten   *Nachrichten von d. königl. Gesellschaft d. Wissenschaften zu Göttingen*
HAA   *Historia abbatum*, auctore anonymo
HAB   *Historia abbatum*, auctore Beda
HE   *Historia ecclesiastica*
HS(S)   Handschrift(en)
H&S   Haddan, A. W., and W. Stubbs. *Councils and Ecclesiastical Documents Relating to Great Britain and Ireland.* Oxford 1871.
HV   *Historische Vierteljahrschrift*
IER   *Irish Ecclesiastical Record*
JEGP   *Jnl. of English and Germanic Philology*

[xiii]

ABBREVIATIONS

JEH   *Jnl. of Eccesiastical History*
Jnl.   Journal
Jrb.   Jahrbuch
JRS   *Jnl. of Roman Studies*
Jrht   Jahrhundert
JTS   *Jnl. of Theological Studies*
MAe   *Medium aevum*
MGH   *Monumenta germaniae historica*
MLN   *Modern Language Notes*
MP   *Modern Philology*
MS(S)   manuscript(s), manuscrit(s)
Munich SB   *Sitzungsberichte d. königl. bayerischen Akademie d. Wissenschaften*
NA   *Neues Archiv d. Gesellschaft f. ältere deutsche Geschichtskunde*
N.F.   neue Folge
N&Q   *Notes and Queries*
N.S.   New Series, etc.
PBA   *Proceedings of the British Academy*
PG, PL   *Patrologia graeca, latina,* ed. J. P. Migne (reference is to column numbers)
PQ   *Philological Quarterly*
RB   *Revue bénédictine*
RHE   *Revue d'histoire ecclésiastique*
RS   *Rolls Series* (Rerum britannicarum medii aevi scriptores, or Chronicles and Memorials of Great Britain and Ireland during the Middle Ages)
RSR   *Recherches de science religieuse*
SMGB   *Studien und Mitteilungen zur Geschichte d. Benediktiner-Ordens und seiner Zweige*
TLS   *Times Literary Supplement*
TQ   *Theologische Quartalschrift*
VA   *Vita anonyma (Sancti Cuthberti)*
Vienna SB   *Sitzungsberichte d. kaiserl. Akademie d. Wissenschaften in Wien*
VM, VP   *Vita metrica (prosa) sancti Cuthberti,* auctore Beda
...x...   Between ... and ...
ZCP   *Zt. f. celtische Philologie*
ZDG   *Zt. f. deutsche Geistesgeschichte*
Zt.   Zeitschrift

A history of

Anglo-Latin Literature

vol. 1: 597-740

introduction:

British Latin before 597

The Roman Occupation (0.1)

Before Caesar's invasion in 55 B.C., Britain appears to have felt the influence of the classical world very little. The British Isles are mentioned only by Herodotus, Aristotle, and Polybius, all of whom wrote in Greek. Contact with Rome was gained through scattered traders and adventurers, who—though they are unlikely to have communicated much of Roman language and culture to the Britons—brought back quasi-fictional reports of a savage land with great mineral wealth.

On the basis of such information Caesar determined to annex the island to his expanding Empire. His reasons were military, political, and economic. The occupation of Britain would break the assistance offered by British Celts to their Gaulish kinsmen across the Channel, and British slaves, metals, and tribute would add impressively to the booty flowing into Rome. Caesar invaded in 55 B.C. and again, more successfully, in 54 B.C. (see *De bello gallico* IV. 20-36; V. 8-23). He subjected a number of Celtic tribes and exacted tribute. Civil wars in Rome and uprisings in Gaul, however, forced him to give up his project of the conquest of all Britain, and in 54 B.C. he retired permanently to the Continent. The next, and far more consequential, Roman invasion of Britain took place almost a hundred years later.

The impact of Caesar's invasions and brief occupation, however, was considerable, and even after his withdrawal Britain remained in much closer contact with Rome than before his invasion. Trade grew rapidly, and Celtic kings feared the possibility of a new invasion to put the re-

[3]

sources of Britain once again under the direct control of Rome. In 26 B.C. they were forced to pay tribute to Augustus to forestall an invasion, and Augustus' successor Tiberius claimed Britain as part of his Empire when he came to power in A.D. 14. British coins of this period show the influence of classical civilization in their design—Pegasus, the Sphinx, Hercules, a centaur, Medusa decorate them—and the British king Cunobelinus (Cymbeline; died ca. A.D. 43) styled himself "Rex" on a coin.

In A.D. 43 the Emperor Claudius invaded Britain and began the full-scale occupation which was to continue for almost 400 years. It was the practice throughout the Empire to encourage subject peoples to adopt Roman ways, a policy which reached its zenith when, in A.D. 213, all freeborn inhabitants of the Empire were granted Roman citizenship. The practice of romanization was slowest to make itself felt in language, an essentially conservative feature of human intercourse, and in remote areas Latin was never made a part of the life of the subject people: in the high Pyrenees, for example, the Basque spoken when Spain and France were conquered is spoken today. Nevertheless, Latin was quite rapidly adopted in areas where Roman influence was strongest, as the modern French and Spanish languages testify, and the Western Church may have insisted on the use of Latin, not through any distaste for the vernacular—in Syria and Egypt the native dialect became the official Church tongue—but because Latin was, in effect, a vernacular itself.

The Roman heritage did not, as it had in France and Spain, become a part of the language of Britain, perhaps because the Celtic inhabitants, not long after they obtained their release from Rome, were overrun by Germanic invaders. The occupation did, however, profoundly influence the linguistic and, to a lesser extent, the literary habits of the Britons in the colonized south of the island. It may have had similar, though less distinct, effects in the militarized north. The evidence of this influence, though meager, provides some idea of the linguistic romanization of town and country, gentry and workers, in their study of classical letters and in their own speech and writing.

The linguistic romanization of the British aristocracy proceeded through administrative and cultural channels. The Romans made a practice of enlisting "client kings," native rulers who cooperated with Roman officials, to implement the occupation. There were a number of such client kings during the Roman occupation of Britain, of whom one of the most loyal and hence powerful was Cogidumnus, who styled himself "Tiberius Claudius Cogidumnus, rex et legatus Augusti in Britannia." Through this practice the native aristocracy participated in Roman rule and, it may be assumed, rapidly became familiar with the language of that administration. Within thirty-five years of the Claudian invasion the Roman General Agricola, by then Governor of Britain, was furthering the romanization of the island culturally:

> Jam vero principum filios liberalibus artibus erudire, et ingenia Britannorum studiis Gallorum anteferre, ut qui modo linguam Romanam abnuebant, eloquentiam concupiscerent.[1]
>
> (Tacitus, *Agricola*, ch. 21)

By A.D. 109 Plutarch could write, as a matter of course, about "Demetrius, the grammarian of Britain, returning home to Tarsus" (*De defectu oraculorum*, ch. 2), perhaps the same Demetrius who left a Greek inscription at York. Martial had already boasted (ca. A.D. 96):

> Dicitur et nostros cantare Britannia versus.[2]
>
> (*Epig.* xi.3)

[1] Moreover he trained the sons of the chiefs in the liberal arts and preferred the natural ability of the Britons to the skill of the Gauls, so that those who had disliked the Latin language sought a command of it.

[2] And Britain is said to sing my verses.

[5]

About A.D. 120 Juvenal added:

> Gallia causidicos docuit facunda Britannos;
> De conducendo loquitur jam rhetore Thule.[3]
>
> (*Sat.* xv.111-12)

This interest and apparent fluency in the Roman tongue
the aristocracy of the towns must have shared with their
country-dwelling counterparts, who were no less dependent on the Roman overlords and no less likely to be proud
of their own Latin accomplishments.

Among the laboring classes, however, it is not so clear
that townsman and countryman fared alike. There is evidence that the laboring classes of even a fairly small urban
center like Calleva Atrebatum (Silchester) had some
command of written Latin. Scratched inscriptions—graffiti
—in cursive script, discovered on a number of items during archaeological excavations at Silchester, demonstrate
this practical, even casual, fluency. One brick-maker
wearily declared "satis" (enough). Another leaves the
tantalizing fragment ". . . puellam" (girl). A third writes
—this time on a tile—"Pertacus perfidus, Campester Lucilianus, Campanus, conticuere omnes,"[4] noteworthy for
its Virgilian tag (*Aeneid* II.1).

A good number of tiles, bricks, and pipes record the
maker's name. Silchester is the best-explored site of the
kind, but there are examples from others: the accusation
"fur" (thief), found on a piece of pottery at Silchester,
turns up again on a potsherd from Dorchester (Dorset).
A London tile reveals that the disgruntled "Austalis
di[e]bus XIII vagatur sib[i] cotidim". In Plaxtol, Kent, a
tile-maker inscribed each tile by rolling it, while still soft,
with a carved piece of wood, recording his name as a trade-

---

[3] Eloquent Gaul has trained the British advocates, and Thule
talks of hiring a rhetorician.

[4] Faithless Pertacus, Campester Lucilianus, Campanus, they all
fell silent.

mark. In Ickleton, Cambs., two pieces of an urn yielded the convivial "[ex ha]c amici bibun[t]."[5]

It need not be thought that these graffiti are the work of Italian immigrants, for the immigrants were not of the laboring class. They were, rather, merchants, land-traders, money-lenders—substantial members of the community. The graffiti imply a literate and romanized working class, at least in the urban centers, and indeed there is no Celtic inscription from the area and period of the occupation in Britain, although such remain in Gaul: the Celtic languages were no doubt spoken, but Latin was the exclusive language for writing. About the country laborers there is no evidence either way; it cannot even be shown that they were literate. It is quite possible that they were not, and that their spoken language was Celtic. Latin survivals in later Celtic vocabulary do not assist in solving the riddle; they are too few, their derivation from Latin is too uncertain, and it is not always possible to show that they did not stem from Church Latin of the eighth or later centuries.

Some characteristics of the Latin source of words which were borrowed during the Roman occupation, however, can be identified. The borrowings from the spoken language of the Romans, Vulgar Latin, show that, while their dialect shared many features with that of Gaul, it had distinctive features of its own, some of which—including, for example, the classical Latin system of inherent vowel quantity—seem to have been markedly conservative in comparison with continental practice. The conservatism of this source suggests that it was principally an upper-class dialect, perhaps even one artificially maintained in the kind of rhetorical schools mentioned by Tacitus, Juvenal, and others.

Britain was from an early period a settlement of vet-

[5] Austalis has been wandering off every day for a fortnight. Friends drink from this.

[7]

erans and the Roman veterans became to a considerable extent a part of the country in which they settled, as did to a lesser degree the troops on active duty. In the chartered town Camulodunum (Colchester), founded for the veteran legionaries by the governor Ostorius Scapula about A.D. 50, a theatre was built before the town defenses were begun. Theatres existed also at Verulamium (St. Albans), Petuaria (Brough), and elsewhere. The colonizing veterans brought with them not only the language of Rome but also the theatrical entertainments with which to beguile the years of their retirement. The descendants of these veterans, often the descendants of a Roman-Celtic marriage, for the most part remained in Britain after the final withdrawal of the legions, which in any case left much of the Roman system of government at first relatively undisturbed.

Even in the remote areas of the west and north, inscriptions on funerary monuments betoken a continuing knowledge of Latin language and life: Latin titles like *magistratus* and *protector* are found from the late fifth and mid-sixth centuries, even an equally late inscription in hexameters. Patrick's father was a *decurion*; the Welshman Gildas calls Latin "nostra lingua" (my language). The inscriptions also suggest, especially where accompanied by an Ogam transliteration, that Latin was still in at least some places commonly spoken as late as A.D. 500. But the Saxon advances extinguished these remnants of latinity, and no Saxon forms of British names can be shown to have come through British Latin.

The British Church (0.2)

Contemporary for most of its history with the Roman occupation of Britain, an outcome and a rival of Roman military strength in the island, the British Church was a significant agency for the introduction and preservation of latinity in Britain. The date of its foundation is unknown. Later interpretations have vested early documents with the meaning that Britain was visited and converted by Apostles—Peter, Paul, James the Great, Simon, or Philip; medieval traditions attribute the conversion to a disciple, Aristobulus or Joseph of Arimathea. It has been suggested that British captives taken to Rome during the first century might have brought the Christian religion with them on their return home; King Caradoc and Bran the Voyager are thought the likeliest possibilities. A medieval tradition reports that a British king, Lucius, sent to Pope Eleutherus for missionaries, and that his request was answered in 185 when Faganus and Damianus came from Rome and effected the conversion of the island. In support of these interpretations and legends are adduced apparent early references to Christianity in Britain: the Pudens and Claudia of Martial (*Epig.* IV.13, and XI.53) are identified with the same names in II Tim. 4.21. The evidence for all the theories which argue for Christianity in Britain before the end of the second century is slight; they cannot be proved nor, by the same token, can they be disproved.

The first reasonably reliable reference to Christianity in Britain is by Tertullian:

> In quem enim alium universae gentes crediderunt nisi in Christum? . . . Britannorum inaccessa Romanis loca, Christo vero subdita. . . .[6]
>
> (*Adv. Judaeos*, ch. 7)

Tertullian's reference to British Christianity some time in the first decade of the third century appears in a vehement passage amid the names of other nations, and some scholars have been inclined to discount it as a rhetorical exaggeration: Britain had not yet lost its exotic associations,

---

[6] In whom else do all the nations believe, but in Christ? Even the portions of Britain invulnerable to the Romans have been conquered by Christ.

least of all in Tertullian's Africa. But the apparent reference in the same passage to the Roman occupation and the uprisings of 183-208 lend a suggestion of authenticity. It is, furthermore, probable that the Church had indeed been increasingly accepted in Britain during the last quarter of the second century, first among the Roman army and later among the Britons themselves. Particularly severe repression of Christianity in Lyons and Vienne around A.D. 177 might have contributed to the influx of the religion from the Continent. It must have spread quickly: references to the British Church during the third century appear in Origen and in the early fourth-century works of Eusebius and Lactantius. In the fourth century Britain was represented by episcopal delegates to a number of major Councils—Arles, 314; Arminium, 359; possibly Sardica, between 344 and 347; Nicaea, 325. The Church in what became England provided Ninian and Patrick, the missionaries who, in the late fourth and early fifth centuries, converted Scotland and Ireland. An Irish Christian, Columban, went to the Continent in the late sixth century and founded monasteries at Bobbio and Luxeuil. Christians in Britain were persecuted under the Diocletianic edict of 303, among them Alban at Verulamium, even though Constantius, the governor of Britain in that day, was not ill-disposed toward the faith. His son Constantine, brought up in Britain, won the imperial throne with the backing of the legions stationed in Britain, became a Christian, and issued in 313 the Edict of Milan, which granted Christians freedom to practice their faith. It is not possible to estimate the extent of the influence of Christianity in Britain during the four hundred years or so before the arrival of St. Augustine in 597. It was in any case, as contemporary documents and archaeological remains show, a widespread if not a universal cult in Britain during the fourth, fifth, and sixth centuries. There is evidence of Christianity in all parts of England, in

Wales, and far into the north; Alban, whose station in life was not mentioned—we may assume it was not prominent, for in his inconspicuous house a Christian found refuge from the Diocletianic persecution—was a townsman, while the aristocratic country villa at Lullingstone had a Christian chapel. Christianity was practiced by Romans and Britons, high and low, in town and country.

It was during the implantation of Christianity in Britain that the Church began to discard Greek as the primary liturgical language for the West. Tertullian himself, whose work occupies the first volumes of Migne's *Patrologia latina,* already illustrates in his vocabulary a received tradition of Latin theological terminology. There is a suggestion of the latinity of the British Church in the name "Eborius,"—Bishop of York at Arles in 314—an early example of a bishop who signs in the name of his see. Britain's Bible was in Latin, although not the translation of Jerome; Gildas in the sixth century still learned the *Vetus latina,* more than a century after Jerome's death, and the British Christians Fastidius and Pelagius show familiarity with both versions. The British Church after the fourth century was relatively isolated from continental Christianity. Little of Continental exegesis, hagiography, and other work in Latin may have circulated before 597, but British Christianity practiced a Latin liturgy and read Latin scriptures. The earliest MSS in Welsh (from the eighth century) employ an ecclesiastical vocabulary made up in good measure of loan-words from Latin. After the advent of monachism in Britain, probably in A.D. 429, when Germanus of Auxerre conducted a mission in the island, centers grew up where the study and recitation of liturgy and Scripture constituted the principal communal activity. For this purpose, if for none other, British Christians were instructed in Latin. Four have left substantial evidence of insular latinity in their writings: Pelagius, Patrick, Gildas, and Fastidius.

There is a letter signed by one Vinisius, and a few fragmentary inscriptions.

Epistola Vinisii (0.3)

The letter from Vinisius to Nigra is of interest chiefly because it represents, aside from Gildas, the only considerable literary relic of pre-Augustinian Christianity in Britain. Pelagius wrote on the Continent; Fastidius' work is difficult to identify; Patrick spent most of his life in exile. The letter of Vinisius, discovered at Bath, is an exception to the rule that the evidence of British Christianity lies exclusively in external documents. It was written as a palimpsest on a piece of lead some 3″ by 1¾″, in all probability in answer to a letter written on the same piece of lead. This kind of exchange was common enough on wax, but the area between Bath and the Severn, where the author may have lived, was rich in lead mines, and the material may have been both handier and more readily available than wax.

Even with missing or illegible words supplied, the text runs to less than fifty words. Vinisius sends his greetings to Nigra, wishes her the grace of the Lord Jesus Christ, and says that news of her difficulties with her husband have reached him; he advises her to be steadfast. On the reverse side he tells her that one Biliconus, a dog of Arius, is coming from Viriconium (i.e., Wroxeter?), and that, his heresy notwithstanding, he is to be taken into the fold, "tu lucem ora Christum" (Pray to Christ, the Light). In his last line Vinisius names the bearer of the message, one Apulicus, and the plural "lamnas" (plates, leaves) suggests that there were other messages traveling with it.

Of some interest is the phrase "Inimicus Christi Biliconum . . . misit . . . canem Arii."[7] Biliconus is a latinized Celtic name—perhaps Irish, because the Welsh form

[7] The enemy of Christ has sent Biliconus, a dog of Arius.

would more probably be Bilicunus. It means "good dog," and recalls other Celtic dog-names, of which Cunobelinus is the most familiar. The letter, although in Latin, shows that the author knew at least enough Celtic to recognize the meaning of Biliconus' name, and that he expected his recipient to recognize it as well, for his phrase "canem Arii" (dog of Arius) depends on it. Are we to assume that the letter was one between Celtic-speaking Christians, who employed Latin only as a self-conscious formality? Or, on the other hand, does the pun on Biliconus' name suggest nothing more than a recollection of an ancestral tongue, now all but out of use? Or are the correspondents genuinely bilingual? There is nothing in the letter to answer the questions which it raises.

The editor of the letter of Vinisius has dated it during the lifetime of Arius, probably shortly before the heresiarch's death in 336. He bases his opinion on the form "canem Arii," which he thinks might rather have been "canem Arianum" (an Arian dog) after 336, and on the suggested reception of an acknowledged heretic in a Christian community, which he thinks could not have taken place later in the century when Arianism became a widespread problem.

Pelagius (0.4)

It is certain that Pelagius was born in the British Isles, but not so certain quite where and when. Jerome calls him *Scotus* (i.e., Irish) more than once, but it may be merely a term of abuse. Writers who see a link between the doctrines of druidism and those of Pelagianism believe he may have been Welsh. But it is hard to credit either Ireland or Wales with a Church active enough to produce a dangerous heretic during the third quarter of the fourth century, when Pelagius must have been born. The terms *Britto* and *Britannicus* by which other writers call him most prob-

[13]

ably refer to Roman Britain, that is, generally, England and part of Wales. Little is known of his background. He seems to have had a good education, but he lacks the hereditary cognomen of an aristocrat. What is most important for this investigation, however, is that it is not possible to show how much of his education, his ideas, and his latinity were developed before he left Britain for Rome, where he is found in 405. But Jerome speaks of their "old friendship" in 414, when he had not been in Rome for almost thirty years; unless Pelagius had seen Jerome in Palestine, he must have been in Rome by 385. Pelagius is last heard of in 418, and there is no way of knowing how old he was then or how much longer he lived. It can only be assumed that, because his contemporaries speak of him often as a Briton, his arrival in Rome was as an adult whose characteristic intellectual equipment was already well-formed, and to this conclusion the theory of druidic influence in his doctrines lends weight. To regard Pelagius as a British writer, in short, is to assent to the opinion of his age.

The doctrines which constitute Pelagianism are somewhat ill-defined. For one thing, Pelagius—who always considered himself orthodox—was anxious not to fall outside the Church, and he modified at least the language of his opinions several times during his life. For another, his disciples, chiefly Caelestius, were not always his direct intellectual descendants. It can, however, be stated fairly that Pelagius denied the orthodox meaning of original sin. He held that sin involved consent of the will, and so inherited sin was not sin in a meaningful sense of the word. From this, and from scriptural exhortations to lead a perfect life, he concluded that man could, through the exercise of his free will, live without sinning. Baptism, it followed, was an aid to higher sanctification, but not a requirement; so was divine grace. Pelagius returned again and again to the power of the human will to perfect itself. He did not, it should be noted, say that such a sinless man had lived, and he certainly did not say that he was such a man; but he insisted on the theoretical possibility. Pelagius lived a doubly hard life. He imposed on himself the strictest rigors of asceticism, and sought to impose them (successfully, to an extent) on the Roman society of his day; and he was called upon again and again to defend himself against charges of heresy. In a number of cases his adversary was no less than Augustine of Hippo, the foremost doctrinal polemicist of the day, yet Pelagius venerated Augustine and sought to resolve his differences with him, and Augustine could still talk with sorrow of his "desideratissimus frater Pelagius." These quarrels, which took place intermittently from 405 to 418, increasingly involved the Church in both the East and the West. Ultimately the cause of orthodoxy won, and Pelagius was excommunicated and banished from Rome. A heretic in spite of himself, he renewed his attempts at reconciliation with Augustine, but the Christian world was by now united against him.

Pelagius' heresy is, no doubt, one of the reasons much of his writing has been lost, and much more transmitted in fragments or under other names. It is unlikely that the riddle of his literary remains will ever be solved. His most recent and thorough student, de Plinval, offers the following canon:

I: AUTHENTIC WORKS

    i. Commentary on St. Paul, *Expositiones xiii epistolarum Pauli.*

    ii. Treatises: *De vita christiana*; *De divitiis*; *De malis doctoribus et operibus fidei*; *De divina lege*; *De castitate*; *De possibilitate non peccandi* (frag.); *Libellus fidei*; *De virginitate.*

    iii. Letters: *Si Deus ac dominus noster* (recip. anon.); *to Claudia*; *to Oceanus*; *to Marcella*; *to Celantia*; *to Demetriada.*

II: PROBABLY PELAGIAN

    i. *De vera circumcisione*; *De induratione cordis Pharaonis.*

[15]

ii.   Letters: *Qui Aethiopem*; *Ad te surgo*; *Audi filia*; *Humanae referunt litterae*; to the daughters of Gerontius.

III: FRAGMENTS OF WORKS MENTIONED BY OTHER AUTHORS

i.   *Eclogarum liber* (Jerome, *Dialogus adversus Pelagianos* 1).

ii.   *De natura* (Augustine, *De natura et gratia*).

iii.   *De trinitate*.

iv.   *De libero arbitrio* (Augustine, *De gratia Christi et de peccato originali*).

v.   *Letters to Livania* (Jerome, *Dial.* III.16; Mercator, *Com. Caelesti* IV.3, and fragment *RB*, 34[1922], 265-75).

vi.   *Comment. in Canticum canticorum* and *De bono constantiae* (Bede, *In Cantica canticorum allegorica expositio*).

Jerome, who had harped on Pelagius' barbaric background, called him nonetheless "homo latinissimus" (a most latinate man). The epithet was deserved. Pelagius knew Lucretius, Virgil, Horace, and Juvenal, and probably Terence, Cicero, Sallust, and Ovid, although he does not hesitate to damn most of them, and all his verbal echoes of Virgil go back to the fourth book of the *Aeneid*. He had read Augustine, of course, and Jerome, Rufinus, Ambrosiaster, Chrysostom, and probably Theodore of Mopsuestia. He defended himself, successfully, in Greek on one occasion. But he declined to make the classics his model. He showed a flair for neologisms (*malesecura, aurotextrina, subuti*), a distaste for the demands of classical prose rhythm, a distrust for syllogism as a rhetorical device, a fondness for the "open" rather than the "closed" periodic sentence.

He was capable of making distinctions in Aristotelian terms, and did so when it served his purpose, but his argument follows his own rules most of the time:

> Quia "non peccare" nostrum est, possumus peccare et non peccare. Quia vero "posse non peccare" nostrum non est et si voluerimus non posse non peccare, non possumus non posse non peccare.[8]   (*De nat.*, ch. 57)

[8] Because "not to sin" depends on us, we can sin or not sin. But because "to be able not to sin" does not depend on us, even

Like the more formal logicians of his day, Pelagius
would begin his discussions with a definition of the terms
he was to consider:

> Multi nostrorum illum absolute atque integre definiunt inno-
> centem qui ne in eo quidem nulli noceat quod prodesse
> desistat,[9]   (*Ad Cel.*, ch. 7)

but even this definition takes a practical rather than an
absolute ideal basis, and in *De divitiis* Pelagius begins by
rejecting a condemnation of riches themselves and taking
as his subject the inordinate love of riches. In this, as in
other matters, Pelagius was concerned with human condition, not primarily with the abstract verity. So his argument is typically exemplary, and he practices what might
be called hortatory logic. The argument *quanto magis* is
encountered again and again: if the Patriarchs practiced
justice under the Old Law, how much more should Christians do so who are enlightened by the revealed truths of
divine charity?

Pelagius' sentence structure was similarly controlled by
the immediate demands of his argument. If he required
extended expression, he would employ periodic phrases
to aid his coherence, but he did not feel obliged thereby
to conform to the "closed" period of classical Latin. He
preferred, on such occasions, to indulge in a kind of verbal
opulence:

> Si igitur odio atque invidia possidemur, si cupiditati et
> avaritiae cedimus, si praesentia commoda futuris praeferimus,
> per spatiosam viam incedimus; habemus enim ad haec comi-
> tem multitudinem et late similium stipamur agminibus. Si
> iracundiae libidinem explere volumus, si injuriam vindicare;
> si maledicenti maledicimus et adversum inimicum inimico

---

though we should wish not to be able not to sin, we cannot not
be able not to sin.
   [9] Many of our thinkers define that man as absolutely and entirely
free of harm to others, who does not give injury even in a case
where his restraint is of no advantage to him.

animo sumus; aeque cum plurimis ferimur. Si vel adulamur ipsi vel adulantem libenter audimus, si vero gratiam impendimus et magis offendere timemus animos hominum quam non ex animo loqui, de multorum item via sumus.[10]

(Ad Cel., ch. 11)

At the same time, he was capable of brevity and pithiness.

Vanitas est omne quod quandoque finitur *(Exp. Rom.* VIII.20). Non est vulgare quod quaerimus; non debet vulgare esse quod vivimus *(De malis doct.,* ch. 24). Optimus est in omni re modus, et laudabilis ubique mensura *(Ad Dem.,* ch. 21).[11]

Pelagius' language and logic were familiar tools to him, and he had little pride in them as accomplishments in their own right.

Fastidius and Faustus (0.5)

All that is known of Fastidius is found in chapter 56 (between the entries for Celestine, *sedit* 422-432, and for Cyril of Alexandria, *sedit* 412 to post 429) of Gennadius' *De scriptoribus ecclesiasticis,* a work of the late fifth century:

Fastidius, Britannorum episcopus, scripsit ad Fatalem quendam de vita christiana librum unum et alium de viduitate servanda sana et Deo digna doctrina.[12]

[10] If therefore we are possessed by hate and envy, if we give way to cupidity and avarice, if we prefer present comforts to future ones, we enter upon the wide way; we have on it many a comrade and we are crowded about with a throng of those who are like us. If we wish to satisfy our love of anger, if we wish to avenge an injury; if we slander slanderers and take against our enemies with a hard heart; in like manner we do it in great company. If we are either adored, or gladly listen to adoration, if indeed we lavish favors and fear more to offend the minds of men than not to speak from the mind, we shall likewise be on the path of many.

[11] All that is vain which will ever be brought to an end; what we seek is not common, what we live should not be common; moderation is best in all things, and measure is everywhere to be praised.

[12] Fastidius, bishop of the Britons, wrote a book on the Christian

The passage is not without its problems. Are we to regard *De vita christiana* and *De viduitate servanda* as titles or simply as descriptions, if indeed the audience of Gennadius would have seen a difference? Is it certain that "Britannorum" refers to the British, and not to the Bretons? (In the eighth-century Corbie MS of Gennadius, the word "Britto" replaces "Britannorum episcopus.") What are we to make of "sana et Deo digna doctrina" from semi-Pelagian Gennadius, who attacked Pelagius in his *De viris illustribus*, when the works traditionally thought to be Fastidius' are Pelagian in character? Fastidius has disappeared, and has left, besides the trace quoted above, only a few scattered manuscript attributions of a much later date. Any discussion of him must consist largely of hypothesis.

In 1890 Caspari printed from manuscripts and older editions a number of letters and homilies of uncertain attribution but, apparently, the work of one man. He considered the possibility that the author was Fastidius, but rejected it on the assumption that the *De vita christiana* once attributed to Augustine of Hippo was, in fact, the work mentioned by Gennadius, and this work had little in common with the documents in his book. Later, Morin suggested that the *De vita christiana* mentioned by Gennadius was instead the first letter in Caspari's edition, and that the contents of that book were, consequently, by Fastidius. He ventured to suggest, moreover, that the opusculum *De viduitate servanda* printed among the works of Caesarius of Arles in *PL* 67.1094-1098, was in fact the work of Fastidius mentioned by Gennadius. Another Caesarian work, beginning *Rogo vos, fili,* he also admitted as quite possibly Fastidius'. Later, Morin found this work was more probably a recension by Cae-

---

life to a certain Fatalis, and another on keeping widowhood, wholesome in doctrine and godly.

sarius of a longer original by Fastidius, the *De vita chris-tiana* mentioned by Gennadius, which Morin had dis-covered and printed. The first letter in Caspari's edition was, then, not the work Morin at first had thought, but he continued to hold that it, like the rest of the works in the edition, was by Fastidius. Meanwhile, other scholars had joined in the controversy; Baer, who would have added the pseudo-Augustinian *De vita christiana* to Fas-tidius' canon; Kirmer, who would have five more works still, borrowed from the canon of Pelagius; Haslehurst, whose edition and translation of the documents in ques-tion offer a summary of the problems of the scholarship up to 1927. To accept the canon finally offered by Morin is but to render to the most authoritative scholar in the field the respect due his opinions. It is also to subtract the latter six works from the canon of Pelagius as de Plinval gives it:

Honorificentiae tuae;	*De possibilitate non peccandi;*
Admoneo te, ut de salute;	*De castitate;*
Humanae referunt litterae;	*De malis doctoribus;*
Audi filia;	*De divitiis.*

Not much can be learned about the author of the canon above from internal evidence, even had we the fullest confidence in the integrity of the canon itself. He writes as one far from home, whose trip to Rome was punctuated by his conversion in Sicily. The title "Britannorum epis-copus" given him by Gennadius suggests that Fastidius returned from this trip to Rome a Pelagian Christian and soon held an important post in the Church. He seems to have written in the first third of the fifth century, to judge from his place in Gennadius' list. He would, then, have brought from his trip word from the city to which the last of the legions had shortly before retired. The style and content of his works need not be studied as a thing apart from the Pelagian corpus, for de Plinval was himself not able to distinguish them from the work of the heresiarch.

With Fastidius might be mentioned Faustus, Bishop of Riez, France. Alcimus Avitus calls him "ortu Britannum, habitaculo Regiensem"[13] (*Epist. ad Gundobadum regum, PL* 59.219), and by this distinction Alcimus probably means that Faustus was British, although he may have meant Breton. In either case, Faustus was in Gaul as a very young man. He lived after 485, yet he was elected abbot of the monastery at Lerins in 433, and from these two dates it has been supposed that he was born not long before 410. Even assuming that his British nationality was certain, we could not say whether Latin was his native tongue or part of his formal education, and whether that education took place in Britain or in Gaul. All of his works, it seems, were composed after his arrival at Lerins. They consist of a long tract, *De gratia*; a shorter one, *De spiritu sancto*; twelve letters of varying length, and a quantity of sermons. Two other tracts, *De ratione fidei* and *De symbolo*, have been edited under his name, and may be his; a number of other writings, once attributed to Faustus, are not now thought part of his canon. He left, nevertheless, a large quantity of writings, most of them semi-Pelagian in doctrine, which might provide unequaled evidence about native British latinity in the early fifth century if it were certain that his education was not entirely Gaulish.

Patrick (o.6)

St. Patrick was born in Britain about 373, the son of a deacon and the grandson of a presbyter. His father, as a free member of the Empire, was a Roman citizen, and a decurion, that is a member of the municipal council. It is likely that Patrick's mother tongue was British, but he speaks of Irish as a foreign language.

[13] British by birth, dwelling in Riez.

At the age of sixteen he was taken captive by Irish pirates, and was a shepherd slave in Ireland until he was twenty-two. He escaped from Ireland, probably to Gaul. After a few years he returned to Britain, and it was there that he felt a vocation to return to Ireland and serve the cause of Christianity. His mission met with some opposition even in Britain, but he was consecrated a bishop and set out on his undertaking. The Ireland to which he returned had, for an uncertain time, contained scattered Christian settlements, especially in the south. Patrick organized the settlements, brought them the sacraments of ordination and confirmation, extended Christianity into areas where it was unknown, and most important of all put Irish Christianity directly in touch with the continental Church. His mission was successful despite the hardships of the land and the active hostility of the people among whom he worked. He died in 461, leaving two Latin works generally held to be authentic, the *Confessio* and the *Epistola ad Coroticum*, and one probable Irish poem, *Faed Fiada*. (According to Carney's interpretation of the evidence, Patrick was born about 423, never traveled to Gaul, followed Palladius—the first "Patrick" —as missionary bishop in Ireland, and died about 493.)

The *Confessio* is an autobiography, spiritual and— where it will assist the spiritual—historical. Its authenticity has been challenged, but most scholars accept it as Patrick's, although even the best MSS have imperfect texts. The theory of a later forger, in any case, is untenable. Quotation of biblical texts reflects accurately the state of scriptural learning in Britain in the mid-fifth century; the prose is confessedly inelegant; the doctrine supports no sectarian or political cause. It seems unlikely that a forger could have contrived to omit any careless anachronism, or that he would have been able to observe the mixture of a *Vetus latina* Old Testament and largely Hieronymian New Testament which the author cites. It is hard to see what the purpose of such a forgery would have been, if not to glorify Patrick or promote the claims of this party or that see, and the rude prose is hardly appropriate for that purpose. There are, in addition to these negative reasons, several more positive ones: the *Confessio* is quoted by writers working in the century after St. Patrick's death, and it demonstrates a kind of humility which even the most objectively historical critics have considered impressive.

The *Confessio* was written in Patrick's old age. Its title stems neither from a recital of youthful errors, although there is a hint of that, nor from any doctrinal affirmation, although two creeds are embedded in it. It is, rather, Patrick's answer to those who had argued against his mission from the first, to those who had resisted it in Ireland, and to those who had imputed to him unworthy motives. It is Patrick's confession that at every stage his inspiration, his guide, and his strength were drawn directly from divine sources. It contains, moreover, illuminating passages in which Patrick comments on his own latinity. Patrick founded several schools during his travels in Ireland, but it cannot be shown that they had anything more than theological ends in view; even the report of one biographer that Patrick "scripsit abecedarium" may mean only that he prepared a kind of alphabetical catechism. Patrick speaks of himself as "peccator rusticissimus" (ch. 1) and "peccator indoctus" (ch. 62; *Epist.*, ch. 1).[14] In themselves these might be dismissed as conventional gestures of humility, as might phrases like "propter rusticitatem meam" (ch. 46), "me pauperculum pupillum idiotam" (ch. 35), or the biblical allusion (II Cor. 11:6) "Nam etsi imperitus sum in omnibus" (ch. 49).[15] More convincing is the long passage early in the work in which he explains his rusticity:

[14] An inelegant (unlearned) sinner.
[15] On account of my lack of polish; me, a poor little ignorant orphan; for although I am ignorant in all things.

[23]

Quapropter olim cogitavi scribere, sed et usque nunc hae-
sitavi; timui enim ne incederem in linguam hominum, quia
non didici sicut et ceteri, qui optime itaque jura et sacras
litteras utraque pari modo combiberunt et sermones illorum
ex infantia numquam mutarunt, sed magis ad perfectum semper addiderunt. Nam sermo et loquela nostra translata est in
linguam alienam, sicut facile potest probari ex saliva scripturae meae qualiter sum ego in sermonibus instructus atque
eruditus, *quia*, inquit, *sapiens per linguam dinoscetur et
sensus et scientia et doctrina veritatis.*

Sed quid prodest excusatio juxta veritatem, praesertim cum
praesumptione, quatenus modo ipse appeto in senectute mea
quod in juventute non comparavi? Quod obstiterunt pec-
cata mea ut confirmarem quod ante perlegeram. Sed quis me
credit etsi dixero quod ante praefatus sum?

Adolescens, immo paene puer inverbis, capturam dedi, antequam scirem quid appetere vel quid vitare debueram. Unde
ergo hodie erubesco et vehementer pertimeo denudare imperi-
tiam meam, quia disertis brevitate sermone explicare nequeo,
sicut enim spiritus gestit et animus, et sensus monstrat af-
fectus.

Sed si itaque datum mihi fuisset sicut et ceteris, verumtamen
non silerem propter retributionem, et si forte videtur apud
aliquantos me in hoc praeponere cum mea inscientia et
tardiori lingua, sed etiam scriptum est enim: *Linguae balbu-
tientes velociter discent loqui pacem.* Quanto magis nos appetere debemus, *qui sumus*, inquit, *epistola Christi in salutem usque ad ultimum terrae*, et si non diserta, sed ratum
et fortissimum *scripta in cordibus vestris non atramento sed
spiritu Dei vivi.* Et iterum spiritus testatur *et rusticationem
ab altissimo creatam.*

Unde ego primus rusticus profuga indoctus scilicet, qui nescio
in posterum providere, sed illud scio certissime quia utique
priusquam humiliarer ego eram velut lapis qui jacet in luto
profundo: et venit qui potens est et in sua misericordia sustulit
me et quidem scilicet sursum allevavit et collocavit me in
summo pariete; et inde fortiter debueram exclamare ad retri-
buendum quoque aliquid domino pro tantis beneficiis ejus hic
et in aeternum, quae mens hominum aestimare non potest.

Unde autem admiramini itaque magni et pusilli qui timetis
Deum et vos dominicati rhetorici audite et scrutamini. Quis

me stultum excitavit de medio eorum qui videntur esse sapientes et legis periti et potentes in sermone et in omni re, et
me quidem, detestabilis hujus mundi, prae ceteris inspiravit
si talis essem—dummodo autem—ut cum metu et reverentia
et sine querella fideliter prodessem genti ad quam caritas
Christi transtulit et donavit me in vita mea, si dignus fuero,
denique ut cum humilitate et veraciter deservirem illis.[16]

(chs. 9-13)

[16] For this reason I have long intended to write, but have hesitated until now; I was afraid lest I fall into the talk of men,
because I have not studied like the others, who have thoroughly
taken in both the law and the sacred Scriptures alike and from
their infancy have never changed their language, but always increased it to perfection. For my message and my language are
translated into a foreign tongue, as can easily be proved from the
flavor of my writing how I am trained and learned in discourse,
For, it is written, by the tongue wisdom is discerned: and understanding, and knowledge, and learning, by the word of the wise
[Ecclus. 4:29].

But what aid is an excuse, though true, especially if with pre-
sumption, since now in my old age I seek for that which I did not
acquire in youth? My sins prevented me from learning what I had
previously read through. But who believes me though I say again
what I said before? In youth, indeed almost as a boy who had not
learned to speak, I was taken captive, before I knew what I ought
to seek and what avoid.

Wherefore today I blush and greatly fear to bare my ignorance,
for in a brief discourse to the eloquent I cannot explain in the way
my spirit and mind wish, and so that the meaning reveals what I
feel.

But if it had been given to me as to others, I should not have been
silent for fear of retribution, and even if it seems to some that I
put myself forward with my unwisdom and slow tongue, it is
nonetheless written: The tongue of stammerers shall speak readily
and plain [Isa. 32:4]. How much more should we seek this for
ourselves, who are, it is said, a letter of Christ for salvation unto
the ends of the earth [cf. II Cor. 3:2], and if not eloquent, yet
confirmed and most strong written in your hearts not with ink
but with the spirit of the living God [II Cor. 3:3]. And furthermore the Spirit testifies even rusticity was created by the most
high [Ecclus. 7:16, misunderstanding *rusticationem*, "husbandry"].

Wherefore I, perhaps indeed once unlearned, an exile, untrained,
who does not know how to provide for the future, yet this I know
most certainly that always before I was humiliated I was like the

It is not always possible to tell what difficulties in the *Confessio* stem from Patrick's uneasy latinity, and what from subsequent mutilations of the text, but it is clear that his concern in writing the language was not with elegance, though he just as clearly knew that such a thing existed. For him the most meaningful ornamentation was scriptural, and he cites Scripture both in direct quotations and in passing allusions. We shall see that Patrick's followers in Ireland were anything but his successors in literary self-effacement. In the *Confessio,* however, it is possible to read an extended Latin work by a fifth-century Briton, albeit one who spent most of his adult life speaking a foreign tongue in exile.

The other Latin work of Patrick, the *Epistola ad Coroticum,* is in the nature of a rebuke, and it tells us little new about the author save in the most conventional terms. A company of Irish neophytes, wearing the white garments of confirmation and with the chrism still wet on their heads, were set upon by a band of Scottish pirates who slaughtered some of them and took others captive. The pirates were themselves Christians, or people of a christianized tribe, but in all probability had fallen back into their old ways. Patrick sends them the letter to persuade them to release the captives, and to warn the faithful

---

stone that lies in deep mud: and the Almighty came and in His mercy lifted me up and indeed raised me on high, and set me atop the wall; and therefore I ought to exclaim loudly to render also something to the Lord for all His benefits to me here and in eternity, which the mind of men cannot estimate.

Wherefore, then, be astonished, great and little ones who fear God, and you, the learned leisure class, listen and study this. Who was it that stirred up the dullard, me, from the midst of those who seem to be wise and learned in the law and powerful in their speech and in everything, and inspired me, hateful to this world, before the others (if I could) that I with fear and reverence and without complaint should faithfully serve the nation to whom the love of Christ carried and delivered me in my life, if I were worthy, so that humbly and truly I should serve them.

to have nothing to do with the pirates until they do. Once again, he relies heavily on Scripture for his rhetoric. Of some interest is the passage "Non mea verba sed Dei et apostolorum atque prophetarum quod ego Latinum exposui, qui numquam mentiti sunt" (ch. 20).[17]

Gildas (0.7)

The earliest life of Gildas was written in the eleventh century, some five hundred years after his death, although the earliest mention of him—by Columban in a letter to Pope Gregory the Great—was written about 600. He was a revered figure among the scholars of the eighth century; however, we have much testimony and little information about him, and even the canon of his works is not at all clear. His anonymous eleventh-century biographer, though unreliable, is more to be trusted than Caradoc of Llan-Carvan, a twelfth-century Welsh monk who wrote the second fabulous account of the historian's life. The earlier biographer of the two was a monk at Ruys, a monastery in Brittany which claimed Gildas as its founder. He reports that Gildas was born in the Strathclyde of noble Christian parents. Gildas received his early training in Wales under St. Illtud, in Ireland, and on the Continent. He traveled to Rome, returned more than once to Ireland and, it is assumed, to Britain. He died in 570; the date of his birth must have been about 500, but he says nothing more of it than that it took place in the same year as the battle of Mons Badonicus.

The best-known work of Gildas is his *Liber querulus de excidio Britanniae*. Also ascribed to him is a Latin poem, the *Lorica Gildae*, of a genre common in the early middle ages but far from certainly his. There are fragments of some lost letters and a penitential; but these

[17] It is not my words that I have set forth in Latin, but those of God and the Apostles and prophets, who never lied.

again have not the authority which recommends the *De excidio* on which, in any case, his reputation would rest. Although it has been shown that the *De excidio* is not so poor an historical document as had once been thought, it must be realized that its author had no intention of recording history when he wrote it. It falls into three parts, of which only the first (chs. 1-26) makes any attempt at historical review at all, and that for homiletic, not historical, ends. (Bede quotes, and may have known, only this first part, but it does not follow that the second and third parts are spurious.) Having recounted the past depravity of the British nation, Gildas turns to his own times. In chs. 27-63 he condemns secular authority on the island, pointing in particular to five princes and reciting their crimes. He gives weight to his declamation by very extensive citation of Scripture. In part three (chs. 64-110), he turns his attention to ecclesiastical authority and, although he does not name specific targets for his abuse, he follows the plan of part two by citing first the crimes he is condemning and then the scriptural texts which foretell their punishment. In the chapters following 26 there are, to be sure, incidental references which have been of value to students of history, but—as in the first 26 chapters—they are there to support the homiletic theme. The anonymous biographer (ch. 19) refers to the *De excidio,* which he quotes, as "epistolaris libellus" (a small epistolary book), and Gildas himself called it "epistola" (a letter, ch. 1) where he described its intent: "non tam fortissimorum militum enuntiare trucis belli pericula mihi statutum est quam desidiosorum."[18] The book, then, is a letter to his own generation concerning moral deeds, not a record for the future concerning historical events; it is in the twelfth-century life (ch. 5) that he is called "historiographus" (one who writes history).

[18] It is not so much my task to tell of the dangers of the courageous soldiers in cruel warfare, as those of the lazy ones.

Nothing is known of Gildas' education. His first biographer says that as a youth he preferred divine studies to liberal arts, but we later read that he was "commoratus . . . tam saecularibus . . . quam divinis scripturis" (ch. 6).[19] A child put in his care (as the result of a miracle) is "ablactatum liberalibus litterarum studiis erudiendum."[20] The author of the even less trustworthy second life says Gildas "studuit studiosus assidue . . . in artibus septem" (ch. 1)[21] and (ch. 8) tells of his work in education. Gildas' prose, in any case, shows little direct influence of Latin literature outside the Bible, but it is self-consciously rhetorical, even bombastic, in a way that the prose of Pelagius and Patrick—and, of course, Vinisius—was not. For his effects, Gildas relies on highly metaphorical language, on appeals to the reader's emotions, and on heavy employment of scriptural allusion and quotation.

Gildas' syntax often makes his prose turgid, but his figures of speech do much to make it vivid. In describing Britain, he speaks of the mountains, "quorum diversorum colorum flores humanis gressibus pulsati non indecentem ceu picturam eisdem imprimebant, electa veluti sponsa monilibus diversis ornata" (ch. 3).[22] He uses simile freely. He speaks of preachers "quasi vino madidi" (ch. 21), warns of sins "velut quibusdam marinis irruentibus . . . voraris feraliter undis" (ch. 30), professes "quam enim libenter hoc in loco ac si marinis fluctibus jactatus et in optato evectus portu remis . . . quiescerem" (ch. 65), and "quasi," "veluti," "ac si"[23] recur frequently in his prose.

[19] Accustomed to secular as much as to divine writings.
[20] Sent for education in the liberal study of letters.
[21] Studied as a scholar carefully the seven arts.
[22] Of which the flowers of several colors, trodden by the steps of men, give them the appearance, not unseemly, of a picture, like a bride adorned with sundry necklaces.
[23] As though steeped in wine; as though in some invading seas you are fatally engulfed by the waves; how willingly, in this place as though tossed up by the streams of the sea and conveyed to the

[29]

He employs, moreover, language which, while not metaphorical, is certainly pictorial: "Novatus . . . porcus niger" (ch. 67), "ultionis justae . . . ignis" (ch. 24), "trans Tithicam vallem" (ch. 19).[24] Most of this language is employed in vituperation of sinners or sin, and he does not elaborate it for its own sake. He does cite Virgil, however, three times (chs. 6, 17, 25) for purposes which appear to be largely decorative. One quotation from Virgil he introduces "ut in proverbium . . . efferetur," another "ut dicitur,"[25] and he shows some concern to refer to sources outside of Scripture. Three times he quotes from British Christian writers ("nostri", chs. 38, 62, 92), each time for a sententious phrase which Gildas himself could easily have bettered. This, like the two references to Jerome, must be taken with at least some of the figurative language as display. Gildas refers only twice to his own style, once in the first chapter and once in ch. 106: "vili . . . stilo," "despecta ingenii nostri cymbula,"[26] scarcely very much in an age which regarded abject protestations of literary incompetence as an established tradition. He speaks of Latin as "nostra lingua" (ch. 23), but his use of it is by no means unselfconscious. Akin to his use of figurative speech is his ornate rhetoric. He may be referring to pagan literature, maybe only to idle tales in his condemnation of "ineptas saecularium hominum fabulas" (ch. 66) which he contrasts with "praecepta sanctorum."[27]

Gildas is a careful stylist; his prose shows signs of conscious refinement in phrases, in sentences, and in the all-

---

desired port by oars, would I be silent [cf. Aldhelm, p. 91 below]; as though; even as; as if.

[24] Novatus, the black pig; the fire of just revenge; across the ocean valley.

[25] As it is reported in a proverb; as it is said.

[26] Vile style; the despised little skiff of my talent.

[27] Unsuitable tales of secular men; precepts of the saints.

over shape of his work. Chapter 27, which begins the section on corruption in secular power, opens thus:

> Reges habet Britannia, sed tyrannos; judices habet, sed impios; saepe praedantes et concutientes, sed innocentes; vindicantes et patrocinantes, sed reos et latrones; quam plurimas conjuges habentes, sed scortas et adulterantes; crebro jurantes, sed perjurantes; voventes, sed continuo propemodum mentientes; belligerantes, sed civilia et injusta bella agentes.[28]

The first phrases of ch. 66, which opens the section on ecclesiastical corruption, are these:

> Sacerdotes habet Britannia, sed insipientes; quam plurimos ministros, sed impudentes; clericos, sed raptores subdolos; pastores, ut dicuntur, sed occisioni animarum lupos paratos, quippe non commoda plebi providentes, sed proprii plenitudinem ventris quaerentes; ecclesiae domus habentes, sed turpis lucri gratia eas adeuntes; populos docentes, sed praebendo pessima exempla, vitia malosque mores.[29]

These are parallel in more than their general form alone. Both employ wordplay ("belligerantes . . . bella agentes," "jurantes . . . perjurantes"), and extensive rhyme, especially in pairs like "insipientes . . . impudentes," which make use of alliteration as well. The phrase "quam plurimos" and the increasing complexity of the phrases between semicolons are similarly a feature of both paragraphs.

---

[28] Britain has kings, but they are tyrants; she has judges, but godless ones; they plunder and agitate frequently, but against innocent men; they avenge and defend, but criminals and robbers; they have many wives, but whores and adulterers; they often take an oath, but only to break it; they take vows, but they always lie; they make war, but unjustly and on their own people.

[29] Britain has priests, but they are foolish ones; many ministers, but shameless; clergy, but sly robbers; pastors, as they say, but wolves ready for the slaughter of souls, by no means providing what is needful for the people, but seeking the fullness of their own bellies; they have church buildings, but go to them only for the sake of gain; they teach the people, but by giving the worst examples, teach them vices and evil ways.

Gildas uses exclamatory phrases relatively infrequently, considering the nature of his work. One example is in ch. 23: "O altissimam sensus calignem! O desperabilem crudamque mentis hebetudinem!"[30] A longer passage appears in ch. 34:

> O quanta ecclesiae matri laetitia, si non te cunctorum mortalium hostis de sinu quodammodo ejus lugubriter abstraxisset, foret! O quam profusus spei caelestis fomes desperatorum cordibus, te in bonis permanente, inardesceret! O qualia quantaque animam tuam regni Christi praemia in die judicii manerent si non lupus callidus ille agnum ex lupo factum te ab ovili dominico, non vehementer invitum, facturus lupum ex agno sibi similem, rapuisset! O quantam exultationem pio omnium patri Deo sanctorum tua salus servanda praestaret, si non te cunctorum perditorum infaustus pater, veluti magnarum aquila alarum unguiumque daemon, infelici filiorum suorum agmini contra jus fasque rapuisset![31]

Perhaps the most extended example of rhetorical development in the *De excidio* is to be found in chs. 69-75. There Gildas points out the failings of even the good priests of his times by comparing them with their predecessors of the Old and New Testaments and the martyrs of the early Church. This he does by means of the rhetorical question, beginning

---

[30] O most deep cloud upon the understanding! O hopeless and cruel dullness of mind!

[31] O how much gladness there would be for the mother Church, if the enemy of all mortals had not, as it were, lamentably dragged you away from her bosom! O how profuse the tinder of heavenly hope would burn in the hearts of the hopeless, if you were steadfast in good! O what and how many rewards of the kingdom of Christ would await your soul in the day of judgment, if that cunning wolf had (not greatly against your will) not taken you, made a lamb from a wolf, from the Lord's flock, to make you a wolf from a lamb, like himself! O how much joy to the holy God, father of all the saints, your salvation would have furnished, had not the miserable father of all the damned, the devil like an eagle with mighty wings and talons, carried you off to the host of his unhappy children, contrary to everything right and just!

[32]

> Quis rogo eorum ob invidiam melioris hostiae caelestique igni in caelis evectae, ut Abel, occisus?

passing on to

> Quis ob testimonium verum Deo ferendum fullonis vecte cerebro percussus, ut Jacobus primus in novo dumtaxat episcopus testamento, corporaliter interiit?

and concluding with a paragraph which begins

> Quis vestrum, ut sanctus martyr Ignatius Antiochiae urbis episcopus, post admirabiles in Christo actus ob testimonium ejus leonum molis Romae confractus est?[32]

Once again we have evidence of careful balance in the structure of the work; once again the wordplay ("caelestique igni in caelis evectae"), the repeated phrase ("ob testimonium") and the elaborate syntax ("ut Jacobus primus in novo dumtaxat episcopus testamento").

These passages illustrate Gildas' range of sources. The first, of course, is based on Scripture. The second, although it refers to scriptural incident, seems to have been based on Jerome, *De viris illustribus* (ch. 2), where the words "fullonis fuste . . . in cerebro percussus interiit" appear. This work of Jerome, and his *Prolegomena in Jeremiam*, furnished a quantity of material for Gildas. The third passage is based on Rufinus' version of Eusebius' *HE* III.36-37. This history, along with Orosius', also constituted one of Gildas' chief sources, especially for his first 26 chapters. There he confesses that he writes "quantum tamen potuero, non tam ex scriptis patriae scriptorumve monimentis, quippe quae, vel si qua fuerint, aut ignibus

---

[32] Who of them, I ask, was killed like Abel, because of the envy of a better sacrifice, and carried off to heaven by heavenly fire? Who, for bearing true testimony of God, was killed by being brained with a fuller's club, as James, the first bishop in the New Testament, suffered bodily death? Who of you, like the holy martyr Ignatius of the city of Antioch, after wonderful deeds in Christ, in witness of Him was torn to pieces at Rome by the teeth of lions?

[33]

hostium exusta aut civium exilii classe longius deportata,
non compareant; quam transmarina relatione, quae crebris
irrupta intercapedinibus non satis claret" (ch. 4).[33] (The
letter *Agito ter consuli gemitus Britannorum* mentioned
in ch. 20 is too fragmentary to reveal much about the
latinity of Gildas' fellow Britons.)

Gildas' use of Scripture is more systematic than Patrick's, who simply incorporated its language into his own
through long mental habit. The Bible, by the middle of
the sixth century, was in a state of transition, neither its
first nor its last. Gildas' quotations are partly *Vetus
latina*, partly Hieronymian. He depended on Jerome for
most of the Old Testament, but not for Ezechiel, the minor
prophets, the sapiential books, or Job. He preferred the
Vetus latina Gospels, with some corrections of the Vulgate,
but accepted Jerome's version of the Acts and the Catholic
epistles; the Pauline epistles approximate the Vulgate, but
show heavy outside borrowings. The withdrawal of the
Roman legions, Britain's chief (though not sole) contact
with the Continent, had taken place only shortly after the
completion of Jerome's translation. Gildas was, little
doubt, one of those who had early in life committed the
Bible to memory, and his "mixed" texts may represent,
not so much the condition of scriptural manuscripts in
Britain circa A.D. 550, but the combination of what he read
and what he had memorized.

The mixture of scriptural texts and ecclesiastical history
mentioned previously illustrates another aspect of Gildas'
attitude toward Scripture. It is for him a current document, and its meaning is immediate. He can condemn
even the virtuous priests of his day because they are not

[33] So far as I can, not so much out of the writings of my nation,
or the records of authors, since they (if they ever existed) have
either been burned by the fires of our enemies or carried far away
in the ships which took our countrymen, and so are not available;
but more out of the narrative of foreigners, which is unclear because broken by many gaps.

eager martyrs like the Apostles or Abel. His vision of the presence of Scripture is based, in large measure, not on his conviction of its historical pertinence, but on his wholly unhistorical attitude toward it: like the *De excidio*, the Bible's history is still meaningful precisely because it is still morally true. Gildas was a student of the allegorical and typological interpretation of the Bible. So it is that he says, in the passage on ecclesiastical corruption, "Ambulavit Enoch cum Deo et non inveniebatur [Gen. 5:24] in mundi scilicet vanitate" (ch. 69); "Quis victoribus solum et in tricentenario numero, hoc est trinitatis sacramento . . . ut Melchisedech, benedixit?" (ch. 69); "Quis in monte cum Domino locutus . . . tropico sensu, ut Moyses?" (ch. 69).[34] Each of these quotations explains the relevance to the sixth century. Gildas must interpret the quotation from Scripture by continuing it with a *scilicet*; he notes that an Old Testament figure is a *sacramentum*, that is, a figure or sign, of a New Testament—and eternal—concept; and he stresses that he finds the priests of his day wanting in comparison with Moses in the tropological sense. This sense, sometimes also called the moral sense, is the one in which a figurative incident is interpreted when it concerns the interior, spiritual state. The allegorical concerns the exterior state, as when in the same chapter Gildas explains that the Ark is a figure of the Church; the anagogical, third of the traditional three levels of figurative meaning, refers to the eternal state, as in the phrase "celestial Jerusalem." Gildas is, of course, most concerned with the tropological and the allegorical, for he has in mind the individuals and the institutions of Britain, rather than the world to come. So we read:

[34] Enoch walked with God, and was seen no more, that is, in the vanity of the world; who like Melchisedech blessed the victors, singly and three hundred in number (which implies the mystery of the Trinity)? who has spoken with God on the mountain in the tropological sense, like Moses?

[35]

Quis . . . prosterneret . . . unicam filiam, quae propria volup-
tas intellegitur, . . . ut Jepte? (ch. 70)

Quis . . . post idolatriae luci, quod moraliter interpretatum
condensae et fuscae cupiditatis, succisionem silvae . . . ut
Gedeon, processit? (ch. 70)

Quis eorum . . . luxuriosos gentium convivas laudantes deos
suos, id est, sensus, extollentes divitias . . . concussis duabus
virtute brachiorum columnis, quae intelleguntur in voluptati-
bus nequam animae carnisque, quibus domus humanae omnis
nequitiae quodammodo pangitur ac fulcimentatur, tam in-
numerabiles, ut Samson, prostravit?[35] (ch. 71)

He interprets the figurative language of the New Testament in a like manner:

Estote prudentes sicut serpentes et simplices sicut columbae.
Prudentes quidem estis, ut aliquem ore exitiabili mordeatis,
non ut caput vestrum, quod est Christus, objectu quodammodo corporis defendatis, quem totis operum malorum conati-
bus conculcatis. Nec enim simplicitatem columbarum habetis,
quin potius corvino assimilati nigrori ac semel de arca, id est
ecclesia, evolitantes inventis carnalium voluptatum fetoribus
nusquam ad eam puro corde revolastis.[36] (ch. 95)

This attitude toward scriptural material made available to
Gildas a body of homiletic examples which he could use in
his epistle with immediate force. He must have counted on

---

[35] Who has offered up his only daughter, which is understood to
mean his will, like Jephtha? Who went forth, like Gideon, after cut-
ting down the wood, the grove of idolatry, morally interpreted as
meaning of thick and dark desire? Which of them like Samson laid
low so many self-indulgent pagan feasters praising their gods (that
is, the senses), hailing their wealth, when by the strength of his arms
he struck the two columns, which signify the pleasures of the soul
and the flesh, by which the house of every human vice is, so to
speak, fixed and established?

[36] Be ye wise as serpents and simple as doves [Matt. 10:16]. You
are wise, of course, when you bite anyone with a fatal mouth, not
to defend your head, who is Christ, by exposing your body, Whom
by all the efforts of evil works you tread underfoot. Nor have you
the simplicity of doves, for you are instead like the black crows,
who flying once out of the ark, that is the Church, and having found
the carrion of carnal delights, never fly back to it with a pure heart.

this force being felt in his audience; of the 110 chapters in the *De excidio*, at least 56 (chs. 38-63, 76-105) can be regarded as nothing more than anthologies of scriptural passages bearing on the subject at hand, and many other chapters are heavily interwoven with scriptural language. To have given up fully half of his carefully planned work to this kind of wholesale quotation, Gildas must have been confident that its pertinence would have been understood. In ch. 93 he makes clear what he imagines that understanding to be: "Velim quidem haec scripturae sacrae testimonia huic epistolae inserta vel inserenda, sicut nostra mediocritas posset, omnia utcumque historico vel morali sensu interpretari."[37] The burden of the interpretation, as we have seen, is moral.

It is clear that Gildas believes that he will accomplish his purpose better through the use of scriptural citation; they lend his work authority, as he says in ch. 37. Their authority, however, depends both on their divine origin and their present intelligibility, and Gildas capitalizes on this double significance in the most prominent feature of his prose.

Columba and Columban (0.8)

Latin learning in the British Church was, as we have seen, in large measure an aspect of the phenomenon to which the Church itself owed its existence, the Roman occupation. Ireland, however, was never part of the Roman Empire, and yet it appears that Patrick introduced neither Christianity nor latinity into Ireland when he began his mission there in 431. The evidence for a tradition of Latin letters in Ireland before Patrick, and the explana-

---

[37] I could wish indeed that these testimonies of sacred Scripture included in this epistle, or to be included, as my slight ability is able, all should be interpreted according to the historical or the moral sense.

tion of that tradition, has been the source of considerable controversy. Patrick himself (*Conf.*, ch. 13) addresses certain *rhetorici*, and it has been suggested that the spread and influence of Irish learning in the late fifth century must have been based on a strong native tradition. One theory, holding that the tradition need not have been older than Patrick's visit, maintains that in his company of missionaries were Britons and Gauls of considerable scholarship. Others believe that the Irish Christians, put in touch with the continental Church by Patrick, visited the schools in Gaul, where classical education had, in the third and fourth centuries, flourished; manuscript evidence hints at a Gaulish influence in Irish latinity. On the basis of a previously ignored document, Meyer held that the barbarian invasions of Gaul in the late fourth and early fifth century caused the flight of Gaulish scholars, Christian and pagan, to Ireland, where they could expect to find a welcome and refuge among their Celtic cousins. The document in question says, speaking of the barbarian invasions, "omnes sapientes cismarini fugam ceperunt, et in transmarinis, videlicet in Hibernia, et quocumque se receperunt, maximum profectum sapientiae incolis illarum regionum adhibuerunt."[38] If this states the case, and several scholars have believed that it does, then the origin of latinity, at least in the south of Ireland, antedates the mission of Patrick by very nearly half a century. It was, nevertheless, certainly through his influence that the new learning took deep root in Ireland and extended beyond the southern part of the country, for part of Patrick's achievement was to have strengthened, organized, and enlarged the Irish Church.

Finnian, founder of the monastery school at Clonard, is said to have been baptized and educated by one of the

[38] All the learned in Gaul took flight, and retreated across the sea, that is, into Ireland, and wherever they found refuge they supplied great aid to learning among the people of those regions.

disciples of St. Patrick. He must have been active during most of the first half of the sixth century; the Annals of Ulster report that he died in the plague of 549. He is said to have traveled to Britain and to have met there the luminaries of the British Church, David, Gildas, and Cadoc. On his return to Ireland he founded a number of religious communities, in one of which he lectured on Scripture. About 530 he became a hermit in a wild district of Westmeath, but he was—like the Egyptian hermit-scholars— soon surrounded by an even bigger community of his followers. In time, this community became associated with almost every subsequent Irish saint of note, and if the hagiographers are to be believed, Finnian's community at Clonard numbered some 3,000 souls. Clonard had the reputation of producing men of both sanctity and learning, and the program there included, it would appear, everything from acts of extreme mortification to the study of letters, both to the end of obtaining a better grasp of Scripture. It is not certain how influential Finnian's monastic school really may have been. Even if it represents the amalgamation through legend of several such schools, however, it still shows something of the renown and popularity the schools enjoyed by the beginning of the sixth century. It shows as well that the schools had a missionary purpose, for Columba of Iona, the apostle of North Britain, is said to have been a son of Clonard, and Archbishop Ussher characterized Finnian's academy as producing "a stream of saints and doctors, like the Greek warriors from the wooden horse."

The influence of foundations like Clonard is to be seen in the life of one of its pupils, Columba, and in the life of another nearly homonymous saint, Columban, who, though not from the school of Finnian, had nevertheless received a superb education in what must have been a similar school at Bangor. Both saints show the effects of this background in the striking combination of their learning and apostolic zeal, or—in monastic terms—contemplation and activity. Columba had founded two monasteries in Ireland up to the time when his missionary ardor and the enmity of an Irish king caused him to go abroad. He crossed the Irish Sea to what is now Scotland and in 563 obtained from King Conall the island of Hi (Iona), previously the site of a druidical community. There, with twelve companions, he founded his third and most famous monastery. In time Iona had the reputation of one of the paramount seats of learning in the British Isles—indeed, in the West. The scholars from Patrick's foundation at Armagh and Finnian's at Clonard came to Iona, and their pupils went forth from it, and to a degree it would be fair to say that Ireland developed an extramural ecclesiastical center. In this center, and in the centers elsewhere in Britain to which it gave rise, the liberal arts were pursued as an adjunct to scriptural study. Columba was believed to have decorated the Book of Kells; both he and Columban were accomplished poets in Latin. No certain work of Columba remains, although a *Regula* and the hymn *Altus prosator* have long been attributed to him, possibly correctly. Two other hymns, *In te Christe credentium* and *Noli pater*, sometimes attributed to Columba, are probably not his work. *Altus prosator* is a rhythmic, rhyming alphabetical poem, and as such it does not suggest a continuing tradition of classical verse form in sixth-century Irish Latin composition. On the other hand, it is grammatically correct by classical standards, and the fusion of biblical theme and language with a kind of forceful expression illustrates the availability of Latin verse as a living medium for the scholars and poets of the Celtic schools.

> Altus prosator, vetustus
> Dierum et ingenitus
> Erat absque origine
> Primordii et crepidine,
> Est et erit in saecula

Saeculorum infinita;
Cui est unigenitus
Christus et sanctus spiritus
Coaeternus in gloria
Deitatis perpetua.
Non tres deos depromimus,
Sed unum Deum dicimus
Salva fide in personis
Tribus gloriosissimis.

. . . .

Zelus ignis furibundos
Consumet adversarios
Nolentes Christum credere
Deo a patre venisse.
Nos vero evolabimus
Obviam ei protinus
Et sic cum ipso erimus
In diversis ordinibus
Dignitatem pro meritis
Praemiorum perpetuis
Permansuri in gloria
A saeculis in saecula.[39]

Columban was born in Leinster between 530 and 545. Little, other than his training at Bangor in northeast Ireland, is known about his early life. About 590—near the time of Columba's death, about 597—Columban and his twelve companions went to Gaul, perhaps by way of Britain. There he established a community at Anegray, and later others at Luxeuil and Fontaine. It was the monastery at Luxeuil which dominated the others, and which

---

[39] The high Creator, ancient in days and unbegotten, was without a first beginning and an outset, He is and shall be in an infinity of ages; with Whom Christ the only-born and the Holy Spirit are coeternal in the perpetual glory of Godhood. We preach not three gods, but we tell of one God in sound faith, most glorious in three persons. . . . The hot flame shall consume the raging enemies who refuse to believe Christ to have come from God the Father. But we shall fly upward straight towards Him and thus with Him shall be among the diverse orders, to gain dignity of reward for perpetual merit, and to remain in glory for ever and ever.

dominated the attention, ultimately, of much of the Church of Merovingian Gaul. Just as Clonard was said to have fostered every Irish saint of the sixth century, so Luxeuil came to be thought of as the home of every Gaulish saint of the seventh. Columban, especially in his penitential discipline, was influential among laity and monks alike, while his paschal observances drew the continental Church into the British struggle between Roman and Celtic systems. Most important for the purposes of our study is the effect of Luxeuil on the preservation of classical letters. The powerful Gaulish system of schools had, as we have seen, been largely destroyed by the barbarian invasions of about A.D. 400. In A.D. 600 Columban returned to Gaul a form of Gallican learning which had been isolated in Ireland for possibly three or four generations. The evidence of this learning is not so clear in the culture of seventh-century Gaul as it is in the writings of Columban himself. They are, in a sense, outside our province, for most of them seem to have been written after Columban went to the Continent, and he appears to have been at most a visitor to England. But they illustrate another aspect of the kind of latinity which, through the missionary efforts of Irish scholars, was being made available to their students outside Ireland, and particularly in England. A considerable amount of material remains which can with some confidence be ascribed to the saint. Nine of the eleven letters attributed to him, three of them in verse, are now accepted as his work, as are four homilies, the *Regulae*, the *Penitential*, perhaps a little boat-song, and a poem *De mundi transitu*. His Latin is not unlike that of Columba—that is, it is by and large correct but not specifically classical in form—but it shows something more of classical learning. Columban wrote hexameters, and he knew his Virgil and Horace, as the opening of his verse epistle to Seth shows:

[42]

Suscipe, Sethe, libens et perlege mente serena
Dicta Columbani fida te voce monentis;
Quae licet ornatu careant sermonis honesti,
Vota tamen mentisque piae testantur amorem.
Vive Deo fidens, Christi praecepta sequendo,
Dummodo vita manet, dum tempora certa salutis;
Tempus et hora volat, momentis labitur aetas.
Despice, quae pereunt, fugitivae gaudia vitae.
Non fragiles secteris opes et inania lucra,
Nec te sollicitet circumflua copia rerum.
Sint tibi divitiae divinae dogmata legis,
Sanctorumque patrum castae moderamina vitae,
Omnia quae dociles scripserunt ante magistri,
Vel quae doctiloqui cecinerunt carmina vates.
Has cape, divitias semper contemne caducas,
In mentemque tibi veniat tremebunda senectus,
Quam gelidae tandem sequitur violentia mortis.[40]

He may also have had real knowledge of Ovid and Juvenal, perhaps even Statius, Persius, and Lucan; it is never easy to know whether a citation of a classical authority is direct or borrowed from an intermediary source book. He knew his contemporaries and others in the tradition of Christian latinity: Prudentius, Juvencus, Eusebius, Jerome, Sedulius, Dracontius, Ausonius, Gildas, Fortunatus, and Gregory the Great, to whom he wrote about A.D. 600:

[40] Favorably accept, Seth, and read with a serene mind the sayings of Columban warning you with a faithful voice; which, though they lack the ornament of fine language, still testify to the devotion and love of a pious mind. Live trusting in God, by following the precepts of Christ, as long as life remains, as long as the time of salvation is sure; time and the hour fly, the age is eroded away by moments. Despise the joys of a transient life that depart. Do not pursue frail wealth and vain profit, nor let great abundance of things concern you. Let the teachings of divine law be your treasures, and the holy fathers' rules of a chaste life, all that the learned masters have written before, or the songs scholarly poets have sung. Take these, always despise perishable wealth, and into your thoughts let dread old age come, which the violence of cold death follows at last.

[43]

Legi librum tuum pastorale regimen continentem, stilo brevem, doctrina prolixum, mysteriis refertum; melle dulcius egenti opus esse fateor; mihi idcirco sitienti tua largire, per Christum precor, opuscula, quae in Ezechielem miro, ut audivi, elaborasti ingenio. Legi Hieronymi sex in illum libros; sed nec medium exposuit. Sed si dignaris, aliqua nobis de tuis transmitte relectis in civitate, extrema scilicet libri exposita; transmitte et Cantica canticorum ab illo loco, in quo dicit, *Ibo ad montem myrrhae et collem thuris*, usque in finem; aut aliorum aut tuis brevibus, deposco, tracta sententiis; et ut totam exponas obscuritatem Zachariae, absconsam propala, ut tibi occidentalis in his gratias agat caecitas. Importuna postulo et magna sciscitor, quis nesciat? Sed et tu magna habes, quia de parvo minus et de multo plus bene scis esse faenerandum.[41]

(Epist. 1.9)

Although Columban may have been no more than a visitor to Britain, the British—to be more exact, Welsh, for from about A.D. 500 there can be distinguished a Wales and an England—schools took part in a fairly active intercourse with those in Ireland. So Patrick, a Briton, stabilized the Irish Church and fostered the spread of learning there; Finnian was acquainted with Gildas and his contemporaries; Columba established a center of Irish learning in Scotland which influenced much of Eng-

---

[41] I have read your book containing the pastoral rule, brief in style, prolix in doctrine, full of high truths; I declare that the work is sweeter than honey to the needy; wherefore I beg you for Christ's sake to bestow on me, who thirst, your works, which, as I have heard, you have compiled with wonderful skill upon Ezechiel. I have read six books of Jerome on him; but he did not expound even half. But if you would deign to, send us something from what you read out in the city, that is the final expositions of the book; send also the Song of Songs from that passage in which it says, I will go to the mountain of myrrh and to the hill of frankincense [Cant. 4:6], up to the end; treat it, I pray, either with others' comments or with your own brief ones, and that you may expound all the obscurity of Zachariah, display what is concealed, so that in this, western blindness may give thanks to you. I make importunities and ask great things, who knows it not? But you also have great things, for you know well that from a small stock less is to be lent and from a great one more.

land, especially in the north. This learning was, in each case, characteristically latinate, and characteristically non- (but not anti-) classical; that is, the latinity was not an imitation of the classics, but like any living medium it employed the devices of the past for present purposes.

First to establish a school in Britain where the tradition of latinity of the Roman occupation might have been preserved after the end of the occupation itself was Ninian, a princeling of Cumberland who had gone to Rome in 380 and there had received the full benefits of a Roman education. He returned to Britain about 395 and established a church in Galloway which became a cathedral with a school. The cathedral school was maintained chiefly for the cathedral clergy, but a passage in his biography suggests that some of the local laity shared its facilities. It was Pelagius, however, who indirectly brought about the effective reinforcement of the connections between Britain and Rome after the end of the occupation. His death had not hindered the spread of his heresy, and in the early years of the fifth century Pelagianism was, to credit some reports, endemic in Britain. To combat it, Pope Celestine sent two Gaulish bishops, Germanus of Auxerre and Lupus of Troyes, to conduct a mission in the interest of orthodoxy. They made their first visit to Britain in 429, and instituted a school for the study of Scripture and letters in Caerleon, the old Roman *colonia*. The Caerleon foundation became the source of others, just as Iona had in North Britain and Luxeuil in Gaul, and one of these schools was established by Illtud in Glamorganshire. Tradition has it that Illtud had been trained in the liberal arts, and that they formed a portion of the curriculum at his monastery at Llan-Illtud. Be that as it may, those who are said to have studied at Llan-Illtud—Gildas, David, Samson, and, perhaps, Cadoc—manifested that same singular combination of study and activity which we noted in the Irish schools. Other schools were founded by

Cadoc at Llan-Carvan, where Gildas is said to have lectured; by Kentigern at Clwyd, where one third of the
community devoted itself to study while the others labored; at Bangor, near Menevia, by Daniel; at Llandaff,
by Dubric; at Menevia, by David. During the 168 years
between the visit of Germanus and Lupus, and the arrival of Augustine of Canterbury, the Latin culture of
England was largely in the hands of such schools, and of
the Irish scholars who visited them. The end of the arts
studied in these schools was the comprehension of Scripture and the praise of God, and diverse disciplines cooperated in this endeavor. Liturgy, Scripture, classical
letters, the Roman and Celtic vernacular all contributed
to the literature of the British and Irish Church during
the more than one and a half centuries of their virtual
isolation from the Continent.

Hisperica famina (o.9)

The *Hisperica famina* (so called in the colophon to the
Vatican MS) is a loose poem or rhythmic prose narrative
on a number of subjects of interest to a student—though
not necessarily to a monk or priest—which dates in all
probability from the fifth or sixth century and comes from
Britain or, more probably, Ireland. It is difficult to describe because it has no apparent overall form and because
in vocabulary and in style it is extremely obscure. The
author wanders from a discussion of schools and scholars
to the matter of Latin itself:

> Bis senos exploro vechros
> Qui ausonicam lacerant palatham;
> Ex his gemella astant facinora
> Quae verbalem sauciant vipereo tactu struem.
> Alterum barbarico auctu loquelarem inficit tramitem
> Ac gemello stabilitat modulo.
> Quaterna quae nectit specimina
> Inclitos litteraturae addit assiduae apices.
> Statutum toxico rapit scriptum damno.

[46]

Litterales urbanae movet characteres facundiae
Stabilem picturae venenoso obice transmutat tenorem.
Alius clarifero ortus est vechrus solo,
Quo hispericum reguloso ictu violatur eulogium
Sensibiles partiminum corrodit domescas;
Cetera notantur piacula
Quae italicum lecti faminis sauciant obryzum,
Quod ex his propiferum loquelosi tenoris in hac
                    assertione affigis facinus.[42]

(A. text, 116-132)

The form is not metrical, rhythmic, or syllabic, and the first editors printed it as prose. In most cases each line is a clause, and each is unified by the rhyme or assonance of the last word with another:

Ac gemello stabilit modulo.

Here as often, the first word is an adjective, the second a noun. There follow a number of essays, perhaps set-pieces in some school of rhetoric: *de caelo, de mari, de igne, de campo, de vento, de plurimis, de taberna* (a book chest?), *de tabula*. Then come sections *de oratorio* and *de oratione,* which contain a prayer in somewhat simpler language. The fullest text, that of the Vatican MS, ends with a miniature tale, having to do with a hunt, a meal, and the interruption of some vagabonds. The whole recalls nothing so much as a school exercise, but whether the difficulty of the language is the outcome of poor scholarship,

[42] I am delving into twice six faults which affront Roman taste [*palatham*, "the inside of figs," in error for *palatum*]; from these, twin evils spring up which injure the heap of words with a serpent's sting. One blocks the highway of speech with barbaric neologisms and stops it up with a double measure. The four-part compounds which it constructs it adds continuously to the famous peaks of literature. It overcomes established writing with its fatal poison. It shifts the literal characters of polished eloquence, and alters the regular flow of description with a poisoned hindrance. The other, I declare, is the only radical fault, in which hisperic eloquence is injured by a venomous sting. This part corrodes the sensible understanding; other atrocities are noted which injure the pure Latin of written narration, which villainy of yours you propound out of these two in the spoken declaration of discourse.

[47]

youthful exuberance, or a serious interest in extravagant Latin is not altogether possible to say; most scholars believe it is the latter. Sometimes described as hisperic, because of their similarity in vocabulary or style to the *Hisperica famina*, are the so-called *Lorica Gildae*; an alphabetical religious poem *Rubisca*; another, called the *St. Omer Hymn*; and, with far less reason, Gildas' *De excidio* and Columba's *Altus prosator*, some of the writings of Columban and Aldhelm, and one or two other works. Only the *Hisperica famina* is, by its own definition, hisperic, and the nomination of other works to this category depends largely on the critical definition of the term. Hisperic vocabulary consists of borrowings from other languages, notably Greek and Hebrew, words like *orticumetra*; new words formed by the addition of a suffix to old words, like *doctoreus*; words used in an uncommon or unknown sense, like *forceps* for mouth; ecclesiastical words, poetic words, Vulgar Latin words:

> Nam strictus romani tenoris me septricat nexus
> Nec scotigenum aperto forcipe pompo seriem.[43]
>
> (B. text, 67-68)

The style of the *Hisperica famina* is equally fanciful, at one moment redundant, at the next elliptical. The whole offers an obscurity which has led some scholars to believe that the *Hisperica famina*, and hisperic writing in general, reflects the influence, perhaps even the presence, in Ireland of the sixth-century Gaulish grammarian Virgilius Maro, who recommended a useful obscurity to enhance the value a reader would put on a meaning he had arrived at through considerable effort. In any case, it is hard to connect the *Hisperica famina* with the heirs of Patrick or Columban, who, though at the opposite extreme of stylistic competence, never seem to have looked upon language as a cloak for meaning.

---

[43] For the strict entwining of Roman speech hedges me about, nor do I show off Irish talk with an open mouth.

chapter one:

the seventh century

The Augustinian Mission (1.1)

Before the end of the Roman occupation, bands of raiders from the western shore of north Germany had been seeking plunder in Britain. Their raids, chiefly along the southeastern coast of the island, had led in the third century to the building of elaborate Roman defenses along the "Saxon Shore." With the degeneration of Roman rule, Britain became increasingly vulnerable to the raiders, and so by the time the withdrawal was completed—the middle of the fifth century at the latest—the Germanic invaders, made up of men from the tribes of Jutes, Angles, and Saxons, had begun to look upon Britain as the object of settlement. Unlike their Roman predecessors, they not only conquered but in large measure drove out or assimilated the Celtic inhabitants of the island; some survivors fled to Ireland or the Continent, but most took refuge in the traditional areas of Celtic concentration: Cornwall, Wales, Scotland, and, to some extent, the wilderness, the fens, and forests. The Saxons, as we may call them conveniently, had no colonial policy of the Roman sort; they came not to subjugate but to displace the Celts, although the conquest was not complete, even in England, until the ninth century. The tradition of Saxon-Celtic enmity remained largely unchanged throughout the rest of the pre-Norman period, so that a tenth-century Saxon poet celebrating the defeat of a Celtic-Danish alliance by Saxon forces could say that there had not been such a conflict since the first Germanic invaders, "the brave war-smiths," came to vanquish the Britons five hundred years before. This separation of races

[49]

was to influence the success of the mission of St. Augustine and the subsequent relations between British and Roman Christianity.

The Romano-Britons had been to a great extent christianized by the end of the fourth century, at least in the urban centers, but as the urban centers felt the fullest force of the Saxon conquest, the British Church was soon driven from a position from which it might have evangelized the invaders. The missionary activities of the Celtic Church between 450 and 600 were largely on the Continent and in Scotland: the illiterate heathen who had displaced the Celts felt little of them. So it was that Gregory the Great, then praefect at Rome, decided about 575 to evangelize the country. It was not until 596, six years after his elevation to the papacy, that he found an opportunity to put his plan into effect. To head the mission he chose one Augustine, prior of Gregory's own monastery of St. Andrew's in Rome. This monastery included as part of its daily routine the study of Scripture and scriptural exegesis, but probably not secular letters. Gregory himself, founder and past abbot of the monastery, wrote of Benedict:

> Romae liberalibus litterarum studiis traditus fuerat. Sed cum in eis multos ire per abrupta vitiorum cerneret, eum quem quasi in ingressu mundi posuerat, retraxit pedem: ne si quid de scientia ejus attingeret, ipse quoque postmodum in immane praecipitium totus iret. Despectis itaque litterarum studiis, relicta domo rebusque patris, soli Deo placere desiderans, sanctae conversationis habitum quaesivit. Recessit igitur scienter nescius, et sapienter indoctus.[1] (*Dial.* ii, Pref.)

[1] He was sent to Rome for the liberal study of letters. But when he saw many among them go along the descending path of vices, he drew back the foot which he had put as on the entrance to the world, lest—if he should deal with any of its wisdom—he might himself fall straightaway into the fearful gulf. Thus having despised the study of letters and left behind his home and his father's wealth, wishing to please God alone, he sought the garment of holy life. Therefore he withdrew, learnedly unlearned and wisely ignorant.

Gregory also wrote of the moral danger of pagan letters (e.g., *Epist.* XI.54) ; the tradition that he burned profane books, although ill-documented, suggests something of the impression he left, as well as of the regime he must have instituted at St. Andrew's. When it is said, then, that the Gregorian mission under Augustine reestablished the links between England and Rome that had been weakened by the Roman withdrawal and broken by the Saxon invasion, it is only the links between England and the Church of Rome that are meant; the missionaries were not scholars of classical civilization, and that civilization, dead by the end of the sixth century, had become the exclusive domain of scholars.

Augustine and his mission arrived on the coast of Kent early in 597. The Kentish king, Aethelberht, had married a Christian Frankish princess, Bertha, some ten years before, and a Frankish bishop, Liudhard, had accompanied her to her new home. During the course of the first year of the mission, Aethelberht was converted, and after him increasing numbers of his household and subjects. Toward the end of 597 Augustine was consecrated a bishop in Gaul and thereafter the mission prospered for some years; in 601 a body of monks arrived from Rome to supplement the original band, and with them the pallium which enabled Augustine to consecrate bishops to other English sees. Laurentius, a member of the original mission, was made abbot of the monastery of SS. Peter and Paul outside of Canterbury, where Augustine had set up his own see; Justus, a member of the second mission, was the first incumbent of the new Kentish see at Rochester; and Mellitus, also a member of the second mission, was made first Bishop of London. But leaders of the Celtic Church held Augustine's mission, and his authority, to extend only to the English, while Gregory had granted authority to Augustine over the Celtic Church as well. On the two occasions when Augustine met with British churchmen to discuss the matter of his jurisdiction, and to try to end Celtic divergence from Roman custom in a number of liturgical practices, notably the computation of the Easter date, he was rebuffed. The Celtic Church had, despite persecution by the heathen Saxons, experienced a century of institutional and spiritual growth. To their traditional hatred of the people whom Augustine had come to evangelize was added their independent progress in the 150 years of their virtual isolation from Rome. Their refusal to contribute to the Roman mission their resources, including their learning, hampered the development of English latinity through much of the seventh century. Of the two important exceptions to this retarded development, Wilfrid was trained on the Continent, and Aldhelm, in his youth, was trained by Celtic masters. Later, Aldhelm benefited from the increase in English intellectual activity brought about by the partial resolution of the Celtic-Saxon ecclesiastical problem at the Synod of Whitby (664) and the arrival of Theodore of Tarsus (669). Meanwhile, two generations of English Christians had come and gone since the arrival of Augustine.

Augustine died in 604, less than three months after Gregory. He was followed in the archiepiscopal see at Canterbury by Laurentius, whom he had already consecrated as his successor. But King Aethelberht died in 616, and it appeared for a while that even in Kent, where the mission had its greatest success, the spread of Christianity might be reversed. Aethelberht's son was not a Christian, and the dioceses of London and Rochester seemed about to offer martyrdom to their bishops. In preference, Mellitus and Justus fled to the Continent, and Archbishop Laurentius almost joined them. In time, however, Aethelberht's son was converted; Paulinus, a member of the second mission, was consecrated a bishop and sent to Northumbria in 625, where within two years he had converted the court and many of the populace; and the con-

tinental bishops Felix and Birinus commenced work
among the East Angles and West Saxons respectively.
By 627 Laurentius, Mellitus, and Justus had died, and
Honorius—another member of the 597 or 601 mission—
was Archbishop of Canterbury. In 632 King Edwin of
Northumbria died, and the area converted by Paulinus
was returned to heathenism. Paulinus fled to Kent, where
he took over the vacant see of Rochester. At his death in
644, he was succeeded by Ithamar, in all probability the
first native bishop in the forty-seven years since Augustine's arrival. In 653 Honorius died, and he was followed
in the see of Canterbury by another Englishman, Deusdedit (Frithona). It was not until the death of the last of
the original missionaries, and the end of the direct influence of the Augustinian mission, that native clergy began to come to power in the English Church.

The influence of the Augustinian mission continued in,
among other things, the ecclesiastical foundations it left
behind. There were cathedrals in Canterbury, Rochester,
and London—the latter unoccupied until Cedda's mission
to the East Saxons in 653—and another, not completed,
in York, besides the monastery at Canterbury. Taking
into account the attitudes of Gregory and the training of
the monks who carried out his mission, the aloofness of
the Celtic Church and its scholars, and the tardiness of
native clergy in assuming positions of importance in the
English Church, one finds it hard to believe that the cathedral and monastery schools, such as they may have
been, offered much in the way of liberal arts. Bede says
(*HE* III.14) that Ithamar was "de gente Cantuariorum,
sed . . . eruditione antecessoribus suis aequandum,"[2] which
may mean that such an education was unexpected in an
English priest. Cedda himself was a pupil of the Irish
monk Aidan, who had come from Columba's foundation

---

[2] Of the Kentish race, but equal in learning to his predecessors.

at Iona to Lindisfarne in 634 and reestablished Christianity in the area Paulinus had converted and lost. Bede (*HE* IV.I) says that Wighard, the Angle who was nominated to succeed Deusdedit at Canterbury when the latter died in 664, was "vir in ecclesiasticis disciplinis doctissimus,"[3] which suggests something of the curriculum—and the intellectual aspirations—of the native clergy at even such a late date. Bede also tells us something of the linguistic problems of the mission:

> Eo autem tempore miserat Ecgberhtus Cantuariorum rex de Britannia electum ad episcopatus officium virum nomine Wighardum, qui a Romanis beati papae Gregorii discipulis in Cantia fuerat omni ecclesiastica institutione sufficienter edoctus; cupiens eum sibi Romae ordinari episcopum, quatinus suae gentis et linguae habens antistitem, tanto perfectius cum subjectis sibi populis vel verbis imbueretur fidei vel mysteriis; quanto haec non per interpretem, sed per cognati et contribulis viri linguam simul manumque susciperet.[4]

More of the program of Augustine's mission may be inferred from the paucity of its documentary survival and from the list of books traditionally held to have been sent to Augustine from Gregory with the reinforcements of 601.

The documents are few and uninspiring. First is the so-called *Gregorii responsiones ad interrogationes Augustini* (*HE* 1.27; a different text, independent of Bede, also exists). The genuineness of this list of questions and an-

---

[3] A man most learned in ecclesiastical teaching.

[4] Now at that time Egbert, King of Kent, had sent from Britain a man named Wighard, chosen for the office of bishop, who had been well instructed in all ecclesiastical matters by the Roman scholars of the blessed Pope Gregory in Kent; and Egbert desired to have him ordained bishop at Rome, so that having a prelate of his own nation and tongue, he with those subject to him might be that much more perfectly instructed whether in the words or mysteries of the faith; insomuch as he would receive these things, not through an interpreter, but by the tongue and hand of a man of their own family and tribe.

swers on ecclesiastical and sacramental administration has
been doubted. Even if it is genuine, Augustine's hand in
it is very small, and indeed his questions as they appear in
the document Gregory returned with the mission of 601
may be nothing more than Gregory's paraphrase as is
suggested by the form of the first one:

> De episcopis, qualiter cum suis clericis conversentur, vel de
> his, quae fidelium oblationibus accedunt altario; quantae
> debeant fieri portiones et qualiter episcopus agere in ecclesia
> debeat?[5]

This view is supported by the lack of any salutation by
Augustine, and by the brevity of the questions (only one
of the nine is longer than the one quoted) in comparison
with the lengthy answers. Although the list of questions
begins "Prima interrogatio beati Augustini Episcopi Cantuariorum ecclesiae,"[6] the very title "beatus" shows that
this portion of the manuscript is a later addition. Some
manuscripts include a preface: recent scholarship has suggested that this part or all of the work is a forgery per-
petrated by Nothelm. Nothing then remains from the pen
of the first Archbishop of Canterbury which can be identified with certainty as his work. The *Bulla plumbea* (*H&S*
III.58-59) is spurious. Two fragments from MS Vat.
Palat. 577, beginning *Fili hominis, speculatorem* and
Rogamus vos, carissimi filii (*PL* 89.818-820) have
been tentatively identified by Machielsen as portions of
sermons by Augustine. The subject, that of permitted
degrees of consanguinity in marriage, echoes the subject
of *responsio* 5, and the sea imagery argues a familiarity
with Anglo-Saxon literary tradition. A characteristic passage is:

---

[5] Concerning bishops, how should they live with their clergy, and
into how many portions should the things which come to the altar
by the offerings of the faithful be divided, and how should bishops
behave in church?

[6] The first question of blessed Augustine bishop of the church
of the Kentish.

[55]

Ecce, carissimi, qualem ad vos legationem perferimus, non cujuscumque, qui pretio possit redimi, sed cujus sanguini pro vobis fuso estis obnoxii. Admonemus sanctitatem vestram: vivete cum conjugibus licitis, vivete continenter. Nemo se ulterius inclitis maculet. Nemo talibus sociatus, ante poenitentiae dignum servitium ad tanti domini corpus accedat, ne non remedium, sed vulnus accipiat, quia quod indigne sumitur, poena est, non medela.[7]

The passage illustrates the author's reliance on the Bible (1 Cor. 2:29-30) and also recalls Petrus Chrysologus' *Sermo* 34 (*PL* 52.297). It cannot, as Machielsen grants, be positively attributed to Augustine, but it accords with our notions of his thought and style.

Apparently genuine, but of little more help in characterizing the latinity of the mission, is the letter from Archbishop Laurentius of Canterbury, Bishop Mellitus of London, and Bishop Justus of Rochester, written probably shortly after Laurentius became archbishop in 604:

Dominis carissimis fratribus episcopis vel abbatibus per universam Scotiam Laurentius, Mellitus, et Justus episcopi, servi servorum Dei.

Dum nos sedes apostolica more suo, sicut in universo orbe terrarum, in his occiduis partibus ad praedicandum gentibus paganis dirigeret, atque in hanc insulam, quae Britannia nuncupatur, contigit introisse; antequam cognosceremus, credentes, quod juxta morem universalis ecclesiae ingrederentur, in magna reverentia sanctitatis tam Brittones quam Scotos venerati sumus; sed cognoscentes Brittones, Scotos meliores putavimus. Scotos vero per Daganum episcopum in hanc, quam superius memoravimus, insulam, et Columbanum abbatem in Gallis venientem nihil discrepare a Brittonibus in eorum conversatione didicimus. Nam Daganus episcopus

[7] Behold, most beloved ones, what sort of mission we bear to you, not from anyone who can be redeemed for a price, but from One whose debtors you are, Who poured out His blood for you. We admonish your sanctity: live with legitimate wives, live continently. No one stains himself more than the weak-willed. Let no one who is a companion to such people, before suitable servitude of penance, approach the body of the Lord, lest he receive an injury instead of a remedy, for that which is unworthily taken is a pain, not a solace.

ad nos veniens, non solum cibum nobiscum, sed nec in eodem hospitio, quo vescebamur, sumere voluit.[8] (*HE* II.4)

More profitable, or at least more suggestive, for the study of the intellectual pursuits of Augustine's mission, is the list of the books said to have been sent to him by Gregory in 601. The list itself is late—it appears in the fifteenth-century *Historia monasterii S. Augustini Cantuariensis* by the Canterbury monk Thomas of Elmham— but there is no reason to doubt that the list is an accurate local tradition. The collection may have been intact in Thomas' day; a few of the items have been identified on the shelves of Oxford and Cambridge libraries. Thomas first mentions a *Biblia Gregoriana* in two volumes, apparently incomplete, with colored translucent interleaves, next a *Psalterium Augustini, quod sibi misit idem Gregorius*,[9] and another psalter. Both books included hymns as well as psalms, and the latter contained other material— the letters between Pope Damasus and Jerome, for example—in addition. There were two copies of the Gospels, two volumes of hagiography, and one of commentaries on the New Testament. A number of these books, including the volume of commentaries, are said to have been very highly decorated with silver and jewels, which does not

[8] To our dearest brethren the bishops and abbots throughout all Ireland, from Laurence, Mellitus and Justus bishops, servants of the servants of God. When the apostolic see in its accustomed manner as in all parts of the world, sent us to preach to pagan people in these western parts, and it happened that we entered into this island which is called Britain; believing, before we knew, that they walked according to the accustomed way of the universal Church, we venerated with great reverence of holiness the Britons as much as the Irish; but knowing the Britons, we thought the Irish better. Now we have learned from Bishop Dagan coming to this island, which we mentioned before and by the coming of Columban, abbot in France, that the Irish differ not a bit from the Britons in their way of life. For Bishop Dagan, coming to us, would not only not take food with us, but not even in the same house where we were eating.

[9] A psalter of Augustine's, which the same Gregory sent with him.

suggest that they were intended for regular hard use by students. They do, nevertheless, confirm something of the implications of "ecclesiasticis disciplinis doctissimus." The regime of study in the schools of the Augustinian mission consisted of scriptural exegesis and hagiography, in both of which Gregory had excelled. The missionaries conducted their ecclesiastical affairs in the Latin of the Church, and spoke the Low Latin of sixth- and seventh-century Italy; they required the assistance of Frankish interpreters in their first contact with the people they came to evangelize. When they commenced the education of a native clergy, their texts and their models were probably of the kind represented by the donation of Gregory. With the death of Deusdedit, this tradition was interrupted, and with the arrival of Theodore of Tarsus, a new tradition of English scholarship was begun.

Theodore of Canterbury (1.2)

The career of Theodore in England was, in some ways, a restatement of the career of Augustine. In many others, however, it reflected the new age in which he lived and the eastern background from which he came. Theodore was born in Tarsus, in Asia Minor, in A.D. 602. Like Augustine, he was a monk, and he had, in all probability, St. Basil as his spiritual guide, much as Augustine had St. Benedict. But whereas the Benedictine Rule discouraged secular learning, the tradition of St. Basil was to encourage it as "leaves which serve as an ornament and protection for the fruit of Christian doctrine." St. Basil (329-379) had more than once urged the study of profane letters as a preparation for and an adjunct to the study of Scripture, most notably in his *Sermo de legendis libris gentilium* (*PG* 31.563-590). It may have been in a monastery under Basil's influence that Theodore began his studies: the remark of Pope Zachary that Theodore was "Graeco Latinus ante philosophus et Athenis eruditus"[10] suggests that not all of his education had been at Tarsus. He was, in any case, "vir et saeculari et divina litteratura, et Graece instructus et Latine" (*HE* iv.i)[11] and a man of the experience that travel brings when, in 667, he came to Rome; and in these two regards he differs from the cloistered Bible scholar Augustine.

When Wighard died in Rome in 664, Pope Vitalian was left with the problem of replacing the successor to the see of Canterbury. After some time he chose Hadrian, African abbot of a monastery near Naples and a scholar. Hadrian hesitated and suggested instead first a monk, Andrew, who proved to be too ill for the task, and then Theodore, whose learning had brought him the soubriquet "philosophus." Vitalian agreed to this suggestion on the condition that Hadrian would accompany the new Primate to England. When they left Rome for England they had with them the Northumbrian monk Benedict Biscop. On his return to Rome, he was appointed interpreter to Theodore and Hadrian. When the three left Rome in 668, Benedict was forty years old, Theodore was sixty-six, and Hadrian was perhaps about forty-three. They arrived in England the next year, seventy-two years after the arrival of the mission of Augustine, to find the English Church in confusion. The decisions of the Synod of Whitby had made available to the English Church some of the scholars of the Celtic Church, but had alienated many others. The see of York, next to Canterbury the most important in the nation, was in dispute between Wilfrid and Chad, and although Theodore was able to resolve this conflict, York was to be the source of further strife later on. The ecclesiastical government of Wessex was in a turmoil owing to the capriciousness of the king, Kenwalch. Immediately on his arrival in 669 Theodore

[10] A Latin philosopher already learned in Greek and the things of Athens.

[11] A man learned in both secular and divine literature, in Greek and in Latin.

set out to stabilize the Church and to extend its influence. At the Council of Hertford (673) he sought to regulate the ecclesiastical hierarchy, to free the monasteries from the influence of the secular clergy, to establish twice-yearly synods, and generally to unify the English Church under Canterbury.

At the same time as he was setting in order the diocesan organization of England, Theodore was extending ecclesiastical and secular learning among the clergy. He consecrated Putta, a student of Gregorian chant, to the see at Rochester. Both the cathedral and the monastery at Canterbury, of which Hadrian was abbot, must have become seats of learning: Bede says of Hadrian's successor Albinus (*HE* v.20) that he had learned from his master no little Greek, and that he knew Latin as well as his native English, and he makes (*HE* v.8) a similar statement about Tobias, Bishop of Rochester, another pupil of Theodore and Hadrian. So it was that a number of other members of the native clergy found at Canterbury a source of learning the like of which had not existed in Britain before the arrival of Theodore. To judge by the words of Aldhelm, another student of Canterbury, even the Irish scholars came to be taught by Theodore, and took back to Ireland with them what they learned from him. The influence of the knowledge of Theodore and Hadrian spread beyond Canterbury despite, or perhaps because of, the pressure of duty; wherever they went on their ecclesiastical missions

> Et quia litteris sacris simul et saecularibus, ut diximus, abundanter ambo erant instructi, congregata discipulorum caterva, scientiae salutaris cottidie flumina irrigandis eorum cordibus emanabant; ita ut etiam metricae artis, astronomiae, et arithmeticae ecclesiasticae disciplinam inter sacrorum apicum volumina suis auditoribus contraderent.[12]
>
> (*HE* iv.2)

[12] And because both [he and Hadrian], as I have said, were fully learned in secular as well as in holy literature, they gathered a

Like Augustine, Theodore also, according to uncertain tradition, brought a large collection of books with him, including not only a psalter and a collection of homilies, but a copy of Homer as well. But the tradition which is clearest, and which tells us most about the educational interests and activities of Theodore and Hadrian, is not so much to be found in the explicit statements of their contemporaries and disciples as in the work of the men who studied with them and who felt their influence: the comparatively paltry leavings of the Italians Augustine, Laurentius, Mellitus, and Justus, and the slight work of Wilfrid, himself educated on the Continent although an Englishman, pales beside the accomplishment of Aldhelm, and gives some measure of what happened to English intellectual life in 669.

Theodore's own writings seem not to have survived. A letter said to be his is reproduced in ch. 43 of the life of Wilfrid by Eddius Stephanus (q.v.) and the decrees of the Council of Hertford are quoted by Bede (*HE* IV.5). More considerable is the long Penitential to which Theodore's name is often attached, but it is of no help in estimating him as an author. It is not a belle-lettristic work, but rather a pastoral handbook or collection of penances to be prescribed for any of scores of sins, and as such it lies outside the scope of this book. It is, moreover, almost certainly not the work of Theodore himself, but the gist of a number of answers given on several occasions about matters of penitential practice, and edited by Eoda, a Northumbrian disciple of Theodore's. (The two forms of *Capitula Theodori* and the *Canones Theodori* are derivatives by later anonymous authors.) The Penitential does, no doubt, represent something of Theodore's attitude on

---

company of scholars and streams of wholesome knowledge daily issued forth to water their hearts; so that they instructed their hearers in the study of metrical art, astronomy, and ecclesiastical arithmetic, along with the volumes of the sacred writings.

these questions, and it, or the version of it ascribed to Bede, became the standard form for such a work in the Western Church for centuries afterwards. MS cccc 320 includes, at the end of the Penitential, the *Responsiones Gregorii,* and then a short poem which may be the only surviving work of Theodore:

> Te nunc sancte speculator
> Verbi Dei digne dator
> Haeddi pie praesul precor;
> Pontificum ditum decor;
> Pro me tuo peregrino
> Preces funde Theodoro.[13]

> (*H&S* iii.203)

Benedict Biscop (1.3)

The contribution of Bede and of his followers in the Northumbrian school owes much to Benedict Biscop. Born Biscop Baducing about 628, he gave up the prospects to which his noble birth entitled him and at twenty-five made his first visit to Rome. His companion, Wilfrid of York, went only as far as Lyons, where he remained "discedente ab eo austerae mentis duce" (Eddius, ch. 3).[14] Soon after 664 he made a second visit, from which he did not return to England but only as far as the monastery at Lerins, where he took his monastic vows (and perhaps received the name Benedict) and remained for two years studying Scripture. At the death of Deusdedit, when Wighard was sent to obtain the pallium as Archbishop of Canterbury, Benedict joined him at Lerins and accompanied him to Rome. But Wighard died and Theodore was appointed in his place. Benedict was directed to go with Theodore and Hadrian on their journey to England,

[13] Holy bishop, worthy bringer of the word of God, holy bishop of Eddius, to you now I pray; I honor your glorious pontificate; for me, thy wanderer Theodore, offer your prayers.
[14] When that leader of austere mind left him.

and he arrived with them in 669 after an absence of five years. For two years he was abbot of the monastery of SS. Peter and Paul in Canterbury, but in 671 he resigned his post to return once more to Rome. In the following year he came back to England and revisited his native Northumbria; in 673 or 674 he received the grant of land on which he founded the monastery of Wearmouth, where he lodged some of the "libros . . . omnis divinae eruditionis non paucos" (*HAB*, ch. 4)[15] obtained on his most recent trip to Rome. In the construction of the monastery he made a trip to France to obtain stonemasons and glaziers to make the church "juxta Romanorum quem semper amabat morem" (*HAB*, ch. 5).[16] Then he yet again went to Rome, this time with the express purpose of stocking his monastery with ecclesiastical paraphernalia and "innumerabilem librorum omnis generis copiam" (*HAB*, ch. 6).[17] He also brought with him the archchanter John, an abbot in his own right, who taught and wrote about the Roman manner of chanting in the new monastery. In 681 or 682 Benedict founded the associated monastery of Jarrow, and about 682 he made his last trip to Rome, from which he did not return before 686. Once again he brought books and sacred pictures back with him, most of which were used for enlightenment of the brethren, some of which were traded with the king to add to the monastery lands. He died on January 12, 689, after having given orders that the "bibliothecam quam de Roma nobilissimam copiosissimamque advexerat, ad instructionem ecclesiae necessariam, sollicite servari integram, nec per incuriam foedari, aut passim dissipari praecepit" (*HAB,* ch. 11).[18]

[15] Not a few books of all divine wisdom.
[16] According to the Roman fashion, which he always loved.
[17] Innumerable quantity of all kinds of books.
[18] He commanded the most glorious and copious library which he brought from Rome, needful to the teaching of the Church, to be diligently kept whole and complete, and not marred by neglect, nor scattered abroad.

[63]

Bede himself may not have been educated by Benedict
—the phrase (*HE* v.24) "datus sum educandus reverentissimo abbati Benedicto"[19] may have been meant only
loosely—but he appreciated the degree to which the abbot's efforts had made his studies and the intellectual
vigor of the monastery possible:

> Toties mari transito numquam ut est consuetudinis quibus-
> dam vacuus et inutilis rediit sed nunc librorum copiam sanc-
> torum nunc reliquiarum beatorum martyrum Christi munus
> venerabile detulit; nunc architectos ecclesiae fabricandae
> nunc vitrifactores ad fenestras ejusdem ornandas pariter ac
> muniendas nunc cantandi et in ecclesia per totum annum
> ministrandi secum magistros adduxit; nunc epistolam privi-
> legii a domino papa missam qua nostra libertas ab omni
> extrinseca incursione tutaretur apportavit; nunc pincturas
> sanctarum historiarum quae non ad ornamentum solummodo
> ecclesiae verum et ad instructionem intuentium proponer-
> entur advexit videlicet ut qui litterarum lectionem non
> possent, opera domini et salvatoris nostri per ipsarum con-
> tuitum discerent imaginum.[20] (Bede, *Hom.* 1.13)

Benedict left no writing; later tradition (embodied in
Pitseus, *Relatio historica de rebus anglicis*, Paris 1619,
113-114) attributed to him a *Concordia regularum, De
suo privilegio, De celebratione festorum totius anni,* and

[19] I was given to the most reverend Abbot Benedict to be educated.

[20] As often as he crossed the sea, he never returned as is the way
with some people empty-handed and without profit, but now he
carried a quantity of holy books, now the holy gift of the relics
of the blessed martyrs of Christ; now he brought architects for
the church which was to be built, now alike glaziers to decorate and
embellish the windows thereof, now teachers to sing and minister
with him in the church throughout the year; now he introduced
a letter of privilege sent from the Lord Pope by which our freedom
from every outside incursion was protected; now he conveyed
pictures of holy stories which were displayed not only for the
ornamentation of the church but also for the instruction of onlookers, that is those who were not able to read writing, so that
they might know the works of our Lord and savior through look-
ing upon those pictures.

Exhortationes ad monachos. The *Concordia* may have been associated with him because of the remark (*HAA,* ch. 6):

> Denique referre erat solitus, quia regulam, quam docebat, in antiquissimis xvii monasteriis didicerat, et quaeque ubicumque optima vidisset, haec, quasi in sacculo sui pectoris recondita, Britanniamque perlata, nobis sequenda tradiderit.[21]

The *Privilegio* and *Exhortationes* recall Benedict's dying words (*HAB,* ch.11):

> Sed juxta quod regula magni quondam abbatis Benedicti, juxta quod privilegii nostri continent decreta, in conventu vestrae congregationis communi consilio perquiratis, qui secundum vitae meritum et sapientiae doctrinam aptior ad tale ministerium perficiendum digniorque probetur, et quemcumque omnes unanime caritatis inquisitione optimum cognoscentes elegeritis; hunc vobis accito episcopo rogetis abbatem consueta benedictione firmari.[22]

The *De celebratione* appears to attribute to Benedict the kind of writing which Bede describes (*HE* iv.16): John the archchanter wrote "ea quae totius anni circulus in celebratione dierum festorum poscebat."[23] But even with these attributions aside, Benedict is a major figure in the history of Anglo-Latin culture because of the efforts

[21] Finally he was accustomed to bring things back, for the rule which he taught, he had learned in seventeen most ancient monasteries, and whenever he saw something good, that—hidden as though in the purse of his heart, and carried throughout Britain—he gave to us to follow.

[22] But in accordance with what the rule of our erstwhile abbot, the great Benedict, contains and in accordance with what the decrees of our letter of privilege contain, seek out with common consent in the assembly of your congregation the man who, because of the merit of his life and teaching of wisdom, shall be proved better fitted and more worthy for the fulfillment of such a ministry, and whomsoever you all unanimously judging by inquiry of love choose to be the best, him, having summoned the bishop, ask to be confirmed as abbot with the accustomed blessing.

[23] That which is required for the celebration of festival days for the whole cycle of a year.

he made to ally it with continental monasticism and scholarship in general, and in particular because of the library which he assembled so laboriously over the course of almost twenty years. It was this library that nourished the studies of Bede, and it was through it that Benedict was his true teacher.

Wilfrid (1.4)

Wilfrid is one of the most colorful, and at the same time one of the most unattractive, figures of the Anglo-Saxon Church. He was born the son of a Northumbrian thegn in 634, and at fourteen became a member of the court of King Oswy through the effect of his wit and handsome appearance on Queen Eanfled. He later joined the monastery at Lindisfarne. Through the intervention of Queen Eanfled he traveled to Lyons and then on to Rome (ca. 652) and met the Pope; on the return journey he received the tonsure in France, and narrowly escaped martyrdom. On his arrival in England, he was received by King Alhfrith of Deira, who made him Abbot of Ripon. He was ordained by the Gaulish Bishop Agilberht in 663 or 664. He was a leading exponent of the Roman party at the Synod of Whitby, and later in the same year he was elected Bishop of York in succession to Colman, the man he had worsted at Whitby; he was thirty years old. He insisted on consecration in Gaul on the grounds that the English hierarchy was contaminated by Quartodecimian heretics at whose hands the consecration might not be valid. Wilfrid plainly knew that, whatever their Easter teaching, the Irish were not Quartodecimians; but his demand gives significance to the Gaulish tonsure and ordination, which he may have sought—or had recorded —with a view to his later career. On his return from Gaul, delayed by misadventure, he found that Oswy had consecrated Chad in his place at York, and he retired to

Ripon until restored by Theodore in 669. In 678 Theodore
divided the diocese of York in three parts and Wilfrid
went to Rome to appeal against the manner in which his
see had been diminished. Pope Agatho decided in his
favor, but on his return to England, Wilfrid was im-
prisoned by order of King Ecgfrith (680) and then driven
into exile in Sussex (681-686). He was later reconciled
with Theodore and through his intervention was returned
to the abbacy of Ripon and the see of York by King Aldfrith (686-691), whence he was yet again exiled, this
time to Lichfield. In 703 a synod of Canterbury called by
Berhtwald demanded that he resign his see at York, and
he went back to Rome for renewed aid. This time Pope
John found less clearly in his favor than had Agatho,
and called upon Berhtwald to hold another synod to review the case. The parties compromised by returning
Ripon and the see of Hexham to Wilfrid, who occupied
them from then (706) until his death in 709.

Wilfrid's life can be traced in a number of contemporary
documents, notably Bede's *HE* and the life by Eddius
Stephanus (see 2.8). His prominence derives only sec-
ondarily from his role in history, however, and primarily
from the controversy in which his ceaseless self-seeking
involved him. He surrounded himself with pomp and
glory—with relics (but not books) on his visits to Rome,
with some of the first stone-built ecclesiastical architecture
in the north, with a retinue that was the wonder and the
scandal of his time. If he brought the north of England
nearer Rome, it was only because he was rejected by the
north and Rome alone could restore him; the alternative
authority in Canterbury never interceded for him more
than weakly, more often proved to be the source of his
discomfort. His court included, but never rebuked, the
rash young priest who accused Bede of heresy. The only
two documents that bear his name to survive forty-five
years of episcopal rule are the petitions he presented to

Agatho and John in Rome, inserted in the life by Eddius; their subject is their author. They make it easy to understand the reluctance of two generations of English kings, bishops, and archbishops to tolerate his presence:

> Perturbationibus enim nuper in Britannia ortis ex parte eorum, qui contra decreta supradicti beatissimi Agathonis papae illiusque successorum venerabilium patrum sibimet episcopatum et monasteria terrasque cum omnibus meis facultatibus usurpabant, compulsus, hanc sacrosanctam apostolicam sedem appellavi, contestans eos per omnipotentem Deum et beatum Petrum principem apostolorum, ut si quis aliquam contra me accusationem haberet, ad vestram mecum praesentiam judicandus conveniret, sicut beati praedecessoris vestri Sergii papae scripta cernebant. Et ideo petitionum parvitatis meae paginam vestrae gloriosissimae praesentiae pro instanti vobis notissima necessitate offerendam curavi, et cum quibus vestrae solitae clementiae et benignitatis aures pulsare haec continens praesumo, ut omnia rectitudinis pietatisque, quae a beatissimis antecessoribus vestris dominis apostolicis sancto Agathone et electo Benedicto et beato Sergio unanimiter erga meam parvitatem decreta sunt, vos largiflua pietatis benevolentia confirmare dignemini.[24] (ch. 51)

Aldhelm (1.5)

Aldhelm is, with Bede and Alcuin, one of the most important pre-Conquest writers of Anglo-Latin; in size, scope, refinement, and influence his work exceeds by far

[24] For compelled by the troubles originated recently in Britain on the part of those who, contrary to the decrees of the aforesaid most blessed Pope Agatho and of his successors the venerable fathers, have usurped for themselves my bishopric and monasteries and lands with all my privileges, I have appealed to this holy apostolic see, adjuring those men by almighty God and blessed Peter, prince of the Apostles, that if anyone has any accusation against me, he should come with me to your presence to be judged, as the writings of your blessed predecessor Pope Sergius decreed. So I have sought to have delivered in your most glorious presence, on account of my present most obvious need, a document of my unworthy petitions, and with these petitions, I presume about these things to assail the ears of your accustomed clemency and benignity, that you may deign to confirm in your abounding benevolence of piety

that of anyone who wrote before him, and of almost all
those who followed him. He was also abbot of a large
monastery and bishop of a powerful see; yet his biographical remains are unreliable and uncertain. Apart
from a few lines in Bede, the earliest life—by Faricius—
was written more than four hundred years after his death,
probably when the author was residing at Malmesbury;
it was followed before 1125 by the account in the *Gesta
pontificum* by William of Malmesbury, in which the inadequacy of the life by Faricius is mentioned. A fourth
source for the life is the fourteenth-century *Eulogium
historiarum* by another monk of Malmesbury, Thomas,
but it is both too late and too brief to be of great help.
William's account commands the most respect, especially
as it points to the insufficiency of earlier accounts, promises to quote all documentary evidence, and bewails, in
good critical-historical fashion, the scantiness of that evidence. Yet this very lament, and the lateness of the work,
deprive it of much of the confidence which students of
Aldhelm might wish to accord it. Bede says (*HE* v.18)
only that Aldhelm shared with Daniel one of the two
dioceses created when the see of the West Saxons was
divided; that before, when only a priest and abbot of
"Maildufi urbs" (the community of Maeldubh), he composed a book against the paschal error of the Celtic
Church; that he wrote a book on virginity, in two forms,
hexameters and prose, emulating Sedulius; and that he
wrote some other books, "utpote vir undecumque doctissimus: nam et sermone nitidus, et scripturarum, ut dixi,
tam liberalium quam ecclesiasticarum, erat eruditione
mirandus."[25] So any account of Aldhelm's life must be

---

everything of justice and piety that was decreed unanimously on
my unworthy behalf by your most blessed predecessors the apostolic lords St. Agatho, the elect Benedict, and the blessed Sergius.

[25] As he was a most learned man in every way: for he was both
brilliant in his discourse, and admirable, as I have said, for his
reading of liberal as well as divine letters.

based on William's *Gesta pontificum*, with such reserva-
tions as the date and source urge upon the prudent.

Aldhelm was born about 640, the son of the Saxon
Kenten, who was cousin of King Ina of the West Saxons.
When he was about fifteen, his parents sent him to study
with one Maeldubh, an Irish scholar of unknown origin,
who had (about 635) settled in Selwood forest, near
Ingleborn castle, a few miles from Brockenburgh, Wiltshire. In the twenty years between his arrival and the
beginning of Aldhelm's study with him, Maeldubh had
capitalized on his great learning and few books by taking
as pupils the sons of the Saxon nobility. Through Maeldubh, Aldhelm must have been able to draw on the learning which was still, before the arrival of Theodore in
669, largely the monopoly of the Celtic Church. Through
him as well he may have learned his love for the extravagant latinity which was to become his most characteristic
stylistic habit and which was to color much Anglo-Latin
prose of the eighth century. It appears that Aldhelm
did well in the school of Maeldubh, and that he remained
there until about 670, when he was thirty. It was then
that his parents sent him to Canterbury to study with
Theodore's companion Hadrian, where Aldhelm probably
acquired his interest in Greek and Hebrew, although
Maeldubh may have had a hand in that too. Apart from
a brief visit to Wiltshire, Aldhelm remained at Canterbury
until 672, when ill-health forced him to return to Maeldubh. A letter of 675 shows him still longing to leave the
forest for the monastery school, but his own health and,
presumably, the advancing years of Maeldubh prevented
him. Aldhelm's other correspondence from this period
shows that he was gaining a reputation as a scholar and
writer from whom others could secure advice and assistance. He had as well received the monastic tonsure and
holy orders, so that when Maeldubh died—again about
675—Aldhelm was elected by his fellow-pupils as abbot

of the monastic community which they had formed. It is a confusion of the two names by which the place was later known, "Maeldubh-burg" and "Aldhelmes-burg" which produced "Malmesbury."

With the death of his master, Aldhelm surrendered any hope of further formal study and began a life of ecclesiastical toil. He did not, however, give up his writing. When he built the monastery church of SS. Peter and Paul at Malmesbury, he composed a short poem in honor of its consecration. His foundations elsewhere, like his writing, spread his fame; he built monasteries at Frome, Somerset, and Bradford, Wiltshire, both destroyed in the time of William the Conqueror. He extended the estates and the buildings of his own monastery. Around 685 he wrote the treatise *De metris* for Aldfrith, King of Northumbria, and the two books *De virginitate* for Hildelida, Abbess of Barking, near London. And so he continued during the first years of his abbacy, building and writing. About 690 he made a trip to Rome with the permission of Kings Ina of Wessex and Ethelred of Mercia, to obtain privileges for his monasteries. He remained awhile with Pope Sergius and returned about 693 bearing the privileges he had sought. Characteristically, he had built two churches on the journey, one in Dorset before he departed, and another near Frome on his return. In England his work, and especially his correspondence, continued to show the scholarly interests of a mind largely occupied with the concerns of ecclesiastical administration. In 705 both talents were called upon in the book to the Celtic Church which Bede mentioned. In the same year, at the death of Hedda, Bishop of Wessex, the see was divided, with Daniel administering the eastern half from Winchester, and Aldhelm the western section from Sherborne. He remained Abbot of Malmesbury, Bradford, and Frome on the refusal of the monks to recognize anyone in his place. Although some sixty-five years of age,

Aldhelm remained as active as before, obtaining charters in favor of the independence of his beloved monasteries, visiting throughout his enormous diocese, building a huge cathedral church at Sherborne, and maintaining his literary correspondence. He died in 709, aged about seventy.

Carmina ecclesiastica

Only three dates in Aldhelm's life are known with any certainty: his election to the abbacy of Malmesbury in 675, his elevation to the see of Sherborne in 705, and his death in 709. It is therefore convenient to review his writings in the order of their appearance in the monumental edition of Ehwald. There the first are the five *Carmina ecclesiastica* (church poems), hexameter compositions of between 13 and 278 lines celebrating a number of churches, probably on the occasion of their consecration. All five begin with the demonstrative article, suggesting that they were intended to be, or were modeled upon, dedicatory inscriptions. The first is "In basilica sanctorum Petri et Pauli"; the second "In basilica beatae Mariae semper virginis"; the third "In ecclesia Mariae a Bugge exstructa"; the fourth "In duodecim apostolorum aris"; the last "In sancti Mathiae apostoli ecclesia,"[26] of which the third and fourth titles, and the last word of the fifth, are editorial. In all likelihood these are but three poems, with only I and v standing alone. According to the theory of Mazzoni and others, II constitutes a prologue to III, while lines 40-41 of III,

> Qua fulgent arae bis seno nomine sacrae;
> Insuper absidam consecrat virginis arae,[27]

[26] For the church of Saints Peter and Paul; for the church of Blessed Mary, Ever Virgin; for the church of Mary built by Bugga; for the altars of the twelve Apostles; for the church of Saint Matthew the Apostle.

[27] Where sacred altars shine under twelve names; and above, the altar of the Virgin makes the apse holy.

are a clear anticipation of IV. Against this theory is the separate demonstrative beginning of II, III, and IV, "Hanc aulam...," "Hoc templum...," "Hanc...absidam...."[28]

The first of the five (1.7) illustrates much about Aldhelm's poetic practice, especially his overt classicism in referring to God the Father,

> Candida caelorum recludens regna tonantis

(cf. Juvencus, IV.554, "summi per regna tonantis"[29]) and his use of phrases, often whole lines, which appear elsewhere in these and other poems: lines one and two,

> Hic celebranda rudis florescit gloria templi,
> Limpida quae sacri signat vexilla triumphi,

are echoed in II.2,

> Cui veneranda rudis sacrantur culmina templi
> Et nova consurgunt sacris vexilla triumphis,[30]

a practice he carries to the point of using nineteen lines (13-31) from the second ecclesiastical song in his poem *De laudibus virginum* (1691-1709). Also to be noted in the first song is Aldhelm's use of pagan and Christian classics; line three, describing Peter and Paul as "tenebrosi lumina mundi," is part of the tradition that leads from Virgil's "clarissima mundi Lumina" (*Georg.* 1.5)[31] through Arator (II.1219) and Venantius Fortunatus (III, VII.3) to Pope Vitalian (quoted by Bede, *HE* III.29). At line six, "Claviger aetherius," he quotes Arator again (1.899); at line nine, "umectant imbribus ora,"[32] Virgil (*Aeneid* XI.90).

---

[28] This church; this temple; this apse.

[29] Opening the bright realms of the celestial Thunderer; through the realm of the high Thunderer.

[30] Here the famed glory of the new temple comes into flower, which adorns the bright banners of holy victory; to whom the pinnacles of the holy new temple are consecrated, and to whom the new banners rise up in holy victories.

[31] The lights of the shadowy world; brightest lights of the world.

[32] Heavenly key-bearer; they water their mouths with rain.

Another characteristic of Aldhelm's verse is his poetic paraphrase of Scripture, found among the *Carmina ecclesiastica* II.20-22; 23ff.; IV.ii.6; IV.xii.14-15. The latter example

> Dicens, "Ecce, venit dominus cum millibus almis
> Ponere judicium cunctis habitantibus orbem!"

paraphrasing Jude 14ff.,

> dicens, "Ecce, venit dominus in sanctis millibus
> suis, Facere judicium contra omnes . . ."[33]

is a fair example of the kind of change Aldhelm makes in adapting his source to the hexameter line.

The texture of Aldhelm's verse has often been said to be less elaborate than that of his prose. While such is no doubt the case, the verse is ornate enough. His fondness for certain verbal effects leads him, as we have seen, to repeat them: so "Dum mergi meruit baptismi gurgite felix" (III.28); "Omnes certatim merguntur gurgite sacro" (IV.viii.10); "Piscibus insidias nectens sub gurgite ponti" (IV.v.6)[34] culminating in

> Ergo diem ac noctem ponti sub gurgite mersus
> Magna supernarum meruit spectacula rerum.[35]
>
> (IV.ii.7-8)

Similar are the parallelisms, such as

> Turgida cum ratibus sulcabat caerula curvis
>
> . . . .
>
> Algida ventosis crepitabant carbasa flabris.[36]
>
> (III.20, 22)

---

[33] Saying, "Behold, the Lord comes with his thousands of souls to judge the world with all those who dwell therein"; saying, "Behold, the Lord cometh with thousands of his saints, to execute judgment upon all."

[34] When the blessed one was worthy to be submerged in the flood of baptism; all shall certainly be submerged in the holy flood; imprisoning the treachery among the fish under the flood of the deep.

[35] Therefore submerged day and night under the flood of the deep, he earned the great visions of celestial things.

[36] He ploughed the swollen sea with his curved boats . . . the icy sails crackled in the gusty winds.

[74]

To such parallelism is added alliteration (IV.i.11-15),

> Ut sibi salvator vera cum voce spopondit,
> Quando piscantem panda de puppe vocavit.
> Qui ponti pedibus calcavit caerula glauci,
> Sed mare mergentem tumidis non sorbuit undis,
> Dextera dum Christi turgentia marmora pressit,[37]

here, as often in Aldhelm, alliteration on "p" (cf. IV.ii. 10-12, and *Epistola* v, beginning).

The taste for alliteration may have been reinforced by the techniques of Old English vernacular poetry, in which alliteration was the organizing principle; but it may, like Aldhelm's interest in rhyme, have come through the tradition of Latin hymnody. He uses suppressed rhymes like "correptus aegrescit" (III.29) ;[38] slant end-rhyme, like

> Cerneret ut numquam splendentem lumine Phoebum?
> Cruribus atque suris claudum restaurat aegrotum,
> Quem fortuna prius gressu privavit egentem;[39]
>
> (IV.ii.17-19)

and full end-rhyme, like

> Claudum restaurat fretus virtute tonantis
> Et cito sanatis praecepit pergere plantis.[40]
>
> (IV.i.20-21)

Aldhelm's poetic technique, then, mixes classical language and style—he rarely admits a false quantity (but see IV.xiii.6)—with those of later Latin authors and prac-

[37] As the savior truly promised him, when He called the fisherman from the curved stern. He trod the waters of the azure flood with His feet, but the sea did not suck down the wader with swollen waves, when the power of Christ struck the foamy turbulence.

[38] He takes ill.

[39] Did he see the sun glowing with light as never before? And he restores the poor cripple with atrophied legs, the wretch to whom fortune previously denied the power of walking.

[40] The faithful one by the power of the Thunderer restores the cripple and quickly he learns to go forth on feet made well.

tices, suggesting that his literary perspective was fore-shortened, and that pagan and Christian poets were equally "classics," equally models for imitation, to him.

The date of the *Carmina ecclesiastica*—even the identity of the churches for which they were written—is uncertain. Faricius thought that the first was written in Rome but as Ehwald points out, it corresponds to no known Roman basilica. Moreover, Mazzoni has noted, following Cogliani, that there is no reference to the city of Rome, and the word "rudis," which means in Aldhelm "new," would scarcely apply to a Roman church. The poem is not necessarily as late as Aldhelm's trip to Rome, then, and it may be the one which William mentions in connection with the church Aldhelm built at Malmesbury, when he became abbot in 675.

The second—or second, third, and fourth—poem refers to a church built by Bugga. She was a princess of Wessex and daughter of the King Cadwalla whose death is mentioned III.30-32. (She is not to be confused with the friend of St. Boniface, nor with a sister of Aldhelm, nor with a daughter of Abbess Dunne of Withington.) The date of the poem is, most probably, shortly after the death of Cadwalla, ca. 689-690. Nothing about the date of the subject of the fifth poem can be determined.

Epistola ad Acircium

We may now turn to the *Epistola ad Acircium*, although the phrase in it, "alibi poeta dicit 'Petrus apostolicae qui culmina praesidet arcis,' "[41] may refer to his own poem *De virginitate* (line 530), and suggests that *De virginitate* was already finished when the *Epistola* was written. Aldhelm's borrowings from himself are frequent, and they have often been used by scholars who sought to determine the order of his works; but this is

[41] Elsewhere a poet has written, "Peter, who presides over the summit of the apostolic citadel."

[76]

almost the only instance in which the priority of one appearance of a phrase over another can be demonstrated. Of the date of *De virginitate*, see below.

The *Epistola* is dedicated "Acircio aquilonalis,"[42] a double way of referring to the ruler of the north, Aldfrith of Northumbria. Aldhelm says that twenty years had passed since he was sponsor at Aldfrith's baptism. Since Aldfrith did not come to the throne until 685, the poem which refers to him as king cannot be earlier than that; Bönhoff believes that it was composed on the occasion of his tenth anniversary. Aldfrith died in 705. Both Bede (*HE* iv.24, v.12) and Alcuin (*De SS. Eboracensis ecclesiae*, 843-845) testify to the scholarly interests of the king, and Cook has suggested that it was under his patronage that the Old English *Beowulf* was composed. He was married to Cuthburga, daughter of King Ina of Wessex, and so was not only Aldhelm's godson but his cousin by marriage, as well as, in all probability, his one-time student at Malmesbury.

The book's full title, *De metris et aenigmatibus ac pedum regulis* (in some MSS, the words *Liber de septenario, et . . .* [43] are prefixed), outlines the structure of the work. The first of the three parts describes the metrical rules for the hexameter line; the second gives examples of these rules in a hundred riddles; and the third defines and describes the feet of two, three, and four syllables which are used to compose a hexameter. Aldhelm's work is, in large measure, that of a compiler and editor, and there is not—except in the riddles—much of originality in the *Epistola*. But of his many sources, only one, Aldhelm himself, is British, and his remarks in the "Allocutio excusativa ad regem"[44] at the end of the work explain the

[42] To the northwind of the northern kingdom.
[43] On meters, riddles, and the rules for metrical feet; a book on the number seven, and . . . .
[44] Explanatory address to the king.

significance of this limitation. Aldhelm begs Aldfrith to accept the work, for

> constat neminem nostrae stirpis prosapia genitum et Germanicae gentis cunabulis confotum in hujuscemodi negotio ante nostram mediocritatem tantopere desudasse priorumque argumenta ingeniorum juxta metricae artis disciplinam litterarum textui tradidisse praesertim inter tot tantosque saecularium rerum tumultuantes strepitus constitutum et ecclesiastica pastoralis curae sollicitudine depressum, quibus mens meticulosa ac scrupulosa quasi quodam artissimo catenarum repagulo constringitur. Non enim hoc proferendo horrendis superciliorum jaculis me vulnerandum arbitror neque dirissima elationis turgidae falarica confixum perhorresco, si paulisper de gratuita divini muneris gratia, quae singulis quibusque non meritorum praecurrentium praerogativa, sed caelestis beneficii munificentia confertur, fretus domino glorier, siquidem illustris ille, qui dicebat

> > Primus ego in patriam mecum, modo vita supersit,
> > Aonio rediens deducam vertice Musas;
> > Primus Idumaeas referam tibi, Mantua, palmas . . .

> hoc, inquam, ille versificans significari voluit, nullum ante se Latinorum georgica Romulidis scripsisse, quamvis Hesiodus et Homerus et ceteri Graeci disertitudinis facundia freti et Argolicae urbanitatis privilegio praediti quadrifariam agriculturam lingua Pelasga deprompserint.[45]

(ch. 142)

[45] Evidently no man born of the stock of our race and nurtured in the cradle of the Germanic nation has, earlier than my humble self, labored so much at this subject, and has transmitted the arguments of earlier scholars about learning the metrical art in a literary text, especially one set among so many and such confused conflicts of worldly things and weighted down by the ecclesiastical concern of pastoral care, by which the careful and scrupulous mind is fettered as though by the most narrow constraint of chains. For by saying this I do not think that I deserve to be wounded by the fearful shafts of the supercilious, nor do I fear to be pierced by the most dire spear of swollen pride, if relying on the Lord I boast somewhat of the freely given grace of that divine gift (which is conferred on each, not through the prerogative of previous merits, but by the munificence of heavenly goodness), just like that famous one who said: I first, as long as life lasts, shall lead the Muses with me, returning to my own land from the Aonian height; I, O

Mention of Aldfrith's baptism, and of the seven fold gifts of the Holy Spirit which accompany the sacrament, leads Aldhelm to a discussion of the allegorical significance of the number seven which occupies almost half of the first section of the work. He quotes passages from the Old and New Testaments illustrating the significance of the number, and supplements them with examples of the importance of seven in nature and in the arts of men. He concludes,

> Cum igitur tot tantisque sacramentorum vinculis tamque sacratis numerorum nexibus per septiformem spiritus gratiam caritas constringatur . . . et quamvis catholici patres spiritalem sermonum medullam enucleantes latentemque in litteris sensum perscrutantes allegorice ad synagogae typum retulerint, nullatenus tamen sacrosanctae matris personam fuisse historica relatione infitiari noscuntur.[46]

(ch. 4)

Aldhelm apologizes for "epistolarem . . . rusticitatem" and "meam mediocritatem"[47] and hopes that the years of separation from Aldfrith will not have diminished their friendship. He proposes to write a hundred riddles on the model of Symphosius, or like those which so occupied Aristotle's attention. He will allow inanimate objects to

---

Mantua, will first bring back the palms of Idumea to you [Virgil, *Georg.* iii.11-13] . . . by this, I say, he meant to signify in verse that no Roman before him had written a poem on the foundation of Rome, even though Hesiod and Homer and other Greeks, relying on the eloquence of expression and endowed with the special gift of Argolic cultivation, brought forth a fourfold harvest in the ancient Greek tongue.

[46] Although therefore charity is bound up by such and so many chains of symbols and by the holy entwining of numbers through the seven fold grace of the Spirit . . . and although the studious exegetical fathers of the Church have recovered the inmost meaning of discourse and the sense hidden in the letters allegorically applied to the type of the Synagogue, yet they are in no sense known to deny the person of the holy mother to have been present in the historical narrative.

[47] Epistolary lack of polish; my mediocrity.

speak (prosopopoeia), not on classical authority, but on biblical, as in Judges 9:8, IV Kings 14:9, Ps. 95:12, and so forth. He proposes to differ from his model, first in exceeding the three-line form of Symphosius, and second —as he points out later in the verse preface, lines 7-8—in revealing the secrets of his subjects; so each riddle is headed by the solution. They are not riddles at all, but ingenious devices for demonstrating the basic rules of hexameter composition, and before Aldhelm comes to them, he reviews the forms of the hexameter line.

To do so he makes use of the dialogue between student and master which had been popular before him (e.g. Junillus' *Praefatio ad instituta regularia divinae legis*, in Christian times, as well as the Socratic dialogues in pre-Christian) and after him (e.g., Aelfric's *Colloquy*). He signifies the master by a form of the Greek M, the student by the Greek D. Ehwald has observed that the significance of the letters is reversed in Junillus, where M=Μαθητης (the learner), and Δ=Διδασκαλος (the teacher). But Μαθητης in the New Testament is translated as *discipulus* (student) in the Vulgate, and Διδασκαλος as *magister* (teacher), so it does not seem, as Ehwald suggested, that Aldhelm is confused by a poor manuscript of his source, but simply that he is using the Latin equivalents of the Greek words, and transliterating their initial letters into Greek, which—as it happens—gives the reverse of the original arrangement. Aldhelm further differs from Junillus in that it is the student who asks all the questions, and the teacher who answers them. In Aldhelm's arrangement, it is still Δ who questions and M who answers, but it does not appear that this represents a confusion on his part; both arrangements were common enough in medieval grammatical and theological dialogues. The dialogue itself proceeds in this fashion:

> Δ Quot sunt genera versuum in dactylico metro?
> M Quinque. Δ Quid est dactylicum metrum?

M Quod constat dactylo et spondeo.

Δ Nonne plerumque ultimus pes trocheo terminatur? **M** Quia nonnulli metricae artis peritia praediti hunc pedem de versu excludendum censuerunt, quia omnis syllaba in ultimo versu adiaphoros est, id est indifferenter accipitur nec interest, utrum corripiatur an producatur; unde a quibusdam vitiosus versus putatur, qui trocheum admittit. Nam ratio exigit, ut in pleno versu xxiv tempora sint; admisso itaque trocheo minuitur temporum numerus et erunt tempora xxiii, qui est versus colobos. **Δ** Superius dixisti v genera versuum esse in dactylico hexametro; quae sint, nominatim dicito. **M** Hexameter, pentameter, tetrameter, trimeter, dimeter.

Δ Hexameter rectius dicitur an hexamatrus?

M Utrumque ut Evander et Evandrus, quorum unum venit ex Graeca enuntiatione, alterum ex Latina,[48]

(ch. 10)

through a discussion of the arrangement of the hexameter line, the feet, ellipsis, and the caesurae, concluding with six verse examples of which the first two are from Symphosius, the third from Prosper of Aquitaine, the fourth and fifth from Virgil, the last from Paulinus of Nola. Elsewhere Aldhelm also quotes from himself— usually lines he has made up for the sake of an example, but sometimes borrowed from other works—and from Lucan, Juvencus, Sedulius very often; from Arator,

[48] D. How many sorts of verses are there in dactylic meter? M. Five. D. What is the dactylic meter? M. That which is made up of dactyls and spondees. D. Do not some end in a trochee? M. Yes, because some of those gifted with skill in metrical art believe that the last foot is to be excluded from the line, for the syllable in the end of the line is always adiaphoros, that is, it is felt indifferently and is not significant whether it is shortened or lengthened; whence that is thought a defective verse by some, which admits a trochee. Nevertheless, the rule demands that in a full verse there should be twenty-four divisions of time, and if a trochee is admitted the number of divisions is reduced and there will be only twenty-three, which is a curtailed line. D. Above you said that there were five sorts of dactylic hexameter; tell me what they are by name. M. Hexameter, pentameter, tetrameter, trimeter, dimeter. D. Is it more correctly called "hexameter" or "hexametrus"? M. Both, like Evander and Evandrus, of which one comes from the Greek way of saying it, the other from the Latin.

Ovid, Corripus, and Fortunatus frequently; from Terence, Seneca, Persius, Juvenal, Ausonius, Prudentius, Claudian, Sidonius Apollinaris, and Horace less often. His chief source through the grammatical and rhetorical sections is Priscian, and to a lesser extent Priscian's sources, Phocas and Suetonius; Audax, Donatus, Donatus' commentator Sergius, Cassiodorus and his source Pompeius, and others, are also used. Since a good many of Aldhelm's quotations from poetry appear in Priscian as well, it is not possible to be sure how many of them he knew first hand: the scarcity and high cost of books must have thwarted his curiosity frequently. Nonetheless he had an energetic mind and a highly developed poetic talent, and it is not necessary to think that all his wide acquaintance with Latin poetry was gained mainly through selections in other grammars.

The first section ends with a request from the student for the riddles he had been promised. The section is entitled "Aenigmata Aldhelmi." While there are nine MSS of the entire work, there are seventeen others of the riddles alone, including at least one (Leningrad Q.1.15), of the eighth century, older than the earliest MS of the whole *Epistola*. Some of these early MSS of the riddles alone—Karlsruhe 85, for example, of the eighth or ninth century—lack both the acrostic prologue (see below) and the titles of the riddles, so that, with the solutions and the grammatical context missing, they become very different things from the didactic exercises which Aldhelm intended them to be. Their popularity apart from the metrical lessons shows that Aldhelm's intentions were not, perhaps, so pertinent to following centuries as to his own; long after the metrics, which he was proud to be the first of his race to study, became commonplace, the riddles which accompanied it were enjoyed and admired.

The prologue of thirty-six lines is acrostic-telestich,

reading down on both ends of the line "Aldhelmus cecinit millenis versibus odas"[49] (cf. the acrostic and inverted telestich beginning *De virginitate*). There are not a thousand lines—the figure is meant to represent a large number, as in *De virginitate* 2895, "Dum decies denis modulantes millibus odis."[50] Aldhelm asks God to aid him in his task of writing the riddles; he will call on no Castalian nymphs nor seek the peaks of Cynthus or Parnassus, for God inspired the prophet Moses and the psalmist.

> Verum si fuerint bene haec aenigmata versu
> Explosis penitus naevis et rusticitate
> Ritu dactylico recte decursa nec error
> Seduxit vana specie molimina mentis,[51]
>
> (Pref., 25-28)

he will begin his task.

The riddles are not only models of composition of the hexameter line; they are models of short poems. None is as short as Symphosius' three-line riddle; they start from four lines (I-XVII, except VIII), five lines (XVIII-XXVIII, except XIX), six, seven, or eight (XXIX-XLV), and vary from four to twelve (XLVI-XCIV), thirteen, sixteen, and sixteen (XCV-XCVII), and seven (XCVIII-IC), observing a rough kind of progression. The hundredth riddle, *Creatura*, that is, all of Creation, is eighty-three lines long, and as it subsumes everything mentioned in the first ninety-nine, serves as a kind of conclusion to balance the prologue, although it has a typical riddling last line, "Sciscitor inflatos, fungar quo nomine, sophos."[52]

The subjects of Aldhelm's riddles are nature and human art. Of the former, there are the wind, earth, cloud,

[49] Aldhelm wrote poems in a thousand lines.

[50] As ten times ten thousand poems are sung.

[51] If truly these riddles may have the blemishes and lack of polish thoroughly removed from the verse, if they may be completed in the dactylic manner, and error does not pervert the labors of the mind with his false appearance.

[52] I ask the proud wise men by what name I go.

rainbow, moon, pleiades, diamond, silkworm, peacock, sal-
amander (and a number of other animals, including the
minotaur, unicorn, scylla, and elephant), the yew tree,
apple tree, and fig tree. Of the latter, there are the bellows, the organ, file, balance, whetstone, spindle, cauldron,
candle, dagger, mill, sieve, trumpet, and wine cup. The
Tall Lighthouse (xcii) has been thought, without
reason, to represent an edifice known to Aldhelm, although in fact only a few of the subjects give evidence of
the special interests of the author (alphabet, organ, writing tablets, pen, chrismal, bookcase), while the treatment
of a few others (raven, dove, sun, and moon) shows the
same; superficially at least, the riddles are impersonal and
secular.

No order is discernible in the series, although occasional
pairings like the raven and the dove, or the fish and
Colossus are found (lxxi, lxxii) :

> Me pedibus manibusque simul fraudaverat almus
> Arbiter, immensum primo dum pangeret orbem.
> Fulcior haud volitans veloci praepetis ala
> Spiritus alterno vegitat nec corpora flatu.
> Quamvis in caelis convexa cacumina cernam,
> Non tamen undosi contemno marmora ponti.
>
> Omnia membra mihi plasmavit corporis auctor,
> Nec tamen ex isdem membrorum munia sumpsi,
> Pergere nec plantis oculis nec cernere possum,
> Quamquam nunc patulae constent sub fronte fenestrae.
> Nullus anhelanti procedit viscere flatus
> Spicula nec geminis nitor torquere lacertis.
> Heu! frustra factor confinxit corpus inorme,
> Totis membrorum dum frauder sensibus intus.[53]

[53] The fair Judge, when first He made the great world, cheated
me of hands and feet at once. I am not supported in flight by the
wing of a swift bird nor does the wind liven my body with repeated
blasts. Although I may look upon the high vaults of heaven, yet I
do not scorn the foamy surface of the billowing sea. The Maker
of my body fashioned all my members, but I have had no service
from them, I cannot walk with my feet or see with my eyes,
though now windows stand open under my brows. No breath

There are certain kinds of tricks, although the practice—
in the original, at least—of putting titles on the riddles
makes trickery a bit pointless. Aldhelm capitalizes on the
paradoxes that can be spun on the idea of a pregnant
sow, "Nunc mihi sunt oculi bis seni in corpore solo/ Bis
ternumque caput. . . ,"[54] and he plays with clues hidden
in the alphabet: "Littera tollatur: post haec sine prole
manebo," *corbus/ orbus* (LXIII); "Littera quindecima
praestat, quod pars domus adsto,"[55] *aries/paries* (LXXXVI).
He refers to the (supposed) Greek etymology of a word
(*nycticorax*, XXXV; *heliotropus*, LI) or the classical authors who have written about it ("Facundum constat
quondam cecinisse poetam. . . ," VII).[56] Many of these
characteristics are borrowed from Symphosius, and became part of the English literary tradition largely through
Aldhelm's work. They found their way into the vernacular
in the riddles of the Exeter Book, for many of which
Aldhelm seems to have been the inspiration, and sometimes the source, and in later Latin verse in the riddles of
Tatwine, Hwaetberht, and Boniface. It was in opening
out the form from the three lines of Symphosius to his
own four to sixteen; in making the homely objects of
everyday life, as well as the exotic beasts of legend and
the mighty phenomena of nature, the subjects of his riddles; and in placing before his readers a contemporary
example of a writer practicing a "classical" form, that
Aldhelm had his greatest influence in the riddles. The
evidence of the rest of the *Epistola*, and of the surviving
MSS, is that his intention in this matter was otherwise,
and that it counted for little.

---

comes from my panting viscera, nor do I strive to throw darts with
my twin arms. Alas! In vain my Maker made me a great body,
since within it I lack all feeling of my parts.
[54] Now I have twelve eyes and six heads in a single body.
[55] A letter is taken away; after that I am left without progeny.
If the fifteenth letter is present, I am part of a house.
[56] An eloquent poet is known to have written once.

Magister goes on to describe the four feet of two syllables, the eight feet of three syllables, and the sixteen feet
of four syllables. For each foot Aldhelm gives a number of
words as examples, as well as hints on which inflections
most commonly offer examples of a given foot. In the
discussion of ionicus minor, magister gets sidetracked into
listing the traditional sounds of animals and things (following chiefly Suetonius):

> Δ Pande exempla vocis confusae de diversis rerum naturis
> congesta! M Haec sunt species vocis confusae, ut majorum
> auctoritas tradidit. Nam apes ambizant vel bombizant, aquilae
> clangunt, anseres crinciunt vel trinsiunt, aves minuriunt vel
> vernant vel vernicant, accipitres pipant vel plipiant, anates
> teritisant, arietes crissitant vel blaterant, asini oncant vel
> rudunt, apri frendunt, arma crepant, aes tinnit, amphora
> profusa bilibit, boves mugiunt vel reboant, cornices butant,
> . . . tigrides raccant, tubae clangiunt, tauri mugiunt, vul-
> tures pionpant, venti flant vel tremunt vel sibilant, ursi
> urgant vel saeviunt, vulpes ejulant, verres quiritant; item
> homines loquuntur, rustici jubilant et reliqua similia. Haec
> genera vocum non ad ionicum pertinebunt, sed discretionis
> gratia prolata sunt.[57]   (ch. 131)

He passes on from the discussion of metrical feet to a
look at the effect of compounding prepositions with verbs,
and a short chapter on prosody—"prosodia est signum
sermonis iter rectum faciens legenti"[58]—including the ten
marks (acutus, gravis, circumflexus, longa, brevis, dasia,

[57] D. Give examples of the confused [as distinct from "articu-
late"] voice, made up of different sorts of things. M. Here are
the kinds of discordant voice, as the authority of most writers
gives them. Bees hum or buzz, eagles scream, geese cackle or hiss,
birds tweet or twitter or chirp, hawks pipe or whistle, ducks quack,
rams bellow or bleat, asses whinny or bray, boars gnash their
teeth, weapons rattle, copper tinkles, an empty jar rings, cows moo
or call, crows caw . . . tigers roar, trumpets blast, bulls moo,
vultures whistle, winds blow or rattle or whistle, bears threaten
or rage, wolves howl, boars scream; also men speak, countryfolk
sport, and the like for the rest. These sorts of words have nothing
to do with the ionic, but are offered for the sake of tasteful use.
[58] Prosody is a figure to aid in the right way of reading.

psili, apostrophus, hyphen, hypodiastoli) and the four characteristics which they signify: tone, beat, respiration, and
"passio . . . vox passibilis conjuncta et unita et divisibilia
discernens. . . ."[59] His last chapter in the rhetoric deals
with synzigia.

Part of the "Allocutio excusativa ad regem," notable
for its rhyming prose, has already been quoted. In it
Aldhelm calls upon Aldfrith not only to rule his country
justly and well, but to emulate that Theodosius who
copied out the entirety of Priscian's grammar by hand,
and chiefly to remember that life is brief, eternity long.

De virginitate

The two works called *De virginitate*—they are sometimes distinguished by calling the prose work *De laudibus
virginitatis* and the poem *De laudibus virginum*—are the
"opus geminatum" of which Bede spoke in his short notice
of Aldhelm. It is clear that the prose version was written
first:

> Porro quemadmodum intactae virginitatis gloriam rhetoricis
> relatibus favorabiliter venerari nitebar, sic itidentidem, si
> hoc carneum animae ergastulum ante fatis, ut dicitur, crude-
> scentibus cassabundum non obierit ac dura Parcarum quies et
> ferreus leti somnus palpebrarum convolatus non tricaverit,
> heroicis hexametrorum versibus ejusdem praeconium pudici-
> tiae subtiliter comere Christo cooperante conabor et, velut
> jactis jam rhetoricis fundamentis et constructis prosae parieti-
> bus, cum tegulis trochaicis et dactylicis metrorum imbricibus
> firmissimum culmen caelesti confisus suffragio imponam,[60]

[59] Feeling . . . a voice of feeling, expressing things in a unified
way while observing the different items.
[60] Moreover, just as I strove to venerate the glory of true virginity favorably in literary narratives, so likewise, if this tottering
fleshly prison of the soul does not first, as the saying goes, perish
through the animosity of the Fates, and if the painful repose of
the Parcas and the iron sleep of death, the shutting of the eyelids,
does not afflict me, I shall strive to compose the praise of the same
modesty suitably in heroic verses of hexameter with the aid of
Christ, and, just as once I did upon the settled foundations of

[87]

he says in ch. 60 of the prose work, and

> Da pius auxilium clemens, ut carmine possim
> Inclita sanctorum modulari gesta priorum,
> Ut prius ex prosa laudabat littera castos;
> Sic modo heroica stipulentur carmina laudem,
> Ut fasti seriem memini dixisse priorem
> Et dudum prompsit voto spondente libellus![61]

(lines 17-22)

But the date of the two is another matter, resting largely on the interpretation of

> Fateor caritati vestrae, quod hoc opusculum, licet constet minusculum, pastoralis curae sarcina gravatus negotiorumque terrenorum ponderibus oppressus ita perniciter, ut sategistis, dictare vobisque destinare nequiverim, quia securae quietis spatium et morosam dictandi intercapidinem scrupulosa ecclesiastici regiminis sollicitudo denegabat et tumultuans saecularium strepitus obturbabat.[62]

(ch. 59)

If "pastoralis" is taken literally, then the prose work cannot be earlier than 705, when Aldhelm was elevated to the episcopacy. Bönhoff, on this assumption, dates it at the first half of 706, with the verse version seeing completion by summer 707 (cf. verses 336ff.). Wildman notes that

---

rhetoric and among the established walls of prose, now I shall add the most firm roof-ridge with trochaic and dactylic roofing tiles, confident of heaven's help.

[61] Give help, O holy and merciful one, so that I may be able to sing in a poem the famous deeds of bygone saints, as before I praised the chaste ones in words of prose; thus may the heroic poetry call forth praise, as (I remember) the earlier sequence of festivals spoke it, and as the little book recently uttered it as a promised offering.

[62] I declare to your charity that, however small it may be, I have been unable to write and send this little work to you quickly enough to satisfy you, borne down as I was by the burden of pastoral care and oppressed by the weight of earthly matters, because scrupulous concern for the administration of the Church ruled out any space of secure quiet and lengthy interval for composition, and the disturbing call of worldly things deafened me.

Aldhelm quotes five lines of the poem in his letter to
Ehfrith, and in the same letter he refers to Theodore of
Canterbury as still alive. Since Theodore died in 690,
Wildman would place the poem before that date, the prose
even earlier. But Mazzoni rejects the dating of this or any
work on the basis of quoted lines. He points out that the
verse quotations in chs. 20 and 36 of the prose work re-
appear in the poem and although he does not seem to have
known that these lines are from Sedulius' *Carmen
paschale*, his argument is still valid: Aldhelm may, in
the lines he reproduces in the letter to Ehfrith, not be
quoting from himself at all, but rather from an earlier,
thus far unidentified, poet. Mazzoni prefers to ignore the
evidence of repeated lines as too indefinite and contra-
dictory, then, and to look at other internal evidence. He
interprets the phrases "ad pontificale . . . conciliabulum
fraternis sodalium catervis comitatus"[63] as referring to the
council of 694, and concludes that the prose cannot be
earlier. He notes too that the letter of Cellanus of
Peronne, praising Aldhelm's literary fame, does not mention a heroic poem, and since the letter from Cellanus
calls Aldhelm an archimandrite—i.e., an abbot—we must
date it before he became a bishop in 705. Mazzoni says,
reasonably enough, that "pontificalis curae" could as easily
apply to the duties of an abbot as to those of a bishop; but
he does not take into account the possibility that the
poem, written for a group of Barking nuns, did not reach
Peronne for sometime after its composition, or the fact
that the letter from Cellanus in any case survives in a
fragment of only a few lines. The materials for dating
the "opus geminatum," then, are several, but they lead to
conflicting conclusions. There is, in fact, no real authority
for assigning any date in particular to the double work.
When Cook talks about characteristics of Aldhelm's later

[63] A companion at the bishops' council in the brotherly crowds
of membership.

prose style as a criterion for determining the authenticity of a charter, he is using very shaky evidence.

The work is, as Bede's phrase suggests, by and large the same thing in two literary forms. There are, however, some variations in contents and treatment. Aldhelm's sources for both treatises include his usual pagan and Christian "classical" models, and in addition the already large body of hagiography that had grown up in the West. It comprised original compositions in Latin and translations into Latin from Greek, notably Gregory's *Dialogues* in the first class and Rufinus' translation and continuation of Eusebius' *Historia ecclesiastica*, and his translation of the *Historia monachorum*, in the second. Several of the women saints especially seem to have been included for the benefit of nuns at Barking who had taken their names—Justina, Thecla, and Eulalia.

Aldhelm's description of the life of these nuns, many of whom came from royal or at least noble families, implies a high level of learning among female religious at the end of the seventh century: "Uberrimam . . . verborum facundiam ac virginalem urbanitatis disertitudinem magnopere admirarer,"[64] and the language he uses in the remainder of his work, if he meant it to be understood, confirms that impression:

> Nunc quadrifaria evangelicae relationis dicta mysticis catholicorum patrum commentariis exposita et ad medullam usque spiritaliter enucleata ac quadriformis ecclesiasticae traditionis normulis secundum historiam, allegoriam, tropologiam, anagogen digesta solerter indagando, nunc priscas historiographorum fabulas et chronographorum seriem, qui fortuitas praeteritorum permutationes temporum tenaci memoriae textu tradiderunt, rite rimando, nunc grammaticorum et orthographorum disciplinas . . . tonis temporibus trutinatas, pedibus poeticis compactas, per cola et commata hoc est penti-

[64] I wonder greatly at the most copious fluency of words and the virginal eloquence of polish.

[90]

memerin et heptimemerin diremptas, immo centenis metrorum generibus sequestratim discretas sagaciter inquirendo.[65]

(ch. 4)

The nuns, he says, are like bees in their diligence and their industry, and he cites scriptural and patristic authorities for the comparison. The consciousness of his audience returns at the conclusion of both works:

> Rimosa namque fragilis ingenii barca dirae tempestatis turbine quassata, licet laborante lacertorum remigio, optatum silentii portum sero attigit; sed tamen nostrae rusticitatis stipulatio superno Christi patrocinio freta fiducialiter confidit, quod nostrarum carbasa antennarum prosperis ventorum flaminibus sinuata quasi inter Scyllam soloecismi et barbarismi barathrum indisruptis rudentibus feliciter transfretaverint, scopulosas quoque labdacismi collisiones et myotacismi voragines incautos quosque sine grammaticorum gubernaculo repertos ad erroris naufragia truciter trudentes minime perhorruerint.[66]
> (ch. 59)

[65] Now by skillful exploration, the fourfold meaning of the evangelical narrative is revealed in the mystical commentaries of the Catholic fathers and spiritually laid bare to the marrow, and divided into the fourfold levels of ecclesiastical tradition according to the historical, allegorical, tropological, and anagogical senses; by due examination now of the early tales of historians, and the lists of chronologers, who have reported the chance changes of bygone times in the tenacious text of memory, now of the teaching of grammarians and orthographers . . . weighed in accents and divisions of time, full of poetic feet, divided by parts of verse and caesuras, that is, after two and a half or three and a half feet, and indeed separated distinctly into a hundred sorts of meter.

[66] Now the cracked boat of my frail invention has been shaken by the fierce wind, by the laboring oar of the muscles, in late evening it comes to the desired port of silence; but still the faithful prayer of my rusticity confidently relies on the heavenly gift of Christ, with which the sails of our sailyards, bellied by the prosperous blowing of the winds, as though between the Scylla of solecism and the Charybdis of barbarism, have happily crossed the sea with ropes unbroken, careless of wreck on the rocks of too many L's and the whirlpools of too many M's and which, found without the pilot of the grammarians, wildly pressing close to the shipwreck of error, were hardly afraid.

[91]

Jam tempus cogit currentes cludere versus
Rustica magnificis condentem carmina sanctis,
Terminus aequoreo dum venit margine metri;
Ponti spumosas ut nauta transfretat undas,
Maxima permodica emensus mox caerula lintre
Attigit optatum lassus de gurgite litus
Turgida ventosis deponens carbasa malis
Antennasque simul solvens de parte rudentum.
Ancora fluctivagam nunc sistat metrica barcam,
Ut saltem in portu quassatus navita flustris
Ad requiem tendens optata sorte fruatur![67]

(lines 2801-2811)

The pattern of the metrical *De virginitate*, as the parallel passages suggest, follows fairly closely that of the prose. An addition, however, sometimes printed separately, is the section *De octo vitiis principalibus*. Another addition in the hexameter version is the preface, in which Aldhelm again introduces an acrostic and telestich, as he had done in the preface to his riddles. This time the phrase is "Metrica tirones nunc promant carmina castos,"[68] which appears in the first line, in the acrostic reading down, in the telestich reading up, and in the last (38th) line reading backward, "Sotsac animrac tnamorp cnun senorit acirtem," which is meaningless and metrically imperfect. Aldhelm could, in his poetry as well as in his prose, invent more difficulties for himself and his reader than even his ingenuity could solve. Nonetheless, he was not simply a well-trained and ingenious poet. He was capable of fresh, correct, compelling versification which, even when it praises an ideal almost forgotten, is perfectly memorable:

[67] Now the time draws close to end the running verses forming the unpolished poem about magnificent saints, when the port nears on the watery shore of meter; as the sailor crosses the foamy waves of the sea, the weary traveler on the great ocean in a tiny skiff arrives at the desired shore from the flood, putting away the sails full of evil winds and at the same time unbinding them from the sailyards. Now the metrical anchor checks the sea-wandering boat, so that the sailor finally in port, shaken by the sea tides, going to his rest, may enjoy his chosen lot.

[68] Now the metrical songs describe the chaste youths.

Vinea frugiferis ut constat gloria campis,
Pampinus immensos dum gignit palmite botros
Vinitor et spoliat frondentes falcibus antes;
Sidera praeclaro cedunt ut lumine solis,
Lustrat dum terras obliquo tramite Titan
Cuncta supernorum convincens astra polorum:
Sic quoque virginitas, quae sanctos inclita comit,
Omnia sanctorum transcendens, praemia supplet.[69]

(lines 177-184)

Letters

Ehwald prints ten letters by Aldhelm. The first, addressed to Leutherius, Bishop of Winchester, was written
while Aldhelm was still a student at Canterbury, that is,
before 675; Ehwald dates it 671. Aldhelm expresses his
regret that he will not be able to be at Malmesbury for
Christmas. His studies, he says, keep him at Canterbury:

> Sed de his prolixo ambitu verborum ratiocinari stricta
> epistolaris angustia minime sinit, quomodo videlicet ipsius
> metricae artis clandestina instrumenta litteris, logis, pedibus,
> poeticis figuris, versibus, tonis, temporibus conglomerentur,
> pathetica quoque septenae divisionis disciplina hoc est
> acephalos, lagaros, procilios cum ceteris qualiter varietur, qui
> versus monoschemi, qui pentaschemi, qui decaschemi certa
> pedum mensura trutinentur et qualiter catalectici vel
> brachicatalectici seu hypercatalectici versus sagaci argumenta-
> tione colligantur.[70]

[69] Just like the viney glory of the fruitful plain, when the vine-
leaf puts forth immense grapes on the shoot, and the vinedresser
strips the leafy rows with his sickle; just like the stars which go
about in the bright light of the sun, when Titan travels over the
world on his slanting path, defeating all the stars of the furthest
poles: so also famous virginity, which adorns the saints, supplies
their every gift beyond compare.

[70] But the narrow limits of a letter hardly permit me to give you
an account of these things in a prolix circuit of words, that is, in
what manner the abstruse methods of the same metric art are
combined together in letters, words, feet, poetic forms, verses,
stresses, quantities; and also how the discipline of metrical form
is varied in seven divisions, that is headless, "thin-waisted" [with
an internal short syllable for a long one] and "bulging" [having
an extra internal syllable], along with the others; which lines are

CHAPTER ONE

The second letter, only a fragment, is nevertheless of great interest:

REVERENTISSIMO PATRI MEAEQUE RUDIS INFANTIAE VENERANDO PRAECEPTORI HADRIANO ALDHELMUS VERNACU-LUS FAMILIAE CHRISTI ET VESTRAE PIETATIS SUPPLEX ALUM-NUS SALUTEM.

Fateor, mi carissime, quem gratia purae dilectionis am-plector, postquam a sodali contubernio vestro ante triennium circiter discedens a Cantia sequestrabar, quod nostra parvitas hactenus ad consortium vestrum ardenti desiderio flagrabat, quod etiam jamdudum cogitarem, quemadmodum in votis est, adimplens perficere, si rerum ratio ac temporum vicis-situdo pateretur, et nisi me diversa impedimentorum obstacula retardarent praesertimque corporeae fragilitatis valitudine medullitus tabentia membra coquente non sinerer, qua quondam, dum post prima elementa iterum apud vos essem, domum redire coactus sum. . . .[71]

It must have been written shortly after Aldhelm's return to Malmesbury, probably in 675. The phrase "rudis in-fantia," it has often been pointed out, does not refer to Aldhelm's literal infancy; William of Malmesbury is

---

judged as having only one form, which as having five possible forms, which as having ten possible forms, according to a certain measure of feet; and how lines are classified by keen reasoning into those wanting a syllable or a foot, or having an extra foot, at the end.

[71] To Hadrian, the most reverend father and the venerable teacher of my recent youth, Aldhelm, member of the family of Christ, a pupil desirous of your blessing, sends greeting. I confess, my most dear one, whom I embrace with the affection of pure love, that since I was cut off from residence in your friendly society on leaving Kent about three years ago, my littleness has burned with the ardent desire for your company, and that I have long intended, so far as my wishes are concerned, to carry out the desire, if the way of things and the vicissitude of times would permit it, and if the several obstacles of hindrances did not prevent me, and particularly if I were not stopped by the illness of fleshly weakness, burning to the marrow my wasting limbs, by which before, when I was with you again after my first studies, I was forced to return home. . . .

clearly wrong in saying that Aldhelm was sent to Canterbury to study under Theodore and Hadrian before he came to Malmesbury and Maeldubh. The general scholarly opinion, that "rudis infantia" is only a figure of speech for Aldhelm's intellectual childhood, is hardly flattering to Maeldubh. Aldhelm was about thirty when he went to study with Hadrian, and he had been a student of Maeldubh for fifteen years before that. "Rudis" may mean here, as it does elsewhere in Aldhelm, "new" and in that case the phrase refers only to Aldhelm's most recent teacher, Hadrian.

The third letter, like the first two, reveals something about Aldhelm's education in liberal arts. It is addressed to Wihtfrid, an otherwise unknown student, perhaps a priest ("venerandus"), who had gone to Ireland to study secular letters. Aldhelm's attitude toward this pursuit is stated at the beginning:

> Absurdum enim arbitror, spreta rudis ac veteris instrumenti inextricabili norma per lubrica dumosi ruris diverticula, immo per discolos philosophorum anfractus iter carpere seu certe aporiatis vitreorum fontium limpidis laticibus palustres pontias lutulentasque lymphas siticulose potare, in quis atra bufonum turma catervatim scatet atque garrulitas ranarum crepitans coaxat.[72]

The letter is incomplete, but it seems to show both a knowledge and an abhorrence of pagan literature.

The fourth letter is the one mentioned by Bede in which Aldhelm addressed the Welsh king Geruntius in an effort to correct British ecclesiastical practices, especially the tonsure and paschal reckoning, which were not in accordance with those of the English Church. It was writ-

---

[72] I think it foolish that, despising the inseparable way of the Old and New Testaments, you take your way through the slippery paths of thorny country, that is through the evil-tempered winding of the philosophers, or—rejecting the pure pools of glassy fountains—drink fenny waters and muddy liquid in which the black hoard of toads abounds and the croaking sound of frogs resounds.

ten in 680, sixteen years after the Synod of Whitby, and it shows both the persistence of the problems which that Synod was convened to solve, and the violence of the feelings which those problems excited:

> Propter communem caelestis patriae sortem et angelicae sodalitatis collegium subnixis precibus et flexis poplitibus vestram fraternitatem adjurantes suppliciter efflagitamus, ut ulterius doctrinam et decreta beati Petri contumaci cordis supercilio et protervo pectore non abominemini et traditionem ecclesiae Romanae propter prisca priorum statuta vestrorum nequaquam tyrannica freti pertinacia arroganter aspernemini. Petrus namque Dei filium beata voce confessus audire meruit: *Tu es Petrus et super hanc petram aedificabo ecclesiam meam et portae inferni non praevalebunt adversus eam et tibi dabo claves regni caelorum* usque *solutum et in caelo.* Si ergo Petro claves caelestis regni a Christo collatae sunt, de quo poeta ait
> Claviger aetherius, portam qui pandit in aethra,
> quis ecclesiae ejus statuta principalia spernens et doctrinae mandata contemnens per caelestis paradisi portam gratulabundus ingreditur? [73]

As this selection suggests, Aldhelm uses much of the space in this long, although fragmentary, letter to quote scriptural and occasionally historical authorities. The line

[73] On account of our common share in the heavenly kingdom and the company of the angelic community, with submissive prayers and begging on bended knees we suppliantly entreat your brotherhood, that you no longer abominate the teaching and decrees of the blessed Peter with supercilious contumacy of heart and violent breast, and no more arrogantly scorn the tradition of the Roman Church on account of old rules of your forebears, relying on tyrannic stubbornness. For Peter, having confessed the Son of God with his blessed voice, was worthy to hear "Thou art Peter, and upon this rock I will build my Church. And the gates of hell shall not prevail against it. And I will give to thee the keys of the kingdom of heaven" and so forth up to "loosed also in heaven" [Matt. 16:18-19]. If therefore the keys of the heavenly kingdom were given by Christ to Peter, of whom the poet said:
Key-bearer of heaven, who opens the gate in the skies,
who, spurning the chief decrees of his Church and despising the mandate of his teaching, shall enter joyfully the gate of the celestial paradise?

Claviger aetherius, portam qui pandit in aethra

appears also in *Carmina ecclesiastica* 1.6; iv.i.2; in the prose *De virginitate* ch. LV; and in the *De metris*. In the latter two instances, the line is again introduced as the work of "poeta." The line itself has been called Aldhelm's, but it is borrowed from two of Arator's and the combination may have been found by Aldhelm in a lost intermediary. As the passage quoted above shows, too, Aldhelm's prose is here much more straightforward than in works where his literary surface was as important as his message. This variation between matter and manner is, however, not surprising in a writer who is, as Aldhelm was aware of being, a literary pioneer.

In the fifth letter Aldhelm returns to a subject which bears more directly on the history of Anglo-Latin. This letter, addressed to one Ehfrith and written shortly before 690 reproves the addressee for going to Ireland for his literary education. It is not, as it was in no. 3, simply to warn him against the dangers of secular letters, but rather to point out that in Theodore and Hadrian England had teachers who outstripped any in Ireland—indeed, the Irish themselves came to Canterbury to study. The letter opens with a burst of Aldhelmian prose, calculated no doubt to impress Ehfrith with what Canterbury could do for a man's latinity:

> Primitus pantorum procerum praetorumque pio potissimum paternoque praesertim privilegio panegyricum poemataque passim prosatori sub polo promulgantes stridula vocum symphonia et melodiae cantilenaeque carmine modulaturi hymnizemus. . . .[74]

It ends almost as enigmatically:

[74] First let those of us who are to sing in the poetry of melody and music, bursting forth under heaven in a shrill consonance of voices, sing a panegyric to the greatly holy and most fatherly covenant of our chieftains and leaders, and a poem about the Creator of all things. . . .

Digna fiat fante Glingio: gurgo fugax fambulo!
Neu timeat scriptor terrentis ludicra linguae!
Sic semper cupiunt scriptorum carpere cartas,
Ut caper hirsutus rodet cum dente racemos;
Nec tamen emendant titubantis gramma poetae.[75]

The problem of the first line has been solved by Traube and, more thoroughly, by Mazzoni, who discovered in the work of Virgilius Maro Grammaticus, a sixth-century French grammarian who was popular with—and may even have visited—the Irish scholars, the following lines:

Verumtamen ne in illud Glengi incidam, quod cuidam conflictum fugienti dicere fidenter ausus est: Gurgo, inquit, fugax fabulo dignus est,[76]

on the basis of which Mazzoni emends the line to read

Dignus fiat, fante Glengo, Gurgo fugax fabulo,[77]

in which Ehfrith is being equated with Gurgo.

Mazzoni's solution seems to resolve the problems, and should not be dismissed simply because he refers to Ehfrid as "Alfredo" throughout, probably following Hahn. The name, indeed, has brought forth a number of interpretations and identifications. The most recent and most thorough is that of A. S. Cook, who thinks the Latin form equals OE Atfrith (Eahfrith) and that man was the same Atfrith who was Abbot of Glastonbury 719-729.

The sixth letter is a very brief one addressed to the nun Sigegith, written about 705. The seventh, even briefer because it survives in a fragment of only a few words, deserves quotation along with the letter it answers:

[75] As Glingius said, let it be worthy, avoiding the eddies of gossip! Nor should the writer fear the scorn of a frightening tongue! Thus they always seek to slander the writings of authors, just as the hairy goat chews the cluster of grapes with his teeth; yet they should not alter the writings of a stammering poet.

[76] Nonetheless, I should not break into the saying of Glengus, which dared to say faithfully, contrary to some: Gurgo, he said, is worthy to avoid scandal.

[77] According to Glengus, Gurgo is worthy to avoid scandal.

DOMINO LECTRICIBUS DITATO STUDIIS MELLLIFLUISQUE ORNATO LUCUBRATIUNCULIS ALDHELMO ARCHIMANDRITAE, SAXONUM MIRIFICE REPERIENTI IN ORIS, QUOD NONNULLI CUM LABORIBUS ET SUDORIBUS IN ALIENO AERE VIX LUCRANTUR, CELLANUS IN HIBERNENSI INSULA NATUS, IN EXTREMO FRANCORUM LIMITIS LATENS ANGULO EXUL, FAMOSAE COLONIAE CHRISTI EXTREMUM ET VILE MANCIPIUM, IN TOTA ET TUTA TRINITATE SALUTEM.

. . . Quasi pennigero volatu ad nostrae paupertatis accessit aures vestrae latinitatis panegyricus rumor, quem agilium lectorum non horrescunt auditus, sine sanna aut amurcali impostura notus propter alburnum dictricis Romaniae decorem. Etsi te praesentem non meruimus audire, tuos tamen bona lance constructos legimus fastos diversorum deliciis florum depictos; sed si peregrini triste reficere vis corculum, paucos transmitte sermunculos illius pulcherrimae labiae tuae, de cujus fonte purissimo dulces dirivati rivi multorum possint reficere mentes, ad locum, ubi dominus Furseus in sancto et integro pausat corpore. . . .[78]

Noteworthy in Aldhelm's reply is the alliteration, now binding words in groups of two or three after the fashion of Old English poetry and later prose. (King Alfred is said to have admired the vernacular works of Aldhelm, but none have survived.)

[78] To my lord Aldhelm the archimandrite, enriched in the study of letters, adorned by honey-bearing work by night, marvelously the discoverer in the land of the Saxons of that which some in foreign parts hardly obtain by labor and effort, Cellanus, born in the island of Ireland, an exile dwelling in an extreme corner of the boundaries of the Franks, the lowest and meanest servant of Christ, sends greetings from a famous settlement, in the Trinity whole and sure. . . .
The praiseful tale of your latinity has come to the ears of my humble self as though in flight of feathered wing, you whom the audience of quick-witted readers does not alarm, without mockery or oily imposture, famous on account of the Alburnian polish of your Latin composition. Though we are not worthy to hear you present among us, we nevertheless read your writings constructed in the fine manner, painted with the delights of diverse flowers; but if you would refresh the sad heart of a pilgrim, send me a few of the little sermons from those most fair lips of yours, the sweet rivers derived from the most pure fountain of which may refresh the minds of many, in the place where Lord Fursey rests in holy and incorrupt body. . . .

Miror, quod me tantillum homunculum de famoso et flori-
gero Francorum rure vestrae frunitae fraternitatis industria
interpellat Saxonicae prolis prosapia genitum et sub arctoo
axe teneris confotum cunabulis. . . .[79]

The eighth letter is to Aethilwald, his pupil, and was
written about 705. The addressee is warned to avoid the
sinful pleasures of youth, especially those of profane letters; Aldhelm points out that "in lege divina vel omnis
vel paene omnis verborum textus artis omnino gram-
maticae ratione consistit."[80] The ninth letter is addressed
to the anti-Wilfrid abbots (see 1.4) on Wilfrid's behalf. Only a fragment, it was written in 705 or 706, and
shows something of the relative simplicity of Aldhelm's
"purposeful" prose. The last of Aldhelm's letters, written
sometime after his elevation to the episcopacy, is addressed to Winberht, abbot of Nutshalling, Hants, and
friend of King Ina. Only the first few lines remain, in
which Aldhelm asks that land granted to the monastery
at Malmesbury by Baldred and now occupied by King
Ina be restored to the monastery. (The authenticity of
this letter has been doubted.)

Among lost works of Aldhelm may be the rhythmic
poems requested by Lull in his letter (745-746) to Deal-
win: "Similiter obsecro, ut mihi Aldhelmi episcopi aliqua
opuscula seu prosarum seu metrorum aut rhythmicorum
dirigere digneris ad consolationem peregrinationis meae
et ob memoriam ipsius beati antestitis."[81]

---

[79] I wonder that from the renowned and flower-bearing fields of
the Franks, the activity of your charming fraternity accosts me,
such a humble man, born of the Saxon race, and cherished in the
tender cradle under a northern sky. . . .

[80] In the divine law, all or almost all the sorts of the arts of language exist in a wholly grammatical form.

[81] Likewise I beg you, that you be good enough to send to me
some little works of Bishop Aldhelm either prose or poetry or
rhythmic verse, for the comfort of my journeying and in memory
of that blessed bishop.

chapter two:

Bede

Life (2.1)

The only direct and authoritative statement about Bede's life is contained in the closing lines of his *HE* (v.24):

Haec de historia ecclesiastica Britanniarum, et maxime gentis Anglorum, prout vel ex litteris antiquorum, vel ex traditione majorum, vel ex mea ipse cognitione scire potui, domino adjuvante digessi Beda famulus Christi, et presbyter monasterii beatorum apostolorum Petri et Pauli, quod est ad Viuraemuda, et Ingyruum.

Qui natus in territorio ejusdem monasterii, cum essem annorum septem, cura propinquorum datus sum educandus reverentissimo abbati Benedicto, ac deinde Ceolfrido; cunctumque ex eo tempus vitae in ejusdem monasterii habitatione peragens, omnem meditandis scripturis operam dedi; atque inter observantiam disciplinae regularis, et cottidianam cantandi in ecclesia curam, semper aut discere, aut docere, aut scribere dulce habui.

Nono decimo autem vitae meae anno diaconatum, tricesimo gradum presbyteratus, utrumque per ministerium reverentissimi episcopi Joannis, jubente Ceolfrido abbate, suscepi.

Ex quo tempore accepti presbyteratus usque ad annum aetatis meae LIX, haec in scripturam sanctam meae meorumque necessitati ex opusculis venerabilium patrum breviter annotare, sive etiam ad formam sensus et interpretationis eorum superadicere curavi.[1]

[1] These things about the ecclesiastical history of Britain, and especially of the English nation, as I could learn either from the writings of the ancients, or the tradition of the elders, or from my own knowledge, with the aid of the Lord I, Bede, a servant of Christ and priest of the monastery of the blessed Apostles Peter and Paul, which is at Wearmouth and Jarrow, have arranged in order.

Who, born in the territory of the same monastery, was given by

A few other remarks in the writings of Bede and his contemporaries throw further light on his life. In the preface
to the *VM* he says of the miracles he is to relate,

> Ex quibus unum est quod in me ipso, sicut jam tibi dixi, per
> linguae curationem, dum miracula ejus canerem, expertus
> sum.[2]

In the *HAA*, ch. 14, is described a *puerulus* (little boy),
at the time of the writing a priest in the same monastery, who with the Abbot Ceolfrid survived the plague
of 685 and sang the antiphons at divine service until a
new choir had been recruited and trained. There is, however, no foundation in fact for the traditional assumption
that the *puerulus* was Bede, nor would it add materially to
modern knowledge and understanding of him if such a
foundation were discovered.

The date of Bede's birth is not known. The *Vita*, attributed in part only, and on doubtful authority, to his
disciple Cuthbert, says 677. In the passage from *HE*
quoted above, the phrase, "ex quo tempore accepti presbyteratus [i.e., thirty] usque ad annum aetatis meae quinquagesimum nonum" cannot be reasonably linked with

---

neighbors when I was seven years old to be educated by the most
reverend Abbot Benedict, and later Ceolfrid; and spending thereafter the whole course of my life dwelling in the same monastery, I
turned every effort to the study of Scripture; and along with the
observance of the monastic discipline and the daily service of singing in Church, I have always loved either to learn, or to teach, or
to write.

In the nineteenth year of my life I received the diaconate; in the
thirtieth, the degree of priest, both through the ministry of the
most reverend Bishop John at the command of Abbot Ceolfrid.

From the time that I took the priesthood until the fifty-ninth
year of my age, I have striven to annotate briefly the following
books of sacred Scripture out of the works of the venerable fathers,
or to add on to them according to the manner of their meaning
and interpretation, for my own need and that of those about me.

[2] Out of which there is one of which I have experienced through
the healing of my tongue, as I have already told you, when I wrote
a poem about his miracles.

the list of works which follows, for that list is clearly not chronological: the grammatical works at the end must have been among his earliest compositions. The *HE* was finished in 731 (v.23: "Hic est impraesentiarum universae status Britanniae, anno . . . dominicae . . . incarnationis . . . septingentesimo tricesimo primo"),[3] and his death probably took place in 735; but as it is not possible to link *HE* v.24 with these dates, it is not possible to be certain of his birthdate. The suggestion that he was fifty-nine in 731, and so was born in 672 or 673, is therefore incorrectly founded, but probably represents fairly the case in general terms. Only the *Retractatio*, a few poems, and two letters are now attributed to Bede but not among the works he lists in 731 (*De locis sanctis* is not in the list, but is mentioned in *HE* v.17) ; the assumption that he was less active during the period 732-735, owing to old age, is natural, and of course we are certain that he was no *less* than fifty-nine in 731.

But Bede's statements, bare as they are, require comment. "Cunctumque ex eo tempus vitae in ejusdem monasterii habitatione peragens" must mean that he was never monk of another; that he did travel outside Wearmouth is shown by his words "ad vestrae . . . fraternitatis praesentiam" in the preface to the *VP*, addressed to Eadfrith of Lindisfarne, and in his reminder to Egbert of York, in the dated letter of November 5, 734, "Memini te hesterno dixisse anno, cum tecum aliquot diebus legendi gratia in monasterio tuo demorarer."[4] (See also *Epist. ad Wihthedum*, ch. 1.) So Bede may have given up writing after the *HE*, but he was still reasonably well and even visiting outside his monastery almost until his death. Both of these visits had to do with study; there is no reason to

[3] Here rests the state of all Britain, in the year of Our Lord's incarnation 731.
[4] I recall that you said last year, when I remained several days in your monastery for the sake of reading. . . .

think that they were rare, although it is clear that Bede could also borrow materials for his work from other monasteries without leaving his own (cf. *Epist. ad Albinum*). But he did not go to Rome; the letter (*PL* 90.113) of Pope Sergius on which the tradition of his Roman trip (or at least of an invitation to make one) is based is ambiguous on this point, and it is hard to believe that Bede would have made no mention of such an experience, e.g. in *De locis sanctis*.

Bede studied under "frater quidam de his, qui me in scripturis erudiebant . . . vocabulo Trumberht" (*HE* iv.3),[5] and his studies, like those of most of his contemporaries, must have been founded on the comprehension of Scripture. In addition, he learned the subordinate but indispensable "stenographic" chores of scholarship: "me operis labori supposui in quo ut innumera monasticae servitutis retinacula praeteream ipse mihi dictator simul notarius et librarius" (*In Lucam*, Prol.).[6]

According to the *Epistola Cuthberti de obitu Bedae*, Bede died on Wednesday, May 25 (the day before Ascension Day, but described as Ascension Day by Cuthbert because he died in the evening, canonically the Thursday), and 735 is the only probable year in which these days coincided. There is some problem about this account, for although it is that of an eyewitness, the two works it describes as having occupied Bede's attention to the very moment of his death—a volume of extracts from Isidore of Seville and a translation of part of the Gospel of St. John into English—do not survive; the Isidore has left no trace, and the Old English Gospel of St. John cannot be Bede's. The chronicles differ widely on the date of the death, varying from 730 to 737; and although many MSS

[5] A certain brother, of those who taught me Scripture, named Trumberht.

[6] I subjected myself to that burden of work in which, as in numberless bonds of monastic servitude which I shall pass over, I was at the same time author, scribe, and librarian.

of the account of Cuthbert survive, the earliest is of the
ninth century. For this reason, as well as that of the difficulty of the two "lost" works by the most popular author
of his age, it may be prudent to withhold absolute cre-
dence in any matter for which the *Epistola Cuthberti*
is the sole authority.

But even without the evidence of the *Epistola Cuthberti*, and setting aside many of the traditional anecdotes
of Bede's life as apocryphal, we are left with very nearly
all we need to know or can expect to know about him. We
know when he died, and at about what age, and that
almost all of his life was spent at Jarrow, and what kind
of interest might occasion an infrequent trip from the
monastery. We know what his life within it was like. He
was almost entirely aloof from controversy (but see *Epist.
ad Plegwinam*) and Church intrigue at a time when both
were widespread, and for over half a century he was virtually always to be found within a space a mere few hundred yards on a side. Such a life need not and cannot produce a detailed biographical record.

Exegetical Works (2.2)

Explanatio Apocalypsis

The work is prefaced by an *Epistola* to "frater Eusebius," also known as Hwaetberht, the same who became abbot in 716; the work was therefore written before
that date, and is probably the earliest of Bede's exegetical
treatises. It is mentioned in the preface to *Exp.*
(ca. 709). In the *Epistola* Bede outlines the seven fold
division of the Apocalypse (although his work is in three
parts) and then goes on to review the seven exegetical
rules of the heretic Tyconius, a Donatist, whose technique
he nevertheless will follow, for it is applicable, not only
in this book, but in all the canonical scriptures. Bede
concludes his introduction

Nostrae siquidem, id est Anglorum, gentis inertiae con-
sulendum ratus, quae et non dudum, id est, temporibus beati
Gregorii papae, semen accepit fidei, et idem quantum ad
lectionem tepide satis excoluit, non solum dilucidare
sensus, verum sententias quoque stringere, disposui.[7]

Bede's approach in this work, as in most of his exegesis,
is to comment phrase by phrase on the text he is treating,
usually (save in *De eo quod ait Isaias, De mansionibus
filiorum Israel,* and *Liber in regum libros quaestionum
XXX*) from beginning to end. In this work, he is dealing
with a frankly mystical text, and his desire is by and large
to relate it to the real world:

> *Quae oportet fieri cito.* Id est, quae in praesenti tempore sunt
> ecclesiae ventura. *Et significavit.* Mysticis eamdem Apoc-
> alypsim dictis innexuit, ne cunctis manifesta vilesceret.[8]

But from time to time he indulges his more usual habit of
treating literal description as figurative:

> *Joannes septem, etc.* Per has septem ecclesias omni ecclesiae
> scribit. Solet enim universitas septenario numero designari,
> quod septem diebus cunctum hoc saeculi tempus evolvatur.[9]

The work begins with a twenty-two line poem celebrating
the vision of John, and, in many manuscripts, ends with
an epilogue. It looks back on a long tradition of exegesis,
including Primasius and others along with Tyconius, and
forward to Alcuin, Haimo, and Remigius, who depended

---

[7] Bearing in mind the laziness of our people, that is, the English,
who received the seed of faith not a little while ago, that is, in the
time of blessed Pope Gregory, and how in reading they had culti-
vated it but little, I have arranged not only to illuminate the literal
meaning, but also to touch upon the higher meaning as well.

[8] Which must shortly come to pass [Apoc. 1:1]. That is, which
are to come to the Church in the present time. And he signified.
He wrapped the Apocalypse in mystical sayings, lest open to all it
should be contemned.

[9] John to the seven, etc. [Apoc. 1:4]. By these seven churches he
means the whole Church. For it is usual for a universal to be signified by the number seven, as the whole time-span of the world is
unfolded in seven days.

upon it for their own commentaries. Bede was, in this fashion, an influential medium for the transmission of patristic learning to the later middle ages, a medium enhanced by the wide distribution of this and much of his other exegesis. There are seventy-five or so extant manuscripts of *Apoc.*, not a few of them from the eighth or early ninth century.

Actuum apostolorum expositio

Bede dedicates this work "Accan episcopo" and mentions in it a "frater Eusebius,"[10] names which place the work between the elevation of Acca to the episcopate (708) and the elevation of Eusebius to the abbacy (716). In *Exp.* he assigns twenty regnal years to Samuel and twenty to Saul, an error which he had specifically avoided in *DTL* (703), and which he also corrected in *DTR* (725) and *Retractatio* (725x731). The inclusion of this error in a work of 709 or later can be explained by his use of earlier material in a hastily written ("velocissime") tract. It may be that the "in actus apostolorum libros II"[11] which Bede mentions in *HE* v.24, are *Exp.* and the geographical glossary which accompanies it in most MSS, or *Exp.* (with the glossary) and *Retractatio*; if the latter, then the "libros II" were both written before 731, and the common view that *Retractatio* was written after 731 is mistaken. Moreover Bede remarks in *Retractatio* on Acts 20:14, "Scripsimus in libro primo . . . Mytilenen insulam esse contra Asiam," an observation which does not, however, appear in the main portion of *Exp.*, but does appear in the glossary as "Mytilene: insula contra Asiam. . . ."[12] Thus it is probable that the glossary is authentic, that Bede regarded it and *Exp.* as constituting a first book,

[10] To Bishop Acca; Brother Eusebius.
[11] Two books about the Acts of the Apostles.
[12] I wrote in the first book that Mytilene is an island facing Asia.

and that *Retractatio* is the second book of the two mentioned in *HE*.

In the preface to *Exp.* Bede says that he

> explanationem quoque beati evangelistae Lucae juxta vestigia
> patrum quantum valeam sudoris expendam. Quod quia
> facere necdum potui et operis videlicet immensitate perter-
> ritus et obstrepentium causarum, quas tu melius nosti, neces-
> sitate praepeditus, ne tamen tuae postulationis contemneretur
> auctoritas, quod interim potui feci. Misi enim opusculum in
> Actus apostolorum, quod ante non multos dies editum et
> velocissime quantum tempus dederat, ne tua sacrosancta
> voluntas impediretur, emendatum membranulis indideram,
> ubi ea quae vel mystice gesta vel obscurius dicta videbantur,
> ut potui, dilucidare temptavi. In quo me opusculo, cum alii
> plurimi fidei catholicae scriptores, tum maxime juvavit
> Arator, sanctae romanae ecclesiae subdiaconus, qui ipsum
> ex ordine librum heroico carmine percurrens nonnullos in
> eodem metro allegoriae flores admiscuit, occasionem mihi
> tribuens vel alia ex his colligendi vel eadem planius ex-
> ponendi. "Actus igitur apostolorum," ut beatus Hieronimus
> ait, "nudam quidem sonare videntur historiam et nascentis
> ecclesiae infantiam texere, sed si noverimus scriptorem eorum
> Lucam esse medicum cujus laus in evangelio est, animadverti-
> mus pariter omnia verba illius animae languentis esse me-
> dicinam. . . ."[13]

[13] Will weigh how far my labor may suffice for an explanation as
well of the blessed evangelist Luke, following the paths of the
fathers. For as I have not yet been able to accomplish it, overawed
as I was by the size of the task and hindered by other demanding
matters, which you know about full well; lest the authority of your
command be scorned, however, I have done in the meantime what
I could. I have sent therefore the little work on the Acts of the
Apostles, which not many days before and most hastily as far as
time permitted, lest your holy will be impeded, I had set down
written and corrected on parchment; where either the deeds
seemed mysterious or the words even more obscure, I have, as far
as I was able, attempted to explain them. In which little work, along
with many other writers of Catholic faith, Arator, the subdeacon
of the holy Roman Church, has aided me most, who going through
the same book chapter by chapter in heroic poetry, added not a few
flowers of allegory in the same meter, giving me the opportunity
either to collect others of the same, or to explain the same ones more
clearly. "For the Acts of the Apostles," as the blessed Jerome said,

Thus it must have been written before *Luke*, which was in turn before *Samuel*, of which in turn again three books were finished by 716.

The date of *Retractatio* is probably before 731, as we have seen, and "annos plures" (many years) after *Exp*. Laistner thinks that the maturity of the style and the range of the reading indicate a date late in this period. Bede's purpose is set out in the brief preface, which is not addressed to any particular individual:

> Scimus eximium doctorem ac pontificem Augustinum, cum esset senior, libros retractationum in quaedam sua opuscula quae juvenis condiderat fecisse, ut quae ex tempore melius crebro ex lectionis usu ac munere supernae largitatis didicerat; non ut de prisca confusus imperitia, sed ut de suo magis profectu gavisus monumentis inderet litterarum ac posteris legenda relinqueret. Cujus industriam nobis quoque pro modulo nostro placuit imitari, ut post expositionem Actuum apostolorum, quam ante annos plures rogatu venerabilis episcopi Accae quanta valuimus sollertia conscripsimus, nunc in idem volumen brevem retractationis libellum condamus, studio maxime vel addendi quae minus dicta vel emendandi quae secus quam placuit dicta videbantur.[14]

A typical correction is that of Acts 1 :6,

"appear to speak naked history and to tell of the infancy of the early Church, but if we know that Luke, the writer of them, was the doctor who is praised in the Gospel, we shall be likewise aware that all the words are his medicine for the languishing soul. . . ."

[14] I know that, when he was older, the distinguished teacher and bishop Augustine wrote books of retractions on some of his works which he had written as a youth, as he learned things better in later time out of the practice of frequent reading and the gift of heavenly bounty; not as though erroneous in his early inexperience, but taking pleasure at his greater growth he should publish it in written monuments and leave it to be read by later ages. And it has pleased me to take his labor as a model for myself, so that after my exposition of the Acts of the Apostles, which I wrote as far as my skill enabled me to, many years before, at the request of the venerable Bishop Acca, now I may make a small volume of retractions upon the same book, either by adding what seems to be missing or by correcting what seems to be wrong, with the greatest diligence.

Domine, si in tempore hoc restitues regnum Israel? Non
hujus Israel sed huic Israel, sicut in Graeco manifestum
est, ubi τῷ Ἰσραήλ et non τοῦ Ἰσραήλ scriptum est; quod
facilius intellegeretur, si addito uno verbo diceretur, domine,
si in tempore hoc restitues regnum populo Israel?[15]

Though not a little of *Retractatio* stems from Bede's increasing knowledge of Greek in later life, it never reveals
a critical grasp of Greek as comprehensive as his understanding of Latin. His use of Greek depended on parallel
texts like Bodleian MS Laud Greek 35 of Acts, and it
was always passive.

In epistolas VII catholicas libri singuli

In his preface to *Exp.*, Bede mentions that he is sending "explanatiunculam epistolae beatissimi evangelistae
Joannis, cujus maximam partem ex homiliis sancti Augustini latissima suavitate diffusis compendiosus breviator
excerpsi"[16] to Acca: this one of the seven commentaries
in this group was therefore probably completed not long
before *Exp.*, and the other six appear by the similarity of
style and treatment to date from much the same time.
The set of commentaries was a most popular work, possibly, as Laistner suggests, because it was the only exposition of James, I and II Peter, I, II, and III John, and
Jude available in the Western Church. In the preface to
Exp., Bede mentions his "explanatiunculam" in association with *Apoc.*, and the commentary on the Catholic
Epistles appears with *Exp.*, *Apoc.*, or both, in a number
of the more than one hundred surviving MSS.

[15] Lord, wilt thou at this time restore again the kingdom to
Israel? Not *of* this Israel, but *to* this Israel, as is clear in the Greek,
where "toi Israel"and not "tou Israel" is written; which would have
been more easily understood, if with the addition of one word it had
been said, "Lord, wilt thou at this time restore again the kingdom to the people of Israel?"
[16] A little explanation of the epistle of the most blessed evangelist John, of which I have excerpted the largest part—taking the
shortcut as an epitomizer—from the homilies of St. Augustine, dif-
fused with the most wide-spreading sweetness.

Outside of the book on 1 John, excerpted largely from Augustine's *Tractatus X in Joannis epistolam,* Bede is often writing without a known source, although he does quote from Cyprian and more than once from Jerome's *Contra Jovinianum.* The treatment is theological, for the most part, rather than allegorical, and Bede undertakes in passing refutation of the Pelagian, Arian, and other heresies. He repeatedly comments on the textual history of the scriptural passage he is discussing, as on 1 Peter 4:18:

> Notandum autem quod hanc sententiam beatus Petrus de proverbiis Salomonis juxta veterem dumtaxat editionem assumpsit, pro qua in nostra quae de Hebraicae veritatis fonte descendit, scriptum est. . . .[17]

His purpose throughout is to clarify the immediate meaning of the text rather than to discover further meanings:

> *Pellicientes animas instabiles.* Pellices appellari solent meretrices, sumpto vocabulo a pollutione, vel a pellis suae formositate qua incautos illiciunt. Pelliciunt ergo animas instabiles, qui eas male docendo erroneis variorum dogmatum sectis quasi constuprantium luxibus subdunt.[18]

It is only when the language of the scriptural text is itself figurative that he provides a figurative account of it, as of James 3:4:

> Naves magnae in mari mentes sunt hominum in hac vita, sive bonorum, sive malorum. Venti validi a quibus minantur ipsi appetitus sunt mentium, quibus naturaliter coguntur

[17] It is to be noted that the blessed Peter took this phrase from the proverbs of Solomon according to the old version, for which, in our version, which is descended from the font of Hebrew verity, there is written. . . .

[18] Alluring unstable souls [II Peter 2:14]. Prostitutes are often called "concubines" [*pellices,* from πάλλαξ, not from *pellicio,* "allure"], the word being taken from "pollution," or from the beauty of their skins [*pellis*] by which they entice the incautious. Therefore they allure unstable souls, who by teaching them badly subject them to the erring sects of sundry doctrines as though to the excesses of the debauched.

aliquid agere, per quod vel ad bonum, vel ad malum perveniant finem. Gubernaculum quo hujusmodi naves circumferuntur, ubi impetus dirigentis voluerit, ipsa cordis intentio est, qua electi, transgressis hujus saeculi fluctibus, felicem patriae caelestis portum attingunt, reprobi quasi Scylla vel Charybdi necati fluctuosis vitae hujus erroribus, quos deserere nesciebant, intereunt.[19]

The set of commentaries is without an introduction or a preface, and Bede refers to them only in *HE* and *Exp*. Yet for all this seeming disregard, Bede was in some ways at his best as a biblical scholar and interpreter here: astute and learned, in control of the textual tradition and *vestigia patrum*, at war with heresiarchs, and constantly providing for the needs of himself and those about him.

In evangelium Lucae libri VI

Bede mentions in his *Epistola* to Acca prefacing *Exp*. that the bishop had also requested a commentary on Luke, but distractions and the sheer size of the task had stayed his pen. The finished work must be the last of the early group, perhaps not very long before 716; it is mentioned in the preface to the commentary on Samuel, which we know (see below) Bede wrote in 716. The commentary on Luke begins with a letter from Acca (see 3.7) in which Bede is called "fratri et consacerdoti" (brother and fellow priest), so he must have been at least thirty when it was written; given that he was born in the early 670's, this is natural, for the work cannot be earlier than 709, and probably not much earlier than 716. Acca also says

---

[19] The great ships in the sea are the minds of men in this life, whether good men or evil. The strong winds by which they are driven are the desires of the same minds, by which they are urged to do a thing, through which they will come to a good or a bad end. The helm by which this sort of ship is turned about, wherever the force of the helmsman wishes, is the purpose of heart, by which the elect, when they have crossed the billows of this world, arrive at the safe harbor of the heavenly homeland, while those who are the rejected, slain as though by Scylla and Charybdis in the billowing errors of this life, perish in them, which they knew not how to flee.

"Saepe quidem tuae sanctae fraternitati et absens scribendo et colloquendo praesens suggessi,"[20] which may refer to yet another visit or series of visits by Bede, although it may mean that the bishop himself visited from nearby Hexham in which diocese Wearmouth-Jarrow fell. In his reply Bede says that he has taken much of the commentaries of Ambrose, Augustine, Gregory, and Jerome for his use, and

> Quorum quia operosum erat vocabula interserere per singula et quid a quo auctore sit dictum nominatim ostendere commodum duxi eminus e latere primas nominum litteras imprimere perque has viritim ubi cujusque patrum incipiat ubi sermo quem transtuli desinat intimare sollicitus per omnia ne majorum dicta furari et haec quasi mea propria componere dicar multumque obsecro et per dominum legentes obtestor ut si qui forte nostra haec qualiacumque sunt opuscula transcriptione digna duxerint memorata quoque nominum signa ut in nostro exemplari repperiunt affigere meminerint.[21]

A few of the very many MSS of this work retain this careful practice, but most of them do not.

Once again Bede follows the tradition of which he is perhaps the crowning example, rendering figurative language morally comprehensible, and "historical" narrative figuratively meaningful:

> *Non est enim arbor bona quae facit fructus malos, neque arbor mala faciens fructum bonum.* Contra hypocritam quae

[20] I have frequently suggested it to your holy brotherhood, both in writing when absent and in conversation when with you.

[21] Because it was laborious to insert their names individually and to show by name what thing was said by which author, I have found it convenient to put aside in the margin the first letters of their names and by these to show separately where each of the fathers begins and where the discourse I have transcribed ends, careful throughout lest I be said to have stolen the sayings of my elders and offered them as my own; and I pray greatly and entreat my readers in the Lord that if by chance they regard any of these our little works to be worthy of transcription, the ciphers for the names be also remembered as in our original copy they will find them set down.

coeperat exsequitur. Si veram, inquit, et non fictam vis habere justitiam, quae verbis ostentas etiam factis compensare
curato ut bona existens arbor bonis orneris et fructibus quia,
etsi se fingat hypocrita, non est bonus qui facit opera mala.
Et si reprehendat insontem, non ideo malus est qui facit
opera bona.[22]

Et haec vidua erat, et turba civitatis multa cum illa. Viduam
esse ecclesiam omnis anima quae sponsi dominique sui se
morte redemptam meminit agnoscit. Divino autem nutu
multa dominum turba multa viduam comitabatur ut viso
tanto miraculo multi testes multi Dei fierent laudatores.[23]

Bede is a characteristic figure in the tradition: although
systematic statements of the allegorical method abounded,
the practice was almost always, as here, pragmatic. There
is no compulsion to link levels of meaning, and no pro-
hibition from "mixing" them. In every instance the con-
tingencies of spiritual need, rather than the rules of
exegetical theory, guide his commentary.

In primam partem Samuhelis libri IV

The prologue to Books I-III of the *Allegorica expositio in Samuhelem prophetam* is addressed to Acca
once again, and mentions that the commentary on Luke
is already finished. The *Prohemium* to Book IV begins

[22] For there is no good tree that bringeth forth evil fruit; nor an
evil tree that bringeth forth good fruit [Luke 6:43]. He continues
what he had begun against the hypocrite. He says if you wish to
have true, and not feigned, justice, you should take care to balance
the things set out in words with deeds, so that being like the good
tree you may be decked out with good deeds and fruits, for though
a hypocrite may pretend to be one, he is not a good man who does
evil deeds. And if such a man reprove the innocent, still the innocent man who does good deeds is not evil on that account.

[23] And she was a widow: and a great multitude of the city was
with her [Luke 7:12]. Every soul that recalls that it has been
redeemed by the death of its husband and lord will recognize
that the widow is the Church. But by divine command the great

Tertio in beatum Samuhelem completo volumine putabam
me aliquamdiu reparata per quietem meditandi vel scribendi
voluptate sic demum ad incoationem quarti manum esse
missurum.[24]

The departure of Ceolfrid for Rome in June 716 prevented Bede from returning to his work until the election
to the abbacy of young Hwaetberht in the same year.
Books I-III may thus be dated 715-716, Book IV, 716 or
717. Once again Bede is "patrum vestigia sequens," and
his scheme—although it reached extremes of allegorical
interpretation unusual even for him—is characteristic of
the assumptions on which a great deal of his exegesis
proceeded:

> Prima beati Samuhelis lectio typice designat unum eun-
> demque dominum Jesum Christum synagogae pariter et
> ecclesiae redemptorem semper rectoremque credendum;
> unius de justitia se legis suaeque credulae prolis ubertate
> jactantis, alterius suae longae desolationis injurias humili
> apud ejusdem sui redemptoris misericordiam devotione de-
> flentis ideoque redamantis et redemptoris sublimi consola-
> tione respirantis.[25]

There are only eight surviving MSS of this work;
Laistner concludes that "it would seem as if even medieval
scholars found his allegorizing excessive."

---

multitude followed the Lord and the widow, so that, having seen
such a miracle, the many witnesses might be made many praisers
of God.

[24] Having completed the third volume on blessed Samuel, and
through a time of quiet having renewed my desire for contemplation and writing, thus at length I proposed to set my hand to begin
the fourth.

[25] The first reading in the blessed Samuel represents by typology
one and the same Lord Jesus Christ to be regarded as the redeemer
and ruler of the Synagogue and Church equally forever, the one
priding herself in the justice of the Law and the abundance of her
faithful progeny, the other bewailing the injuries of her long deso-
lation to the mercy of her redeemer with humble devotion and
therefore taking hope in the sublime consolation of her lover and
savior.

[115]

De mansionibus filiorum Israel
De eo quod ait Isaias

These two letters are mentioned by Bede at the end of *HE* as among his *libri epistolarum,* and they differ from most of his exegesis by dealing with only a small portion of a scriptural book, and by treating it in a discursive way rather than verse by verse. They are nonetheless examples of one kind of commentary—of "familiar exegesis"—that he practiced, and they were moreover occasioned by questions arising from other more orthodox commentaries he had written. Both are addressed to Acca. The first begins

> Quasdam mihi pariter, dilectissime antistitum, non tamen unius ejusdemque difficultatis solvendas quaestiones destinando, parumper me ab incoata beati prophetae Samuhelis expositione ad Mosen Isaiamque scrutandos articulum deflectere cogis,[26]

and ends

> De prophetae autem testimonio quod pariter exponendum misisti, si quid Deo concedente memoria dignum sentire poterimus, et ipsum tibi quantocius non celare curabimus.[27]

The second begins

> Quoniam quidem, primae tuae propositioni festinato respondens, secundam, quae mihi videbatur obscurior, opportunius rebar ex témpore considerandam; nunc ergo de illa juxta mei ingenioli sensum, quod catholicae et absque scrupulo fidei dici et intellegi possit exponam. . . . Ad hoc autem quaerendum admonitum te asseris ex lectione tertii nostri in Samuhelem libelli. . . .[28]

[26] By sending to me, most beloved bishop, likewise certain questions to be solved, not however of one and the same difficulty, you force me to turn aside for a while from the exposition I had begun on the blessed prophet Samuel to the study of Moses and Isaiah.

[27] Regarding the testimony of the prophet which you likewise sent for explanation, if I am able to find anything worthy in my memory with the help of God, that too as soon as possible I shall not try to keep from you.

[28] Wherefore indeed, replying to your first request in haste, I

[116]

From this we can see that they belong together; that
De mansionibus came first; and that both came after the
commentary on Isaiah and the third book of the commentary on Samuel. We know (see above) that the first
three books of the *Samuel* were finished before June 716,
and the fourth book begun some time thereafter; but
though the passage which Acca asked about was in Book
III (ch. 2), we cannot conclude that he had not seen
Book IV, and cannot therefore set so certain a *terminus
ad quem* as Ceolfrid's departure in 716. It seems nonetheless, from the mention in the first letter of *Samuel*
and *Isaiah* together that they were fairly recent works,
and the date 716 probably approximates the right one.

In evangelium Marci libri IV

Bede's commentary on Mark is shorter than his commentary on Luke in much the same degree as the Gospel
of Mark is shorter than the Gospel of Luke, which illustrates something of the methodical approach he used,
following his text verse by verse. By his phrase "de qua
tota historia diximus pro captu nostro plenius in expositione libri regum diximus et de mensa ac panibus pro-
positionis in libro expositionis tabernaculi et vasorum
ejus"[29] we know that it was after *Samuel* (ca. 716) and
De tabernaculo, but we do not know the latest date for
the latter. He also says

---

shall return forthwith more opportunely to the second to be considered, which seems to me the more obscure; now therefore I shall
expound, according to the understanding of my small intellect, that
which can be said and interpreted in Catholic faith without uneasy
conscience. . . . You however take for yourself this reminder which
is to be sought in reading my third small book on Samuel. . . .

[29] I have spoken more fully about the entire history in my exposition of the Book of Kings, and I have spoken about the table and
votive breads in my book of exposition of the tabernacle and its
vessels, as far as my understanding allowed.

Sed et nonnulla propria ad imitationem sensus eorum ubi opportunum videbitur interponemus lectoremque supplex obsecro ut, si haec nostra opuscula transcriptione digna duxerit, annotationem quoque nominum eorum quae supra in margine apposita sunt diligens scriptura conservet quo modo in expositione evangelii beati Lucae quam ante annos plurimos auxiliante Dei gratia composuimus constat esse factitatum,[30]

which shows us that it was not soon after *Luke* (well before 716). A date on the order of 720 x 725 should not be far off.

Not a little of the *Mark* has been taken over from the *Luke,* sometimes with small changes. Compare the following commentary on Luke 8:54

Ubi diligens lector inquirat quare verax evangelista dictum salvatoris exponens interposuerit de suo, *tibi dico,* cum in Syro sermone quem posuit non plus sit dictum quam *puella surge,*[31]

with that on the same passage in Mark 5:41,

Quaerat diligens lector quare verax evangelista dictum salvatoris exponens interposuerit de suo, *tibi dico,* cum in Syro sermone quem posuit non plus sit dictum quam *puella surge,* nisi forte propter exprimendam vim dominicae jussionis hoc augendum putavit magis sensum loquentis quam ipsa verba suis curans intimare lectoribus. Nam et familiare constat esse evangelistis atque apostolis cum de veteri testa-

---

[30] But also I introduce many things, where it seems opportune, which are suitable to be copied for their meaning, and I humbly beg the reader, if he thinks this little work of mine worthy of transcription, that he should carefully preserve as well in his writing the notations of the names of the authors quoted which I have set down opposite the passage in the margin, just as was done in the commentary on the Gospel of blessed Luke which, with the aid of the grace of God, I wrote many years ago.

[31] Where the careful reader asks, "Why does the truthful evangelist, setting forth the sayings of the savior, interpose on his own, 'I say unto you,' since in the Syriac which he includes nothing more is said than 'Maid, arise.'"

mento testimonia assumunt magis sensum propheticum
ponere curare quam verba.[32]

In principium Genesis libri IV

The commentary survives in two forms, of which the
earlier and shorter is sometimes called *Hexaemeron*.
Bede's comment "si enim hodierna die, verbi gratia, per
Kalendas Apriles esset luna septima decima"[33] is usually
assumed to refer to the time of its writing, and this would
seem to be 720: other possible years, such as 701, do not
fit so well. But the earlier commentary continues only as
far as Gen. 3, while the indication of date which fixes the
year at 720 is in Bede's discussion of Gen. 8:16 and so
serves only to fix the date of that passage, although it is
likely that the rest of the commentary followed on shortly.
The *Epistola* to Acca which opens the work must have
been part of the original shorter version, for Bede says
"perspectis patrum voluminibus, collegi ex his, ac duobus
in libellis distinxi,"[34] and it is in the form of two books
that the earlier version survives. Later it was made into
Book 1 of the four books of the complete work, although the
last few lines of printed editions, beginning "Quaerit
autem adversarius," are also part of the later revision.
The original plan is clear from his words "perduxi . . .
opus usque dum ejectus Adam de paradiso voluptatis exsi-

[32] The careful reader may ask "Why does the truthful evangelist, setting forth the sayings of the savior, interpose on his own
'I say unto you,' since in the Syriac which he includes nothing more
is said than 'Maid, arise,' unless for the sake of illustrating the
power of the Lord's command he thought this should be added,
seeking to reveal to his readers more the sense of what was said
than the words themselves. For it is perfectly familiar among the
evangelists and Apostles when they take testimonies from the Old
Testament, that they seek more to put the prophetic sense than the
words."

[33] If, for example, today—April first—were the seventeenth day
of the moon.

[34] Having looked through the books of the fathers, I made a
collection out of them, and I separated it into two books.

lium vitae temporalis intravit; aliqua etiam de sequentibus sacrae historiae . . . auxilia vestrae intercessionis comitante, scripturus."[35]

In Esdram et Nehemiam libri II

In the preface to *Genesis*, quoted above, Bede says "librum sancti Esdrae . . . perscrutatus fuero,"[36] so this project must have been, in plan at least, an early one. But in its completed form Bede says "De qua tota prophetiae sententia plenissime, prout potui, disserere in temporum libro curavi,"[37] which means that the finished work is after *De temporum ratione*, 725, and before 731. The work is figurative in the spiritual mode, that is, it sees in the restoration of Jerusalem a figure of the return to grace of the repentant sinner:

> Quapropter, reverendissime antistes Acca, tuis diligenter obsecundans hortamentis, considerando eidem volumini operam dedi. Confidens vero adjutore et consolatore domino ac salvatore nostro Jesu Christo, quia donet nobis propitius, retecto cortice litterae, altius aliud et sacratius in medulla sensus spiritalis invenire; quod videlicet ipsum dominum, ac templum et civitatem ejus, quae nos sumus, propheticis quidem figuris, sed manifesta ratione designet.[38]

De tabernaculo libri III

This work is mentioned in *Mark* and *De templo*, but as *De templo* is late . . . "nuper" (recently) in 731 . . . and

[35] I carried the work on up to the point where Adam, ejected from the paradise of joy, entered into the exile of mundane life; some things from what follows in the sacred history . . . with the aid of your intercession, I have still to write.

[36] I shall have examined the book of holy Ezra.

[37] About the full meaning of the prophecy, as far as I was able, I have striven to write at length in my book on Time.

[38] Wherefore, most reverend Bishop Acca, being diligently obedient to your commands, I have set myself to the labor of considering the same volume. Confident in the true aid and consolation, our Lord and savior Jesus Christ, that He may be kind enough to give me to find the higher and more holy spiritual sense in the inmost

Mark is undatable, but probably in the 720's, no firm date can be assigned to it. Laistner suggests that as it deals with portions of Exodus, it was begun when *Genesis* was finished, i.e. after 720. There is no real preface, although ch. 1 begins

> Locuturi, juvante domino, de figura tabernaculi et vasorum, atque utensilium ejus, primo situm loci, et circumstantias rerum, quomodo sese habuerint, quandoque haec fieri praecepta sint, inspicere atque attentius considerare debemus. *Omnia autem*, sicut apostolus ait, *in figura contingebant illis*: *scripta sunt autem propter nos*. Omnia videlicet, non solum facta vel verba, quae sacris litteris continentur, verum etiam locorum, et horarum, et temporum situs, et ipsarum quoque in quibus gesta, sive dicta sunt circumstantia rerum.[39]

The texts which Bede comments on are Exodus 24:12 to 30:21.

De templo Salomonis

The letter to Albinus which accompanied a copy of *HE* includes the sentence "Sed et aliud, quod te partim desiderare comperi, volumen tibi vice remunerationis aeque ad transcribendum destinavi, videlicet illud, quod de structura templi Salomonis atque allegorica ejus interpretatione nuper edidi."[40] Plummer guesses that the

---

part, having unraveled the literary cortex; which signifies by means of prophetic figures, but in a clear method the same Lord, and His temple and His city, who we are.

[39] As I am going to speak, with the aid of God, about the figure of the tabernacle and its vessels and utensils, first I must carefully examine and give consideration to the site of the place, and the attributes of the things, of what sort they were, and when these laws were made. For as the Apostle said, Now all these things happened to them in figure: and they are written for our correction [I Cor. 10:11]. All, that is, which is contained not only in the deeds or the words of sacred writ, but also in the places, the hours, the seasons, in which they are done or said, are also the attributes of the things as well.

[40] And I have in like manner also sent to you another volume,

"praesentes rerum temporalium angores"[41] mentioned in
the letter to Acca at the beginning of *De templo* are the
troubles which followed the accession of Ceolwulf in 729.
If *nuper* means a year or two, then the work is ca. 729 x 731.
The epistle to Acca (in three late MSS it is addressed to
Nothelm, to whom the *Liber in regum libros quaestionum
XXX* is also addressed) sets forth the purpose of the work:

> Verum quia nova quaeque nonnumquam amplius delectant,
> visum mihi est, opusculum quod de factura templi Dei
> sequens magnorum vestigia tractatorum nuper allegorice
> condideram, tuae sanctitati percurrendum mittere.[42]

The work treats III Kings 5-7 and II Paralip. 2-5, largely
from the mystical signification of the details of the temple,
but occasionally more literally:

> *Ostium lateris medii in parte erat domus dexterae*, etc.
> Quidam hunc locum male intellegentes, putant ostium
> templi a meridie fuisse, non attendentes quia si hoc sig-
> nificare voluisset scriptura, non ita diceret: *ostium lateris
> medii in parte erat domus dexterae*, sed ita potius sim-
> pliciter, *et habebat domus ostium ad meridiem*. Nunc autem
> longe aliud significat. Partem namque domus dexterae,
> latus templi meridianum dicit. In cujus parte orientali
> ostium erat in ipso angulo factum, juxta terram. In quod
> introeuntes, statim ad altiora gradatim ascendebant, habentes
> viam ascensus per ipsa parietis interiora, donec tali itinere
> ad medium coenaculum, et a medio pervenirent ad tertium.
> Haec ita esse non dubitandum, quamlibet scriptura non
> dicat, quia sic ascendentes creberrimas habebant a meridie

---

which I learned you wanted in part, for the sake of having it
copied, in return for your gift; that is, the one I recently composed
on the building of the temple of Solomon and the allegorical interpretation thereof.

[41] The present troubles of worldly things.

[42] Truly, since new things sometimes give more pleasure, I have
it in mind to send to your holiness for perusal the little work which
I recently compiled in the allegorical fashion about the making of
the temple of God, following the paths of the great works on the
subject.

fenestras, quarum luce certum per omnia et sine offensione iter agerent.[43]

The three earliest surviving MSS are of the ninth century, two from the Continent and one from Bury St. Edmunds; but Abbot Ceolfrid sent one to Lull on his request not long after Bede's death.

Liber in regum libros quaestionum XXX

This short work—in one book—is in answer to the request of "dilectissimus frater Nothelmus,"[44] the London priest who "sive litteris mandata, sive ipsius Nothelmi viva voce referenda transmisit" materials from a trip to Rome; "Qui videlicet Nothelmus postea Romam veniens, nonnullas ibi beati Gregorii papae simul et aliorum pontificum epistolas, perscrutato ejusdem sanctae ecclesiae Romanae scrinio, permissu ejus, qui nunc ipsi ecclesiae praeest Gregorii pontificis, invenit, reversusque nobis nostrae historiae inserendas. . . ." (*HE*, pref.)[45] Nothelm's trip has not been dated, but it—

[43] The door for the middle side was on the right hand of the house, etc. [III Kings 6:8]. Some, misunderstanding this passage, think that the door of the temple was on the south side, not bearing in mind that if the Scripture had meant to signify that, it would not have put it thus: The door for the middle side was on the right hand of the house, but rather, more simply, thus: And the house had its door on the south side. Now, however, it says something entirely different. It says that the right hand of the house was the south side of the temple. In the east part of which the door was made at the corner, alongside the ground. Those going into it immediately went to a higher level step by step, having the way of ascent along the inside of the same wall, until by such a route they came to the middle chamber, and from the middle chamber to the third. This is not to be doubted, even though the Scripture does not say that those who went up in this manner had the windows most frequently on the south, by the light of which they made their way surely through it all without stumbling.

[44] Most beloved brother Nothelm.

[45] Brought either in writing, or by the voice of the same Nothelm; the same Nothelm, thereafter going back to Rome, and having, with the permission of the Pontiff Gregory who now rules the Church, searched the archives of the same holy Roman Church, found there

like the *Quaestiones*—must be before 731. He became Archbishop of Canterbury in 735. Laistner thinks that the work may be about 725, before the commentary *In Esdram* and *De templo Salomonis,* on the basis of style and content.

In his dedicatory epistle, Bede says

> Fit etiam ut non omnia quae a patribus scripta sunt ab omnibus possint haberi et ignorentur quaestiones scripturarum a legentibus non quia a doctoribus expositae non sunt sed quia ipsae earum quaestiones vel non habeantur vel habitae non intellegantur a quaerentibus sicut in plurimis eorum quorum a me responsa et petisti et accepisti constat esse factitatum.[46]

The thirty chapters deal with thirty passages from I Kings 2:25 to IV Kings 24:14.

Collectaneum

The *Collectaneum* on the Pauline Epistles which Bede mentions in *HE* v.24 was, it appears, early confused with one by Florus of Lyons (fl. ca. 830-860), and although the confusion had been noted by Mabillon, scholars until the twentieth century continued to regard the Florus work as Bede's, possibly because it was printed among Bede's work by Migne, following Giles. The work by Bede is not, at the present, available in an edition, although it is included in the program of the *Corpus Christianorum*; but studies of the MSS have already contributed to modern knowledge of Bede, especially in expand-

---

a number of letters of blessed Pope Gregory as well as of other popes, and coming back gave them to me to include in my history.

[46] For it is the case that not everything written by the fathers can be made available to everyone, and questions of Scripture are a matter of ignorance to readers, not because they have not been commented upon by the doctors of the Church, but because the questions themselves are not available, or if available are not understood by those who ask them, as was the case with many of those for which you asked and received the answers from me.

ing the notions given by Laistner of Bede's reading in
Augustine, which now appears to have been very extensive indeed. There remain only seven MSS of the Bede
Collectaneum, and it may be that Florus' work eclipsed
it, rare as such a fate is for a Bede *opusculum.* Of the
seven, five are ninth or early tenth century, and the other
two are eleventh and twelfth centuries. Lupus of Fer-
rieres mentions the Bede work in a letter to Hincmar of
Reims in the midst of the ninth century, and his copy
seems to have been a grand one: "Tantus est liber, ut
nec sinu celari, nec pera posset satis commode contineri."[47]
By the twelfth century, however, the Abbot of Mont-
Saint-Michel is concerned about the currency of two collections and the problem of their authorship. If it is true
that Florus' collection supplanted Bede's, it probably did
so within the century or so following Florus' death.

*In librum beati patris Tobiae explanationis
allegoricae liber I*

The only criterion for dating lies in Bede's description
of this work, similar to that of *De templo,* and so perhaps
about the same time, that is, in the two or three years preceding *HE.* The work was very popular, as the seventy-
odd extant MSS show, and it is mentioned in a letter of
Alcuin, who asks the Archbishop of Treves to lend him a
copy. It is very short. Bede begins with a paragraph which
explains his scheme:

> Liber sancti patris Tobiae, et in superficie litterae sa-
> lubris patet legentibus, utpote qui maximis vitae moralis et
> exemplis abundat et monitis. Et si quis eundem etiam
> allegorice novit interpretari, quantum poma foliis, tantum
> interiorem ejus sensum videt simplicitati litterae praestare.
> Maxima namque Christi et ecclesiae sacramenta, si spir-
> italiter intellegitur, in se continere probatur,[48]

[47] Such is the book, that it cannot be kept in the fold of my cloak,
nor can my pouch easily hold it conveniently.
[48] The book of the holy father Tobias offers to its readers much

and he carries it out in this fashion:

> *Sed occiso rege a filiis suis, restituta sunt cuncta sua Tobiae.* Quia superato saepius diabolo, ac suis sceleribus, quae velut pessimam prolem genuit, condemnato, rediebant prospera populo Dei. Quibus altercationibus etiam ecclesiae statum post incarnationem domini fluctuare videmus.[49]

Bede's image of the "fruit among leaves" is a fitting—and traditional—one for the kind of exegesis which pushes aside the surface and wrests the meaning from within, but it is not the only kind he practiced; elsewhere he contributed to a more "literal" tradition of commentary.

In proverbia Salomonis libri III
(Super parabolas Salomonis allegorica expositio)

There is no way to date this work; we know only that it was written before *HE*, that is, before 731. There is no preface or epilogue, but the last portion, *De muliere forti*, in which the chapters are "numbered" by the letters of the Hebrew alphabet, often appears separately. Much of the work is based on an otherwise rarely noted commentary on the psalms by the fifth-century writer Salonius. It is, in the main, an allegorical explanation, verse by verse, of the Book of Proverbs, which Bede refers to as "*Parabolae* Graece, Latine dicuntur *similitudines*; quod

---

that is wholesome in the literal surface, seeing that it abounds with the greatest examples and admonitions of the moral life. And if one is able to interpret it allegorically, he will see that it contains as much inner meaning within the literal simplicity as there are fruit among leaves. It will be found that the greatest mysteries of Christ and the Church are contained within it, if it is understood spiritually.

[49] But the king having been killed by his sons, all things which were his were restored to Tobias [cf. Tobias 1:24-25]. For when the devil was overcome, and with his legions, which he brought forth as the most evil race, condemned, prosperity returned to the people of God. In which struggles we see the state of the Church fluctuate after the incarnation of the Lord.

huic libro vocabulum Salomon ob id imposuit, ut sciremus altius, et non juxta litteram, intellegere quae dicit,"[50] an etymology he may have got from Isidore. Perhaps the best-known commentary in the work, however, is not allegorical; of Prov. 4:3 Bede says,

> Nihil magis ad spem percipiendae sapientiae mentem erigit, quam cum eos quos in sapientia jam clarere miramur, aliquando parvulos et indoctos fuisse meminimus.[51]

A great many manuscripts of the work, including at least four of excerpts and fifteen of *De muliere forti,* survive.

In canticum Habacum liber I

This short work, often called "allegorica expositio" in the MSS, cannot be dated save that it is before 731. It is dedicated in a few opening lines:

> Canticum prophetae Habacuc, quod tibi exponi pedisti, dilectissima in Christo soror, sacramenta dominicae passionis maxime pronuntiat. . . . Sed et incarnationis ipsius, resurrectionis, et ascensionis in caelos, fidei quoque gentium, et perfidiae Judaeorum mystice describit eventum. Contemplatus enim propheta statum praesentis saeculi, viderat pacem peccatorum et afflictiones proborum, viderat impios abundare divitiis, et innocentes cottidianis esse subjectos flagellis; viderat in loco judicii impietatem, et in loco justitiae iniquitatem; viderat lacrimas innocentum et consolatorem neminem, nec posse resistere calumniatorum violentiae cunctorum auxilio destitutos,[52]

[50] What are called parables in Greek, are called similitudes in Latin; which name Solomon gave to this book so that we know we might understand what he said according to the higher meaning, and not the literal.

[51] Nothing encourages the mind of the student of wisdom to hope more than when we remember that those whom we now admire, shining in their learning, once were young and unlearned.

[52] The song of Habakkuk, which you asked me to expound to you, most beloved sister in Christ, principally proclaims the mysteries of the Lord's passion. . . . But it also describes mystically the incarnation itself, the resurrection, the ascension into heaven, as well as the faith of the nations and the perfidy of the Jews. If the prophet could see the state of the present world, he would see peace

and it ends:

> Notandum autem, exposita oratione, sive cantico, Habacuc,
> quia nomen quoque ejus, quod interpretatur *amplexans*,
> sensui ejusdem orationis congruit. Patet enim quia interno
> amore cordis amplexabatur dominum, eique adhaerebat,
> qui in illo se solum gloriari et gaudere testatur. Utinam
> autem fiat, dilectissima soror et virgo Christi, ut etiam nos
> ipsum diligentes tali nomine digni efficiamur. Si enim eum
> toto corde, tota anima, tota virtute amplecti satagimus,
> dignabitur et ipse nos ulnis suae dilectionis amplecti, memor
> sui promissi quo ait: *Qui autem diligit me, diligetur a patre
> meo, et ego diligam eum, et manifestabo ei meipsum*; sicque
> inter illius sponsae merebimur membra numerari, quae suo
> conditori, sponso videlicet caelesti solet laetabunda cantare:
> *Laeva ejus sub capite meo, et dextra illius amplexabitur
> me.*[53]

The identity of the "soror"—almost certainly *in Christo*,
not *in carne*—is unknown. Only a dozen manuscripts
survive; unlike the similarly unpretentious *opusculum* on
Tobias, it seems to have had scant popularity.

---

among sinners and affliction among the just, he would see the un-
holy great in wealth, and the innocent daily brought under the
whip; he would see impiety in the place of judgment, and iniquity
in the place of justice; he would see the tears of the innocent and
none to console them, nor are the destitute by any aid able to resist
the violence of all those who plot against them.

[53] It is to be noted, now that I have explained the prayer or song
of Habakkuk, that his name too, which is interpreted "embracing,"
suits well the meaning of the same prayer. For it is clear that he
embraced the Lord with the inner love of his heart, and clung to
Him, in Whom alone he professed himself to glory and rejoice.
Would that it came to pass, most beloved sister and virgin of
Christ, that we too by such a name should be made worthy to love
Him. For if we strive to embrace Him with our whole heart, whole
soul, whole strength, He likewise deigned to embrace us in the
arms of His love, recalling His promises, Who said: He that loveth
me shall be loved of my Father, and I will love him, and will mani-
fest myself to him [John 14:21]; thus we may merit to be numbered among the members of His brides, who sing to their maker,
that is to their bridegroom in heaven, joyfully: His left hand is
under my head, and His right hand shall embrace me [Cant. 2:6].

In Cantica canticorum libri VII

The date of this work is also unknown, save that it is before 731. The organization is explained at the beginning of Book VII, the last book:

> In expositione Cantici canticorum, quam libris quinque explicavimus (nam primum hujus operis volumen contra Julianum, pro defensione gratiae Dei, quam ille impugnavit, unde et hac destituente periit, specialiter confecimus), ita patrum vestigia secuti sumus, ut interim opuscula dilecti Deo et hominibus papae ac patris nostri Gregorii relinqueremus intacta; jucundius fore legentibus rati, si ea quae in explanationem hujus voluminis per cuncta opuscula sua sparsim disseruit, quia plurima sunt et copiose dicta, quasi in unum collecta volumen, pariter omnia poneremus, quod modo adjuvante domino sumus facturi. Credatur ergo septimus in Cantica canticorum liber, nostro quidem labore collectus, sed beati Gregorii sermonibus et sensu compositus, ut si quis forte sit qui nostra forte opuscula jure spernenda existimet, habeat in promptu legenda ejus dicta, quem constat nullatenus esse spernendum. Si quis vero haec quoque nostra captus amore legat, sicut marmoreis nostrae parvitatis aedificiis aureum tantus architectus culmen imponat.[54]

[54] In the commentary on the Song of Songs, which I have explained in five books (for I wrote specially the first book of this work, against Julian and in defense of the grace of God, which he impugned, and being deprived of which, he died), I have followed the paths of the fathers, except that I have left untouched the works of the pope beloved of God and men, our father Gregory; reckoning that it would be more pleasant for the readers, if that which he scattered throughout all his works—which are many and copiously written—in explanation of this volume, I collected all together alike into a single volume, which with God's aid I now am about to do. Let therefore the seventh book on the Song of Songs be thought of as collected by my labor, but composed from the sermons and interpretations of blessed Gregory, so that if perhaps there is anyone who thinks my little works worthy to be spurned, he may have for immediate reading those sayings of the man who is not at all to be spurned. If on the other hand anyone does read my little works too for the sake of comprehension, let such an architect place the work of Gregory like a golden roof-ridge on the marble buildings of my littleness.

There is no preface or epilogue, but the first and last books, standing somewhat apart from the organization of the middle five books, are sometimes encountered separately in MSS.

The work was popular and frankly derivative, and it provided the medium for the transmission of a great deal of early medieval lore to the later middle ages, not only theological, but "scientific" and literary as well. Of Cant. I :16 he writes, *inter alia*:

> Assimilantur laquearia simplicioribus Christi famulis, qui propriis ecclesiam virtutibus potius exornare, quam doctrinae verbis defendere et contra perversorum dogmatum impetus norunt munire. Dependent autem affixa tignis laquearia, quia necesse est ut quicunque in sancta ecclesia sublimes virtutibus splendere desiderant, summorum patrum dictis atque exemplis, quibus a terrenorum ambitu suspendantur, tota mente inhaereant. Et bene tigna haec cedrina et laquearia dicuntur esse cypressina quia utramque hanc arborem imputribilis naturae, altitudinis eximiae et odoris constat esse praecipui, quod eis apte convenit qui cum apostolo dicere possunt, *Christi bonus odor sumus Deo*, et, *Nostra conversatio in caelis est*, et, *Quis nos separabit a caritate Christi? tribulatio?* et reliqua. Sed et hoc, quod odor cedri serpentes interim fugare solet, juxta illud poetae,
>
> > Disce et odorantem stabulis accendere cedrum,
> > Galbanoque agitare graves nidore chelydros:
>
> ejusdem laquearibus altis, id est, doctoribus congruenter aptatur, qui virtute verbi caelestis solent venenata haereticorum dogmata repellere, eosque a simplicium seductione fugare,[55]

[55] The "rafters" are likened to the simpler servants of Christ, who know better how to furnish the Church with their virtues, than to protect it against the blow of perverse teaching and to defend it with the words of doctrine. For rafters when they are fixed hang from a beam of wood, because it is necessary that some exalted ones in the holy Church should wish to shine with virtues, with the sayings and examples of the greatest fathers, by which they are suspended from the circuit of worldly things, and to which they cleave with their whole minds. And well these beams are said to be cedar and the rafters cypress, because both of these trees are of the

with its tag from Virgil (*Georg.* III.414, 415).

De locis sanctis

Although Bede does not mention *De locis sanctis* in the list of his works (*HE* v.24), he says earlier, while discussing the Irish priest Adamnanus (*HE* v.15),

> Scripsit idem vir de locis sanctis librum legentibus multis utillimum. . . . De cujus scriptis aliqua decerpere, ac nostrae huic historiae inserere commodum fore legentibus reor.[56]

At the end of the excerpts (*HE* v.17), Bede adds

> Haec de opusculis excerpta praefati scriptoris ad sensum quidem verborum illius, sed brevioribus strictisque comprehensa sermonibus, nostris ad utilitatem legentium historiis indere placuit. Plura voluminis illius, siqui scire delectat, vel in ipso illo volumine, vel in eo, quod de illo dudum strictim excerpsimus, epitomate requirat.[57]

The end of the work itself reads

---

kind that does not rot, distinguished by great height and odor, which is most like unto those who can say, with the Apostle, For we are the good odor of Christ unto God [II Cor. 2:15] and But our conversation is in heaven [Philip. 3:20] and Who then shall separate us from the love of Christ? Shall tribulation? [Rom. 8:35] and the rest. But also the following, that the odor of cedar has the power to put serpents to flight, according to that saying of the poet, "Learn also to burn pungent cedar in the stalls, and to clear out deadly serpents with its yellowish vapor," is fittingly applied to the high rafters, that is, the doctors of the Church, who repel the poisonous teachings of heretics with the power of the heavenly word, and drive them from the seduction of the innocent.

[56] The same man wrote a book on the holy places, most useful to many readers. I believe it may be helpful to readers to excerpt some things from his writings, and to insert them in this history of mine.

[57] This much, taken from the works of the aforesaid writer, according to the meaning of his words, but condensed into briefer and restricted discourse, it has pleased me to put into my history for the help of readers. If anyone wishes to know more of his other works, let him seek it in the volume itself, or in the book which I recently briefly abridged from it.

Haec de locis sanctis, prout potui, fidem historiarum
secutus exposui et maxime dictatus Arculfi, Galliarum
episcopi, quos eruditissimus in scripturis presbyter Adamnanus lacinioso sermone describens tribus libellis compre-
hendit. . . . Ex qua nos aliqua decerpentes veterumque
litteris comparantes tibi legenda transmittimus, obsecrantes
per omnia, ut praesentis saeculi laborem non otio lascivi
torporis, sed lectionis orationisque studio tibi temperare
satagas.[58]

Now in fact the passages in *HE* v.15-17 are a conflation
of Adamnanus' and Bede's works, and it may be the reference there that made him feel that to cite the work again
at the end of the same book would be superfluous. Laistner has pointed out that Bede's *De locis sanctis* is quoted
in the geographical supplement to his commentary on
Acts, and so must be earlier than it, that is, before 709,
although we must give a new meaning to "dudum" to
accept so early a date.

The short work was very popular and survives in
many MSS. It was perhaps more widely copied than
Adamnanus' work because it includes not only material
from his treatise, but other passages from Hegesippus'
Latin abbreviation of Josephus' *Jewish Wars* and some
from the *De situ Judaeae* attributed to Eucherius of
Lyons. A characteristic short chapter is the third:

De Acheldemach, et loco ubi suspensus est Judas.
Portam David egredientibus, fons occurrit in austrum
per vallem directus, ad cujus medietatem ab occasu Judas
se suspendisse narratur. Nam et ficus magna ibi ac vetus-
tissima stat, juxta quod Juvencus ait:

[58] These things about the holy places, as far as I have been able,
I have set forth following the historical facts and taught mostly
by Arculf, the Bishop of the Gauls, whose books Adamnanus, the
priest most learned in writings, compiled in three short volumes,
employing elaborate language. . . . From which borrowing a few
things and arranging them with ancient writing, I have sent them
to you for perusal, begging you throughout that you strive to com-
bine the labor of the present world, not with the inactivity of self-
indulgent torpor, but with the toil of reading and prayer.

Informem rapuit ficus de vertice mortem.

Porro Acheldemach ad australem plagam montis Sion, peregrinos et ignobiles mortuos hodie quoque alios terra tegit, alios inhumatos putrefacit.[59]

Because he does not list it in *HE* v.24, we do not know where Bede would have grouped this work; Laistner places it separately under "Geography," but it seems to fall between exegesis and hagiography in its account of parascriptural tradition.

Hagiography (2.3)

Bede's historical and hagiographical writings are in a fashion intermixed, so that no account of the latter should fail to include *HE*, and no account of the former can ignore their "fabulous" content. The compilers of the invaluable *CPL* list the saints' lives together with the historical works. But in his list at the end of *HE*, Bede groups four saints' lives separately under the heading "de historiis sanctorum," following the letters and preceding the *Historia abbatum monasterii hujus*, which in turn comes before the *HE*. Thus the saints' lives, the lives of the abbots, and *HE* are all termed "historiae," but grouped separately.

The reason for this arrangement lies in the system of the whole list: exegesis in order of canon; epistles; hagiography; biography; history; martyrology and hymns; didactic works. Each item is a different kind, its style and content defined by received tradition and by the role

[59] Regarding Acheldemach, and the place where Judas was hanged. Going out of the Gate of David, there is a fount lying directly south toward the valley, amid which Judas is said to have hanged himself upon his downfall. And a great and exceeding old fig tree stands there, about which Juvencus said: The fig tree has snatched hideous death from the pool. Next Acheldemach, on the south side of mount Sion, covers with its earth today dead pilgrims, humble men and others, and makes still others unburied to rot.

that genre played in the life of the monastery. Martyrology and hymns, for example, are both liturgical. Hagiography is a narrative, like biography and history, but in
this case it is a narrative required by the monastic rule
for pious reading and for the Lections at Matins. The
biography, the *Historia abbatum*, is a narrative which
documents the character (and possessions) of the individual monastery. The *HE* comes the closest to our
modern meaning of historical narrative, and indeed contributed not a little to our sense of that meaning.

Liber vitae et passionis sancti Anastasii
Liber vitae et passionis sancti Felicis confessoris

The life of St. Anastasius has not survived, or, as
Levison says, "has not been as yet discovered," but the
passages in his *Martyrology* and in his later *Chronicle*
which deal with Anastasius may contain some phrases
from his reconstitution of the botched translation (*Mart.,
PL* 94.820; *Chron., PL* 90.566) :

> Reliquiae corporis ejus prius Hierosolymis ad monasterium
> suum, deinde Romam delatae, venerantur in monasterio
> beati Pauli apostoli, quod dicitur ad aquas Salvias.
> Reliquiae beati martyris Anastasii primo monasterium suum,
> deinde Romam, advectae, venerantur in monasterio beati
> Pauli apostoli, quod dicitur ad aquas Salvias.[60]

The *Vita et passio sancti Felicis* is prefaced by the
paragraph,

> Felicissimum beati Felicis triumphum, quem in Nola
> Campaniae civitate, domino adjuvante, promeruit, Paulinus
> ejusdem civitatis episcopus versibus hexametris pulcherrime
> ac plenissime descripsit; qui quia metricis potius quam

---

[60] The relics of his body, taken first to his monastery in Jerusalem,
and thereafter to Rome, are venerated in the monastery of blessed
Paul the Apostle, which is called "Ad Aquas Salvias." The relics
of the blessed martyr Anastasius, taken first to his monastery, later
to Rome, are venerated in the monastery of blessed Paul the
Apostle, which is called "Ad Aquas Salvias."

simplicibus sunt habiles lectoribus, placuit nobis ob pluri-
morum utilitatem eandem sancti confessoris historiam
planioribus dilucidare sermonibus ejusque imitari indus-
triam qui martyrium beati Cassiani de metrico opere
Prudentii in commune apertumque omnibus eloquium
transtulit.[61]

The effect of this treatment can be judged in the following passages, which contrast Felix and his brother:

> Hermia cum fratre sui cognomine patris
> Terrenas divisit opes, caelestia solus
> Obtinuit Felix; geminos sententia discors
> Divisit fratres: Hermiam mundus abegit,
> Felicem Christus sibi sustulit; ille caduca
> Maluit, hic solida; praesentibus ille cohaesit,
> Iste solum caelo vertit, patrimonia regnis;
> Ille heres tantum proprii patris, iste coheres
> Christi. . . .
> Ergo pari dispar fratrum de sanguine sanguis
> Hermias velut asper Edom terrena secutus
> Squaluit in vacua captivus imagine mundi
> Duraque Idumaei praelegit jura parentis,
> In gladio vivens proprio vanaeque laborem
> Militiae sterilem tolerans, qua Caesaris armis
> Succubuit. . . .
>
> (Paulinus, lines 76-101)[62]

[61] Paulinus, the Bishop of Nola, described the most happy triumph
of blessed Felix, which he won with the aid of God in the same city
in Campania, most beautifully and most fully in hexameters; and
because they are manageable more to readers learned in prosody
than to the simple sort, it has pleased me, for the utility of the
majority, to make evident the same life of the holy confessor in
plainer discourse, and to imitate the industry of him who translated
the martyrdom of blessed Cassian from the metrical work of
Prudentius into discourse common and plain to all.

[62] He divided his worldly goods with his brother Hermias, called
by the name of his father, and Felix alone chose heavenly goods; a
difference of opinion separated the twin brothers: the world drove
Hermias, Christ took Felix to Himself; the former preferred temporal things, the latter lasting ones; the former clung to present
things, the latter turned to the heavens, the patrimony of the
kingdom; the former was the inheritor of his own father, the latter
a sharer in the inheritance of Christ. . . . Therefore Hermias, the
differing sibling of the brothers of the same blood, like coarse Edom

Habuit autem et fratrem cognomine sui patris, id est Hermiam, cum quo patrimonium divideret terrenum; qui longe a Felicis moribus agens, atque ideo felicitate indignus perpetua effectus est. Nam terrena solummodo bona diligere studuit, et Caesaris potius quam Christi esse miles elegit.[63]

(Bede, ch. 1)

Bede's rendering involves considerable condensation of Paulinus' four poems into a short work of only ten columns in Migne's reprint, but it adds at the same time emphasis to the spiritual meaning of the narrative by wordplay ("longe a Felicis moribus agens, atque ideo felicitate indignus perpetua effectus est") and rhetorical balance.

Vitae sancti patris Cuthberti

Bede wrote two lives of St. Cuthbert of Lindisfarne (ca. 634-687), the first a metrical version of 979 lines, the second a longer prose version. Both are founded partly on an earlier anonymous prose life (see below, 3.3) written 699 x 705. One well-known passage will illustrate the relationships of the three versions:

Ille vero homo Dei Cuthbert, inobstinata mente appropinquans ad mare usque ad lumbare in mediis fluctibus, jam enim aliquando usque ad ascellas tumultuante et fluctuante tinctus est. Dum autem de mare ascendens, et in arenosis locis litoris flectens genua orabat, venerunt statim post vestigia ejus duo pusilla animalia maritima humiliter proni in terram, lambentes pedes ejus, volutantes tergebant pel-

---

following worldly things, led a squalid life, a captive to the empty pretense of the world, and chose the hard laws of his Jewish father, living by his own sword and bearing the barren labor of vain combat, which succumbs to the arms of Caesar. . . .

[63] He also had a brother, called by the name of their father, that is Hermias, with whom he divided his worldly patrimony; and who, behaving in a manner far from that of Felix, on that account was made unworthy of perpetual happiness. For he practiced the love only of worldly good, and held it better to be a soldier of Caesar than of Christ.

libus suis, et calefacientes odoribus suis. Post servitium autem et ministerio impleto accepta ab eo benedictione, ad cognatas undas maris recesserunt.[64]

(Anon., Bk. II, ch. 3)

At ille egressus monasterio sequente exploratore descendit ad mare, cujus ripae monasterium idem superpositum erat. Ingressusque altitudinem maris, donec ad collum usque et brachia unda tumens assurgeret, pervigiles undisonis in laudibus tenebras noctis exegit. Appropinquante autem diluculo, ascendens in terram denuo coepit in litore flexis genibus orare. Quod dum ageret, venere continuo duo de profundo maris quadrupedia quae vulgo lutraeae vocantur. Haec ante illum strata in arena, anhelitu suo pedes ejus fovere coeperunt, ac villo satagebant extergere. Completoque ministerio, percepta ab eo benedictione patrias sunt relapsa sub undas.[65]   (Bede, ch. 10)

Ad mare deveniunt; collo tenus inditus undis
Marmoreo Cuthbertus agit sub carmine noctem.
Egreditur ponto genibusque in litore fixis
Expandit geminas supplex ad sidera palmas.
Tum maris ecce duo veniunt animalia fundo

[64] But that man of God Cuthbert, going to the sea with his mind resolute, was soaked up to his loincloth amid the waves, and sometimes by the tossing and churning up to his armpits. When he came up out of the sea, and falling to his knees prayed in a sandy place on the shore, quickly there came in his path two small sea animals, humbly making themselves prone on the earth, licking his feet, and rolling about dried them with their skins, warming them with their breath. After this service, and having completed their ministry and accepted his benediction, they returned to their familiar waves of the sea.

[65] And he, leaving the monastery with the spy following, went to the sea, above the shores of which the monastery was set. And he went into the deep part of the sea, until the swelling waves came up around his neck and arms, passing the darkness of the night in praises to the sound of the waves. When dawn came, he went up onto the land and began to pray anew, kneeling on the shore. When he had done which, two quadrupeds, commonly called otters, came up from the depths of the sea. These, prostrate before him on the sand, began to warm his feet with their breath, and strove to dry them with their fur. Having completed their ministry, and having taken from him their blessing, they returned to their watery homeland.

Vatis et ante pedes fulva sternuntur harena;
Hinc gelidas villo flatuque foventia plantas
Aequoreum tergunt sancto de corpore frigus;
Supplice tum nutu sese benedicier orant.
Qui parens votis verbo dextraque ministris
Impendit grates patriasque remittit ad undas
Ac matutino tectis se tempore reddit.[66]

(Bede, 223-234)

Verses 552-555,

Hujus nunc Tyrio venerabile pignus in ostro
Jure datas patrio sceptri jam tractat habenas,
Utque novus Josia fideque animoque magis quam
Annis maturus, nostrum regit inclitus orbem,[67]

have been assumed by Manitius and subsequent scholars
to refer to Osred, who reigned 705-716. The date agrees
with the already mature style which Bede exhibits, and
with the wide range of his reading. Jaager has traced the
influence of Virgil, Arator, Sedulius, Cyprianus Gallus,
Fortunatus, Paulinus of Nola, Dracontius, Prudentius,
Aldhelm, Paulinus of Perigueux, Alcimus Avitus, Damasus, Serenus Sammonicus, Ovid, Horace, Prosper,
Orientius, Augustine, and Persius, in the work, and
Bede's handling of the hexameter line shows technical
skill if not high inspiration. His vocabulary shows some

---

[66] They came to the sea; Cuthbert spent the night covered with
waves up to his marble neck, in song. He came out of the deep and
with his knees upon the shore held out his two hands in supplication
toward the stars. Then behold, two animals came from the depth of
the sea and stretched themselves on the yellow sand before the feet
of the singer; they wiped the ocean cold from his holy body with
their fur and with their breath warmed his icy feet; while suppliantly
they begged with their motion for a blessing. When he had com-
plied and extended his thanks to the faithful ministers with his word
and the blessing of his hand, he returned them to their watery homeland and went back in the morning to his habitation.

[67] Whose venerable pledge now in royal law governs the given
reins with an ancient sceptre, and like a new Josiah more mature in
faith and soul than in years, famous rules our world.

hisperic traits—"altithronus," "armipotens," "belliger," "bellipotens," "celsithronus," "flammiger," "flammivomus"[68]—but it is generally conservative and self-effacing. He uses rhyme sparingly, and then—since it is only once or twice disyllabic—it is not obtrusive. His use of alliteration is similarly restrained ("ut cunctorum nova lux fidei fusa sub axem"), and sometimes appears in enjambement (". . . de nubibus arva. / Africa Cypriani. . ."). The poem, dedicated to the priest John, is entirely directed toward the glorification of the saint, of whose deeds in life Bede had met the eyewitnesses, and of whose miracles after death Bede's own cure ("linguae curationem") was an evidence.

It was probably the verse life which prompted the community at Lindisfarne to ask Bede for a longer history of the saint in prose:

> Sciat autem sanctitas vestra quia vitam ejusdem Deo dilecti patris nostri quam vobis prosa editam dedi, aliquanto quidem brevius, sed eodem tamen ordine rogantibus quibusdam e nostris fratribus heroicis dudum versibus edidi. Quos si vos habere delectat, a nobis exemplar accipere potestis. In cujus operis praefatione promisi me alias de vita et miraculis ejus latius esse scripturum. Quam videlicet promissionem in praesenti opusculo, prout dominus dederit adimplere satago.[69]   (prol.)

The Bishop Eadfrith to whom the work is dedicated died in 721, and Bede's reference to the prose life in *DTR* (725) speaks of it as written "ante aliquot

[68] Enthroned on high; powerful in weapons; fierce in battle; powerful in battle; enthroned on high; making flame; spitting flame.

[69] Your holiness should also know that the same life of our father beloved of God which I have given to you written in prose, I formerly wrote in heroic verse somewhat shorter, but arranged the same, at the request of some of our brethren. If you would like to have which, you can obtain a copy from us. In the preface to this work, I promised that I would write more fully other things about his life and miracles. And, as far as God has enabled me, I strive to fulfill that promise in the present work.

annos" (some years before). He had, moreover, before him the example of such double literary productions as Sedulius' *Carmen* and *Opus paschale* and Aldhelm's two works on virginity.

Bede says in the preface to *HE* that he had two sources for the prose life:

> Inter quae notandum, quod ea, quae de sanctissimo patre et antistite Cuthberto, vel in hoc volumine, vel in libello gestorum ipsius conscripsi, partim ex eis, quae de illo prius a fratribus ecclesiae Lindisfarnensis scripta repperi, assumpsi, simpliciter fidem historiae, quam legebam, accommodans, partim vero ea, quae certissima fidelium virorum attestatione per me ipse cognoscere potui, sollerter adicere curavi.[70]

But his prologue to the *VP* mentions only the eyewitness sources:

> nec sine certissima exquisitione rerum gestarum aliquid de tanto viro scribere, nec tandem ea quae scripseram sine subtili examinatione testium indubiorum passim transcribenda quibusdam dare praesumpsi, quin potius primo diligenter exordium, progressum, et terminum gloriosissimae conversationis ac vitae illius ab his qui noverant investigans. Quorum etiam nomina in ipso libro aliquotiens ob certum cognitae veritatis inditium apponenda judicavi, et sic demum ad schedulas manum mittere incipio. At digesto opusculo sed adhuc in schedulis retento, frequenter et reverentissimo fratri nostro Herefrido presbytero huc adventanti, et aliis qui diutius cum viro Dei conversati vitam illius optime noverant, quae scripsi legenda atque ex tempore praestiti retractanda, ac nonnulla ad arbitrium eorum prout videbantur sedulus emendavi, sicque ablatis omnibus scrupulorum ambagibus ad purum, certam veritatis

[70] Among which things it is to be noted, that those things which I wrote about the most holy father and Bishop Cuthbert either in this volume or in the small book of his deeds, I took partly from those things which I first found written about him by the brothers of the church of Lindisfarne, accepting simply the facts of the history which I read, and partly I have been careful to add with diligence those things which I was able to find out for myself from the certain witness of faithful men.

indaginem simplicibus explicitam sermonibus commendare
membranulis, atque ad vestrae quoque fraternitatis praesentiam asportare curavi, quatinus vestrae auctoritatis
judicio vel emendarentur falsa, vel probarentur vera esse,
quae scripta sunt. Quod cum domino adjuvante patrarem,
et coram senioribus ac doctoribus vestrae congregationis
libellus biduo legeretur, ac sollertissime per singula ad
vestrum pensaretur examen, nullus omnimodis inventus est
sermo qui mutari debuisset, sed cuncta quae scripta erant
communi consilio decernebantur absque ulla ambiguitate
legenda, et his qui religionis studio vellent ad transcribendum esse tradenda. Sed et alia multa nec minora his quae
scripsimus praesentibus nobis ad invicem conferentes, de vita
et virtutibus beati viri superintulistis, quae prorsus memoria
digna videbantur, si non deliberato ac perfecto operi nova
interserere, vel supradicere minus congruum atque in-
decorum esse constaret.[71]

[71] I have not presumed to write anything about so great a man
without certain investigation of the things done, nor did I presume to
give to anyone for copying those things which I had written without careful examination of undoubted witnesses, nay rather, first I
carefully investigated the beginning, progress, and end of his most
glorious customs and life among those who knew. Whose names I
have thought it well to put from time to time into this book, as clear
evidence of how I learned the truth. And when my little work was
made, but still up to then kept in the form of notes, frequently I
showed what I had written both to our most reverend brother, the
priest Herefrith, when he came here, and to others who having
known the man of God for a long time knew his life best, so that
they in their leisure might read it and recast it, and not a few
things, as far as seemed good to them, I carefully emended according to their judgment, and thus I have been studious to commit in
writing the clear, certain inquiry of the truth on parchment, in
simple discourse, free from every obscurity of doubtful matter, and
to send it to the presence of your brotherhood, so that what has
been written might, if false, be emended by the judgment of your
authority, or approved if true. When I had done this with the help
of the Lord, and the little book had been read for two days before
the elders and teachers of your congregation and most carefully
weighed under your examination word by word, not a phrase was
found in all which needed to be changed, but all that was written
was decreed by common consent without any doubt suitable for
reading, and for giving over to those who wished to copy it in the
exercise of their faith. But, conferring together in our presence,
you brought by way of addition many more things, not less im-

Bede keeps his word by referring to these witnesses, more frequently in the beginning of the book than toward the end. The last of them is Herefrith, in whose words the story of Cuthbert's death—perhaps the most striking portion of the *Vita*—is told. Other quotations are inserted, including one from the *Responsiones Gregorii* (see above, 1.1) which he also cited in the *HE*. The connection between the *Vita prosa* and *HE* is close; some MSS incorporate the chapters dealing with Cuthbert (IV.25-30) from *HE* into the *Vita prosa*. The connection between the *Vita prosa* and the *Vita anonyma*, on the other hand, is more difficult to trace. Eight of the miracles in Bede's work are additions to the list in the anonymous life, and the verbal similarities elsewhere are negligible. He often expands the manner of the narration without altering the matter, but he has eliminated many of the names of persons and places, perhaps to enhance the general relevance of the story. He has also rearranged the sequence of his written source. Some, including Plummer, have not admired Bede's revision of the anonymous life, but there is more to the matter than our own attitude toward the differences. Bede believed the book was the work of someone at Lindisfarne; since his version was written under the close supervision of the community there, perhaps no more than twenty years after the first book, it seems probable that he was right. But in these circumstances, how could his version have proved acceptable— even desirable—if the community had been satisfied with the *Vita anonyma* and disappointed with the revision he gave them? The approaching death of the last people who had known Cuthbert; the brevity of the *Vita metrica* and the austerity of the *anonyma*; the growing cult of

---

portant than those which we had written, about the life and virtues of the blessed man, which seemed certainly to be worthy of being remembered, if it had not seemed scarcely fit and proper to add new things or tack them onto a planned and completed work.

Cuthbert and the celebrity of Bede as a writer in the 720's; these were in all probability the circumstances that occasioned the commission, and that explain the survival of Bede's work in thirty-six complete MSS, of the *anonyma* in seven.

Bede regards the miracles, here as elsewhere, as a theologian, not simply as an historian. While he insists on the historical accuracy of the narrative, and checks its details with eyewitnesses, he can write:

> Sicque in duobus miraculis duorum patrum est virtutes imitatus. In phantasticis quidem praevisis et evacuatis incendiis, virtutem reverentissimi et sanctissimi patris Benedicti, qui simulatum ab antiquo hoste quasi ardentis coquinae incendium ab oculis discipulorum orando pepulit. In veris vero aeque victis ac retortis ignium globis, virtutem viri venerabilis Marcellini Anconitani antistitis, qui ardente eadem civitate ipse contra ignem positus orando flammas compescuit, quas tanta civium manus aquam proiciendo nequiverat. Nec mirandum perfectos et fideliter Deo servientes viros tantam contra vim flammarum accipere potestatem, qui cottidiana virtutum industria et incentiva suae carnis edomare, et *omnia tela nequissimi ignea* norunt extinguere. Quibus aptissime congruit illud propheticum, *Cum transieris per ignem non combureris, et flamma non ardebit in te.* At ego et mei similes propriae fragilitatis et inertiae conscii, certi quidem sumus quia contra ignem materialem nil tale audemus, incerti autem an ignem illum inextinguibilem futurae castigationis immunes evadere queamus. Sed potens est et larga pietas salvatoris nostri, quae indignis nobis et nunc ad extinguenda viciorum incendia, et ad evadendas in futuro poenarum flammas, gratiam suae protectionis impendat,[72]   (ch. 14)

[72] Thus he imitated the virtues of two fathers in two miracles. In foreseeing and dismissing the phantom fires, he imitated the miracle of the most reverend and holy father Benedict, who by prayer drove away from the sight of his disciples the fire simulated by the old enemy as though of a burning kitchen. In overcoming and turning aside the real balls of fire, he imitated the miracle of that venerable man, Marcellinus, Bishop of Ancona, who when the same city was afire, positioning himself against the fire restrained through prayer the flames which such a large band of citizens had not been able to

and elsewhere, "Cujus internis id est animi virtutibus, ea quoque quibus foras effulgebat miraculorum signa testimonium dabant" (ch. 26).[73] The importance of the miracle was not that it had effect, but that it had meaning; its similarity with other miracles, not its uniqueness, was the mark of its noteworthiness.

Martyrologium

A martyrology is a table of the dates of the year and the martyrs whose sufferings are observed on each day. Bede's is the principal of these special applications of the calendar, although among his sources is the *Martyrologium Hieronymianum* of the fifth century. He drew on other sources including the *Passiones* and *Vitae* of the individual martyrs, and Cyprian, Eusebius-Rufinus, Jerome himself, Gennadius, Augustine, Gregory, as well as the pseudo-Rufinus *Historia monachorum* and the *Liber pontificalis*. Of his purpose he says, "omnes, quos invenire potui, non solum qua die, verum etiam quo genere certaminis, vel sub quo judice mundum vicerint, diligenter annotare studi" (*HE* v.24).[74] The work was written be-

---

do by throwing water on them. Nor is it to be wondered at that such perfect men, the faithful servants of God, received power over the force of flames, who knew how to tame, by the daily practice of virtues, the fires of their own flesh, and how to extinguish "all the fiery darts of the most wicked one" [Eph. 6:16]. To whom that prophetic saying most aptly applies, "When thou shalt walk in the fire, thou shalt not be burned, and the flames shall not burn in thee" [Isa. 43:2]. But I and those like me, conscious of our own fragility and helplessness, are certain that we dare nothing of the sort against material fire, and are uncertain whether we shall with immunity evade that inextinguishable fire of the punishment to come. But the love of our savior is powerful and abounding, which extends the grace of His protection to our unworthy selves both now to extinguish the fires of our vices, and in the world to come to avoid the flames of punishment.

[73] The signs of his miracles and those things by which he shone outwardly, gave testimony to his inward virtues, that is of his soul.

[74] All those martyrs whom I have been able to find, I have dili-

tween 725, when he composed the *Chronica majora*
which provided the versions of Prosper used in the Martyrology, and 731 when he mentioned it in the last chapter
of *HE*. It was used by later authors, especially Florus of
Lyons, Ado, and Usuard, who often filled in the days on
which Bede recorded no martyrdom, neglecting his careful treatment of sources; they have, for example, no fixed
rule when their sources give discrepant dates, whereas
Bede always prefers the "Jerome" dating in such a di-
lemma, and while Bede may distort his source in the
process of condensing it, his later "editors" distort their
sources in their emphasis on sensational, rather than historical, detail.

Chronology (2.4)

Bede's chronological writings, even more than his historical writings, identified him to medieval scholars and
characterized his reputation among them. They were, by
and large, his nearest approach to active controversy,
and they were his most "international" works.

Chronological writing dealt with two of the great human concerns: man's understanding of the physical cosmos and his performance of his spiritual obligations.
Medieval chronology sought, explicitly or implicitly, to
relate the least fraction of a minute to the moment of
Creation in the past and to the unpredictable future. The
source of this concern was Easter, the principal feast of
the Christian year. Easter—or at least, the historical
Easter, and the anniversaries of the historical Easter in
the first years of the Church—was simultaneous with the
Jewish Passover, and as the earliest Christians were
mostly Jews, no great problems arose from this. But the
internationalization of the Church was the beginning of

---

gently sought to record, not only on what day, but also in what sort
of contest, or under what judge they conquered the world.

difficulties which did not cease to cause bewilderment, division, strife, and even homicide until Bede's time.

The development of these difficulties was long and complicated, but it may be enough to suggest how they came about in general. The Passover is celebrated on the fourteenth day of the Jewish month Nisan, which begins with the first new moon in spring. Thus Passover can be reasonably well ascertained in any year on the basis of the lunar calendar. When the early Church lost its Jewish identity, it soon decided to celebrate Easter on Sunday, and later that the Sunday must not be Nisan 14; it would have to be Nisan 15 or the next Sunday afterward, so that the Easter Sunday was between Nisan 15 and 21. Tradition soon grew that the vernal equinox was the early limit for Nisan 14. Now this sets three different kinds of cycle one on the other: the lunar cycle of 29½ days a month, 354 days in a year; the solar cycle of 365¼ days a year; and the weekly cycle of 52 x 7, making 364 days a year. Easter must satisfy criteria in all three. It is theoretically possible to calculate the Easter date for any future solar year, but either it must be calculated all over for any other future year, or a table must be prepared with all future years entered in it, and such a table—to be infinitely valid—would have to be infinitely long. What was really needed was a table which employed a formula giving a repeating cycle, so that after a certain length of time—the shorter the better—all three units would return to their beginning position. Such a table had, of course, to take into account the disparity between solar, lunar, and hebdomadal time on the "lowest common denominator" principle, and had also to observe such other limiting criteria as earliest and latest possible dates for Easter.

These problems became greater because the issue of authority was joined to them. As early as the second century disagreement between Rome and Alexandria on the

[146]

computation of the Easter date had broken out, and in 314 the Council of Arles considered the question and determined that the date of Easter should be decided by the Roman see and communicated to the faithful world by annual paschal letters. Now the British Church was represented at the Council of Arles, and it seems likely that the table in use in Rome at that time was carried back to Britain by the bishops. But the relative isolation of the British Church from the remainder of the Western World after the mid-fifth century left it with equally ancient, but discordant, traditions of Easter-reckoning. More than anything else it was this discord that kept the two churches apart from 597 until 664, and it was the particularly wide divergence of the two Easters impending in 665 which contributed to the convocation at Whitby in 664 of representatives of the British and Roman parties, whose different calculations had managed well enough side-by-side for some time before.

Thus the question of chronology in Bede's time reflects a serious difficulty which had been most acutely felt in Northumbria, his quarter of his nation, and the ecclesiastical history of the whole country drew its character largely from the problems posed by the Easter question and the possibilities gained by its solution. When we see that, in addition, his chronological studies had drawn him into ecclesiastical strife, not excluding a charge of heresy against him and disharmony with the controversial Wilfrid, we can understand the importance of his computistical works, and of the computistical portions of his historical and exegetical works as well.

De temporibus liber

Bede's first surviving identifiable chronological work— some short anonymous tracts on the subject may also be his—is *De temporibus liber*, which can be dated 703 by references at the beginning and end of ch. 22, and by the passage in ch. 14,

> Si nosse vis quot sunt anni ab incarnatione domini, scito quot fuerint ordines indictionum, utputa quinto anno Tiberii principis XLVI; hos per XV multiplica, fiunt DCXC; adde semper regulares XII, quia quarta indictione secundum Dionysium dominus natus est, et indictionem anni cujus volueris, utputa in praesenti unam; fiunt DCCIII.[75]

It is therefore of much the same date as the school writings, and probably like them meant for the instruction of his pupils; at the beginning of *DTR*, he says that he wrote it at the request of "fratribus quibusdam" (certain brothers) to expand on *DTL*. *DTL* is indeed short, no more than ten pages including the *Chronica minora* which form chs. 17-22. It begins with the smaller units of time, "De momentis et horis" (on moments and hours), and passes on to the day, week, and month, pausing there for a discussion of lunar time. An explanation of the annual cycle leads to one of the paschal reckoning, and then to the largest units, the ages of the world. Chapter 16 is "De mundi aetatibus" (on the ages of the world).

> Sex aetatibus mundi tempora distinguntur. Prima aetas ab Adam usque ad Noe continens generationes decem, annos vero MDCLVI; quae tota periit diluvio, sicut infantiam mergere solet oblivio. Secunda a Noe usque ad Abraham generationes similiter complexa decem, annos autem CCXCII; quae in lingua inventa est, id est Hebraea, a pueritia namque homo incipit nosse loqui post infantiam, quae et nomen inde accepit quod fari, id est loqui, non potest. Tertia ab Abraham usque ad David generationes XIV, annos vero CMXLII, continens; et quod ab adolescentia incipit homo

[75] If you wish to know how many years there have been since the incarnation of the Lord, find out the orders of the indictions there have been, as for example in the fifth year of Prince Tiberius, 46 multiply these by 15, and you have 690; always add the 12 "regulars," because the Lord was born according to Dionysius in the fourth indiction, and the indiction of the year which you want, as for example at present, one; and that makes 703.

posse generare Mattheus generationum ex Abraham sumpsit
exordium, qui etiam pater gentium constitutus est. Quarta
a David usque ad transmigrationem Babylonis generationibus aeque juxta Mattheum xiv, annis autem CDLXXIII,
porrecta, a qua regum tempora coeperunt, juvenilis enim
dignitas regno est habilis. Quinta deinde usque ad adventum
salvatoris in carnem generationibus et ipsa xiv, porro annis
DLXXXIX, extenta, in qua, ut gravi senectute fessa, malis
crebrioribus plebs Hebraea quassatur. Sexta, quae nunc
agitur, nulla generationum vel temporum serie certa sed, ut
aetas decrepita ipsa, totius saeculi morte finienda.[76]

The remaining six chapters are a particular account of
each of the six ages in detail.

The arrangement makes the subject seem straightforward, as it was intended to do, but the work was hotly
controversial. For one thing, it took sides in the centuries-
old paschal dispute, and at a time when the disparity between Roman and Celtic reckoning was threatening new
difficulties in the Easter of 704. Though the Synod of

---

[76] The epochs of the world are divided into six ages. The first
age, from Adam to Noah, containing ten generations, and 1,656
years; in which all perished in the Flood, just as infancy is submerged in forgetfulness. The second age from Noah to Abraham
likewise was made up of ten generations, but 292 years; which is
discovered in its language, that is Hebrew, for from childhood
onward man begins to know how to talk, following his infancy,
which takes its name from the fact that he cannot speak, that is,
talk. The third age, containing fourteen generations, and 942
years, from Abraham to David; and because from his adolescence
man is capable of reproduction, Matthew takes up the beginning of
the generations from Abraham [Matt. 1:1-2], who was made the
father of the nations. The fourth age from David up to the Baby-
lonian exile, extended also to fourteen generations according to
Matthew, and to 473 years, from when the times of the kings began,
for the dignity of a young man is proper for royal authority. The
fifth age extended from then until the advent in the flesh of the
savior in the same fourteen generations, and moreover in 589 years,
in which the Jewish people were shaken by more and more frequent
evils, as though wearied by burdensome old age. The sixth age,
which now reigns, is of uncertain duration in time or generations
but, like extreme old age itself, is to end with the death of the
whole world.

Whitby had decided for Rome against the Irish, the techniques of implementing this decision were difficult to master, and existing texts were confusing and self-contradictory. For another, when in ch. 22 of the *chronica* Bede wrote "Dominus nascitur completis ab Adam annis MMMCMLII, juxta alios MMMMMCXCIX,"[77] he departed so far from the traditional figure of Eusebius and Jerome that he brought upon himself the charge of heresy. A priest named David denounced Bede in the presence of Bishop Wilfrid of York for having denied that Christ became incarnate in the sixth age of the world. True, the traditional reckoning assigned a thousand years to each age, and so Bede's 3,952 did not tally with the tradition; but the tradition was not doctrine, and Bede's *opusculum* was intended to set the tradition straight. Besides, the remark in question appeared in the chapter entitled "De sexta aetate."

Wilfrid did not reject the charge, or send word to Bede that he should reply to it. Indeed, it was not until 708 that an otherwise unknown monk named Plegwin wrote from Hexham to report the situation to Bede, who replied in the *Epistola ad Pleguinam de aetatibus saeculi*:

> Venit ad me ante biduum, frater amantissime, nuntius tuae sanctitatis, qui pacificae quidem salutationis a te laetissima verba detulit. Sed haec tristi mox admixtione confudit, addendo videlicet quod me audires a lascivientibus rusticis inter hereticos per pocula decantari. Exhorrui, fateor, et pallens percunctabar, cujus hereseos arguerer. Respondit quia negarem in sexta aetate saeculi dominum salvatorem in carne venisse. Percunctari ergo coepi quomodo diceretur, utrum quia dominus non venisset in carne cum tamen sexta esset aetas, an quia domino in carne veniente necdum sexta aetas veniret, vel certe aetas septima jam venisset, cum aperta ratione sexta aetas non nisi ab ejus possit incarnatione coepisse. Deprehendique sive hoc sive

[77] The Lord was born 3,952 years after Adam, according to others, 5,199.

illud insimularetur, me in utroque sane fidei et ecclesiasticae unitatis existere consortem.[78]

The letter, very nearly as long as the tract it defends,
seems to have ended the suspicion about Bede's orthodoxy, but he never lost the feelings which the last paragraph barely veils:

> Obsecro sane ut has purgationis meae litteras religioso ac
> doctissimo fratri nostro David porrigas, quatenus eas ille
> coram venerabili domino ac patre nostro, Wilfrido scilicet
> antistite, legere possit ut, quia illo praesente atque audiente
> insipientium sum prius appetitus conviciis, ipso etiam nunc
> audiente ac dejudicante quam immeritus eadem convicia
> sim perpessus appareat. Ipsum quoque David prae ceteris
> rogo ut, juxta exemplum sibi cognominis pueri, furorem
> spiritus nequam a fratre disipiente hortatu sanorum ver-
> borum quasi dulci psalmodiae modulatione sedulus effugare
> contendat; quod utique in illa cena in qua me poculo de-
> brius culpare studuit, ille qui semet potius lectioni intentus
> inculpabilem facere debuerat, perficere nequibat, utpote
> sensus et sententiae meae quam laudabat necdum plene
> conscius. Vere enim dictum est *quia si momorderit serpens
> in silentio, non est habundantia incantatori.*[79]

[78] Two days ago, most beloved brother, the messenger of your
holiness came to me, who carried from you the most happy words
of peaceful salutation. But soon he poured with this a sad mixture,
that is, by adding that you hear me repeatedly mentioned among the
heretics by lascivious rustics in their cups. I confess I was horrified,
and growing pale I inquired of which heresy I was accused. He
replied that I had denied that the Lord our savior had come in the
sixth age of the world. I then set about asking in what manner it
was said, whether that the Lord had not come in the flesh when it
was, however, the sixth age, or that—although He had come in the
flesh—it was not in the sixth age that He had come, or indeed that
the seventh age had already come, when after all the sixth age
could not have been begun except by His incarnation. And I was
surprised whether this or that accusation was made, as in both
points I share the whole faith and ecclesiastical unity.

[79] I beg you greatly that you pass on these letters of my purga-
tion to the religious and most learned brother of ours, David, so
that they may be read before the venerable lord, our father Wilfrid
the bishop, because it was in his presence and hearing that I was
first attacked by the abuse of the unlearned, and therefore now in

De bissexti praeparatione

At an unknown date, but well before 725, Bede wrote a tract "De bissexti praeparatione" on the zodiac. The tract survives in thirteen MSS, and—although it is nowhere attributed to him, and he does not mention it in *HE* v.24—it is almost certainly the work he refers to in *DTR*, ch. 38 "si cui sane quae de signifero et caeli ambitu paucis diximus forte habentur incognita, huic vulgari et fortassis compendiosiori ac manifestiori ratione satisfacere curavimus."[80] Since ch. 38 is itself (with ch. 39) a letter written before its insertion into *DTR* in 725, "De bissexti praeparatione" must antedate them both, but it is probably later than the controversy of 708.

Ad Helmwaldum

The *Epistola ad Helmwaldum de bissexto* which later, without its salutation, was to become chs. 38-39 of *DTR*, was written to an unknown monk probably 708 x 725.

> Quaeris igitur tibi quadrantis annui quem bissextum vocant, rationem breviter ac manifeste, quantum res patitur, explicari, quandamque, ut ita dicam, naturae occultioris abyssum apertarum clavibus litterarum ad promptum liberae

---

his hearing and with his judgment it may appear how unworthily I have suffered the same abuse. And more than the rest I beg the same David that, following the example of the boy of the same name, he will carefully strive to put to flight that wicked rage of the spirit with an exhortation of wholesome words coming from the brother like the melody of sweet psalmody; which certainly, at that dinner at which he set about to blame me when he was stupefied with his cup, he who ought rather to have been striving to make himself blameless by reading, was unable to accomplish, for even when he praised my meaning and my interpretations, he was not fully aware. For truly it is said "If a serpent bite in silence, he is nothing better that backbiteth secretly" [Ecc. 10:11].

[80] If by any chance anyone does not understand what I have written on the zodiac and the course of the heavens in a few words, for such I have sought to make it known and to satisfy him with a longer and clearer explanation.

serenaeque cognitionis educi, nec dignus es a mea parvitate
rogitans sperni, quam tot terrarum marisque spatiis inter-
jacentibus per epistolas alloquendam ac de necessariis con-
sulendam decrevisti.[81]

Chapter 38 begins "De ratione bissexti non nova nunc
cudere sed quae in epistola roganti amico quondam dixi,
etiam his inserere placuit opusculis, ubi post praefationem
congruam ita subjeci."[82] The two chapters of *DTR*, "De
ratione bissexti" and "De mensura crementi bissextilis,"
include a lengthy passage from Augustine's *De trinitate*.
Bede refers to the letter in *HE* v.24 as "de ratione bissexti." The letter as a separate document survives in
one composite eleventh-century MS and in another of the
fifteenth century; its contents were chiefly known through
its insertion in *DTR*.

De temporum ratione

Bede's major work on chronology was the *De temporum ratione* or *De temporibus liber major*, composed
—as he says in chs. 49, 52, and 58—in 725. His reason is
given in the preface as the request of the monks who
"suadebant . . . mihi latius aliqua de temporum statu,
cursu, ac fine disserere."[83] He may also have felt that
the letters to Plegwin and Helmwald had not entirely re-

[81] You ask therefore to have explained to you briefly and clearly,
as far as the subject permits it, the scheme of the fourth part of the
year's duration, which they call the bissextus, and, as I shall say so,
to have certain things brought forth from the gulf of the more
obscure sort by the keys of open letters to the exposition of free
and serene understanding, nor are you worthy to be spurned when
you ask this of my littleness, which you have judged fit to be saluted
by letters across all the intervening space of land and sea, and to
be consulted on necessary matters.

[82] I do not purpose now to forge new things about the scheme of
the bissextus, but rather those things which I wrote in a letter to a
friend who asked me, I purpose to insert in these little works,
where after a suitable preface I have accordingly put them.

[83] Persuaded me to write more fully something about the beginning, course, and end of time.

solved the difficulties of *DTL*; his preparation of the
materials for *HE* may have reminded him of the need for
a larger work on chronology; and the paschal question,
still abroad despite the victories of the Roman party since
the Synod of Whitby, may have encouraged him to include
new documents, like the *Laterculus* of Polemius Silvius,
which had come into his hands since the composition of
DTL (cf. *DTR*, ch. 14). These additional motives probably account for the controversial tone of the work which
is otherwise inconsistent with its professed didactic
purpose.

In outline it follows the progression from the smallest
to the largest units of time which Bede had used in
DTL, and which was already characteristic of computistical works before the earlier tract. The first chapter, which
deals with counting-games and speaking with the fingers,
suggests that the book would have been included in the
curriculum for some of the youngest members of the community, and the repeated allusions to oral explanation
confirm that the monastic student was its primary audience. The ultimate purpose was not, however, simply to
end a paschal controversy; the culmination of the work
in the chapters on the six ages of the world emphasizes
his belief that chronological study, like all other, is ancil-
lary to the study of the Bible, the central document in
medieval scholarship.

Like *DTL*, *DTR* ends with a chronicle, but fittingly a
much expanded one (the later work is well over ten times
the length of the earlier), with details drawn from Jerome,
Orosius, Josephus, Rufinus, and Hegesippus. Under the
entry for 3,952 from the Creation, Bede writes "Jesus
Christus filius Dei sextam mundi aetatem suo con-
secravit adventu,"[84] reaffirming but clarifying his former
doctrine. The chronicle was early separated from the work

[84] Jesus Christ the Son of God consecrated the sixth age of the
world with His coming.

of which it forms chapters 66-71 : there remain 44 MSS of the *Chronica majora* alone against 135 of *DTR*, some of them without the chronicle. Of *DTL* about 45 MSS, and 18 of the *Chronica minora* alone, survive.

In his preface, Bede is fully aware of the secular snares that such an undertaking can conceal:

> Quorum quisque dicta perspexerit, credo mox nostro labori calumniam facere desistet si non hunc tamen lividis quod absit contemplatur obtutibus. Verum utcumque ferant haec mea scripta legentes primo editum pro captu meo libellum tibi, dilectissime abba meus Hwaetberhte, percurrendum atque examinandum offero, multum deprecans ut si quid in eo tu vituperabile deprehenderis statim mihi corrigendum insinues, at ubi ordinate ac rationabiliter actum videris mecum Deo qui donavit et sine quo nihil possumus facere devotus gratias agas. Si quem sane vel illud offendit cur aliquid de hujusmodi negotio temptare praesumpserim, quare de his quae sparsim in veterum scriptis inveniri potuerant ipse novum opus condere studuerim, audiat dicente sancto Augustino quia ideo necesse est plures a pluribus fieri libros diverso stilo non diversa fide, etiam de quaestionibus eisdem, ut ad plurimos res ipsa perveniat; ad alios sic, ad alios autem sic. Audiat et me pro me simpliciter respondentem: cui displicet vel superfluum videtur, quod haec rogatu fratrum undecumque collegi uniusque libelli tenore conclusi, dimittat ea legenda, si qui velint, et ipse de communibus patrum fontibus quae sibi suisque sufficere arbitretur hauriens mecum nihilominus debita fraternitatis intemerata jura custodiat.[85]

[85] Everyone who will have examined their sayings, will, I believe, soon cease casting calumny on my work, if spiteful onlookers do not expect in it what is absent. But however those reading these writings of mine may regard them, first I offer my little book to you, most beloved abbot of mine Hwaetberht, written according to my own understanding, to be perused and examined, praying greatly that if you find anything in it which is blameworthy you immediately let me know it is to be corrected, and where you find it properly and reasonably done, with me you should devoutly give thanks to God Who gave it, without Whom we can do nothing. If this one or that one is offended, wondering why I have presumed to attempt anything of this sort, or why I labored to make a new work on matters which can hardly be found in the writings

But at the end of his book, the subject of his final chapters—"De temporibus Antichristi," "De die judicii," "De septima et octava aetate saeculi futuri"[86]—has influenced the nature of his concern with his work:

> Ergo noster libellus de volubili ac fluctivago temporum lapsu descriptus opportunum de aeterna stabilitate ac stabili aeternitate habeat finem. Quem rogo si qui lectione dignum rati fuerint, me suis in praecibus domino commendent piaque apud Deum et proximos, quantum valent, agant industria, ut post temporales caelestium actionum sudores aeternam cuncti caelestium praemiorum mereamur accipere palmam.[87]

Ad Wihthedum

Bede mentions in *HE* v.24 a letter "de aequinoctio juxta Anatolium."[88] It was written before 731 to an unknown monk named Wihthed, probably after 725, for it is asso-

---

of the ancients themselves, let him hear what St. Augustine says, that it is necessary for many books to be written by many, in diverse styles but not with a diverse faith, about the same questions, so that the same thing may get through to many people, in one way to some, in another to others [*De trinitate* 1.3]. And let him hear me too, answering simply for myself: whoever is displeased or thinks it superfluous, that I have collected these things from everywhere at the request of my brethren and put them together in the discourse of a single book, let him send them away to be read, if any there be who wish to do so, and keep for himself those things from the common sources of the fathers which he thinks will suffice him and his; mine are the unspotted bounden obligations of brotherhood.

[86] On the times of Antichrist; on the judgment day; on the seventh and eighth age of the world to come.

[87] Therefore our book about the rolling and tossing flowing of the times, having told of the eternal stability and stable eternity, has its fitting end. And if anyone has considered it worth reading, them I ask that they commend me to the Lord in their prayers, and that as far as they are capable they act with holy diligence toward God and their neighbors, so that after the temporal labors of heavenly deeds, we may all be worthy to receive the eternal palm of celestial rewards.

[88] About the equinox, according to Anatolius.

ciated in many of its thirty-three surviving MSS with
DTR, but incorporated into it in but two. It is shorter
than *DTL* and concerns itself with the pseudo-Anatolian
Canon which had formed the basis of much Celtic Easter-
reckoning. Bede himself referred to the *Canon* in *DTR*
(ch. 30), when discussing the equinoxes, and there accepted the support of its confirmation; but here he attempts to throw it out of court by casting doubt on the
authenticity of the text, thus undermining its teaching
without directly attacking it. According to Jones, the frequent appeals to the *Canon* in paschal literature virtually
disappear after the *Epistola ad Wihthedum de aequinoctio
vernali.*

Didactic Works (2.5)

Bede mentions five works at the end of his list in *HE*
v.24. The two works *De temporibus* seem to be included
because they share some of the subject matter of *De natura
rerum*; but *De orthographia* and the two parts of the
work on poetry and figurative language are grouped here
because they were written at the same time and for the
same purpose as *De natura rerum.* They are now held to
be Bede's earliest surviving works, more derivative than
those that followed, composed for the daily needs of instruction within the monastery. Their appearance at the
end of the list may reflect Bede's own appraisal of their
restricted originality, scope, and audience.

De natura rerum was probably composed before *DTL*
(703) and perhaps before *De orthographia* and *De metris,
schematibus et tropis.* It is a brief description of the
cosmos, prefaced by a quatrain, and commencing with introductory chapters "De quadrifario Dei opere," "De
mundi formatione," "Quid sit mundus."[89] The discussion

---

[89] About the fourfold work of God; about the formation of the
world; what the world is.

of the elements and firmament includes consideration of
the zodiac and the motions of the heavenly bodies, anticipating the chronological tracts which were to follow,
but much of the material is presented in the precise words
of his authorities: Augustine, Ambrose, Pliny, Isidore;
some of the early MSS preserve source-marks which probably originated with Bede. The work is not so well
organized as his later studies, depending as much as it
does on what was available in the writings of a number
of earlier authors; it may be little more than the "published" form of a teacher's notebook. It survives, however,
in well over one hundred MSS.

De orthographia was probably written before *De metris,
schematibus et tropis,* perhaps 699-701. Only the first
section corresponds with what we would now term or-
thography, consisting of some notes about assimilation of
consonants and the "pro-nominal" use of letters for names.
The remainder of the work is an alphabetical handbook
of usage:

> Arbor omne lignum dicitur, arbusta non nisi fructifera.
> Avenae sterile germen, habenae retinacula jumentorum:
> hoc de habendi potestate, illud de occupandi aviditate
> dictum.
> Accidunt mala, contingunt bona, eveniunt utraque.[90]

The work is heavily indebted to earlier writers like
Diomedes, Caper, and Agroecius, and shows little of
Bede's own capacities. It was later the basis of a work of
the same name by Alcuin with which it is often confused
in the MSS, but at least seventeen of the Bede version do
survive.

---

[90] Every tree is so called, but an orchard is not an orchard unless
fruit-bearing [distinction between *arbor* and *arbusta*]. Oats is the
name given to a barren sprout, reins to the harness for beasts of
burden: the latter is so called because of its power to restrain, the
former because of its avidity to spread [distinction between *avena,*
as though from *aviditas,* and *habena,* from *habeo*]. Bad things
befall; good things happen; both come to pass.

The date of the *De arte metrica*—and, presumably, of
the *De schematibus et tropis* which forms a part of it—
can be deduced from the introductory dedication to
Cuthbert:

> Haec tibi, dulcissime fili et collevita Cuthberte, diligenter
> ex antiquorum opusculis scriptorum excerpere curavi et
> quae sparsim reperta ipse diutino labore collegeram tibi
> collecta obtuli, ut, quemadmodum in divinis litteris sta-
> tutisque ecclesiasticis imbuere studui, ita et in metrica arte,
> quae divinis non est incognita libris, te solerter instruerem.
> Cui etiam de figuris vel modis locutionum, quae a Graecis
> schemata vel tropi dicuntur, parvum subicere libellum non
> incongruum duxi, tuamque dilectionem sedulus exoro ut
> lectioni operam impendas illarum maxime litterarum, in
> quibus nos vitam habere credimus sempiternam.[91]

Laistner, insisting that only a difference of nine or ten
years in the age of the two men could justify the language
of this passage, makes the last years of Bede's diaconate
—701 or 702—the date of the work. The *De arte metrica*
begins in Bede's usual systematic way with the smallest
parts, the letters of the alphabet, and goes on to the syllables and the combinations of them in metrical form,
first in feet and then in entire lines; Aldhelm had followed much the same pattern in his own work *de arte
metrica*. Bede also has a penultimate chapter "De
rhythmo" in which he quotes from Victorinus:

> Videtur autem rhythmus metris esse consimilis, quae est
> verborum modulata compositio, non metrica ratione, sed

[91] I have sought to excerpt these things for you, dearest son and
fellow deacon Cuthbert, diligently from the works of ancient writers,
and what I have collected together by long labor here and there, I
have set out before you in order, so that just as I have striven to
dip into divine writings and ecclesiastical statutes, even so I might
carefully instruct you in the art of meter, which is not unknown in
holy books. And I have thought it to the point to add on a little book
about figures or modes of speaking that the Greeks call schemes or
tropes, and I sedulously beg your loving kindness that you especially
apply yourself to the work of reading those writings in which we
have the grounds for our belief in eternal life.

numero syllabarum ad judicium aurium examinata, ut sunt carmina vulgarium poetarum,[92]

recalling the words of his "bibliography" in *HE* v.24, "Liber hymnorum diverso metro sive rhythmo."[93] His only genuinely critical passage—aside from the remark that "metra alia . . . Porphyrii poetae . . . quia pagana erant, nos tangere non libuit"[94]—is the final chapter, in which he distinguishes three types of poetry :

> Sane quia multa disputavimus de poematibus et metris, commemorandum in calce quia poematos genera sunt tria. Aut enim activum vel imitativum est, quod Graeci dramaticon vel mimeticon appellant; aut enarrativum, quod Graeci exegematicon vel apangelticon nuncupant; aut commune vel mixtum, quod Graeci coenon vel micton vocant. Dramaticon est vel activum, in quo personae loquentes introducuntur sine poetae interlocutione, ut se habent tragoediae et fabulae: drama enim Latine fabula dicitur: quo genere scripta est
>
> > quo de Moeri pedes? an quo via ducit, in urbem?
>
> quo apud nos genere Cantica canticorum scripta sunt, ubi vox alternans Christi et ecclesiae tametsi non hoc interloquente scriptore manifeste reperitur. Exegematicon est vel enarrativum, in quo poeta ipse loquitur sine ullius interpositione personae, ut se habent tres libri Georgici toti et prima pars quarti, item Lucretii carmina et his similia. Quo genere apud nos scriptae sunt parabolae Salomonis et Ecclesiastes, quae in sua lingua, sicut et psalterium, metro constat esse conscripta. Coenon est vel micton, in quo poeta ipse loquitur et personae loquentes introducuntur, ut sunt scripta Ilias et Odyssea Homeri et Aeneidos Virgilii et apud nos historia beati Job, quamvis haec in sua lingua

[92] It seems also that rhythm is similar to meter, which is the modulated composition of words, measured not by metrical rule, but by the number of syllables to the judgment of the ear, as the poems of vernacular poets are.

[93] A book of hymns in diverse meter or rhythm.

[94] The other meters of the poet Porphyrius we should not touch upon, for they were pagan.

non tota poetico, sed partim rhetorico, partim sit metrico
vel rhythmico scripta sermone.[95]

One of the allusions to Homer in the work is through
the medium of Theodorus (fl. 399), and most of the work
is a mixture of Donatus, Pompeius and Servius, Audax,
Victorinus, Diomedes, *et al.*, but the materials have
undergone revision to a greater extent than those in *De
natura rerum* or *De orthographia.* The examples are
chosen more from Christian poets like Sedulius, Prosper,
Juvencus, Prudentius, Fortunatus, and Arator, than from
Terence, Lucan, or even Virgil.

Bede's purpose in writing the supplement *De schematibus et tropis* is to show that all the figures of speech
known to the ancients are employed in the Bible:

sancta scriptura ceteris omnibus scripturis non solum
auctoritate, quia divina est, vel utilitate, quia ad vitam ducit

[95] Indeed, since we have argued many things about poems and
meters, it should be pointed out in the conclusion that there are
three sorts of poems. Either a poem is active or imitative, which
the Greeks call dramatic or mimetic; or it is narrative, which the
Greeks call descriptive or reportorial; or it is common or mixed,
which the Greeks call by the same names. That poem is dramatic
or active, in which speaking persons are introduced without the
interruption of the poet, as in the case of tragedies and fables: for
drama is called fable in Latin: in which sort is written "where are
you going, Moeris? Where does your path lead—to town?" [Virgil,
Eclogues 9.1], and in which sort, among us, the Song of Songs is
written, where the voice of Christ, alternating with that of the
Church without the interruption of the poet, is clearly found. It is
descriptive or narrative, in which the poet himself speaks without
the interpolation of another person, as in all the first three books
of the Georgics and the first part of the fourth book, and likewise in
the poems of Lucretius and ones similar to these. In which sort,
among us, the parables of Solomon and Ecclesiastes are written,
which in their language, like a psalter, are composed in meter. The
common or mixed sort of poem is that in which the poet himself speaks and speaking persons are introduced, as the *Iliad* and
Odyssey of Homer are written, and the *Aeneid* of Virgil, and among
us the history of blessed Job, although the latter is not altogether

[161]

aeternam, sed et antiquitate, et ipsa praeeminet positione dicendi, ideo placuit mihi, collectis de ipsa exemplis, ostendere quia nihil hujusmodi schematum, sive troporum valent praetendere ullis saeculis eloquentiae magistri, quod non illa praecesserit.[96]

Schemes are changes in the order of words, tropes in their meaning; they are the syntactic and semantic figures of speech. In this distinction, in expanding the classification (chiefly on the model of Isidore), and in drawing his examples entirely from Scripture, Bede differs most from his source, Donatus. He lists seventeen schemes, and explains them:

> Paromoen est cum ab eisdem litteris diversa verba sumuntur. Quae nimirum figura, quod ad positionem litterarum pertinet, melius in ea lingua qua scripta est editaque requiretur. Habemus tamen et in nostra translatione, unde demus exemplum.[97]

It is noteworthy that he does not draw on the alliterative technique of the native poetry with which he was familiar to illustrate this passage.

In the second short section, *De tropis*, Bede describes twenty-eight of the type "dictio translata a propria sig-

---

verse in its language, but written partly in prose, partly in a metric or rhythmic discourse.

[96] Holy Scripture towers above all other writings not only by its authority, which is divine, or its utility, which leads us to eternal life, but also by its antiquity, and by its very use of language; and therefore it has pleased me, when the examples of this were collected, to show that the masters of eloquence in any age are able to put forth nothing of schemes or of tropes of this sort, which holy Scripture will not excel.

[97] Paromoen is the scheme in which different words are begun by the same letters. Which figure truly, insofar as it pertains to the position of letters, is best to be sought in that language in which it was written and published. We have an example of it in the Latin translation of the Bible, however, from which we give it [cf. Ps. 117 :26-27; Ps. 57 :5].

nificatione ad non propriam similitudinem,"[98] under thirteen main headings. The chapter "De allegoria" begins:

> Allegoria est tropus quo aliud significatur quam dicitur, ut: *Levate oculos vestros, et videte regiones, quia albae sunt jam ad messem.* Hoc est, intellegite, quia populi sunt jam parati ad credendum. Hujus species multae sunt, ex quibus eminent septem: ironia, antiphrasis, aenigma, charientis mos, paroemia, sarcasmos, asteismos.[99]

The discussion of *asteismos* most closely resembles the modern understanding of allegory, and most concisely sets out Bede's own theory of scriptural allegory as it influenced his exegetical works:

> Asteismos est tropus multiplex, numerosaeque virtutis: nam ἀστεϊσμός putatur quidquid dictum simplicitate rustica caret, et satis faceta urbanitate expolitum est, ut: *Utinam abscindantur qui vos conturbant.* Notandum sane quod allegoria aliquando factis, aliquando verbis tantummodo fit. . . . item allegoria verbi, sive operis, aliquando historicam rem, aliquando typicam, aliquando tropologicam, id est, moralem rationem, aliquando anagogen, hoc est, sensum ad superiora ducentem, figurate denuntiat. Per historiam namque historia figuratur, cum factura primorum sex sive septem dierum, totidem saeculi hujus comparatur aetatibus. Per verbum historia, dum hoc quod dicit Jacob patriarcha, *Catulus leonis Juda, ad praedam, fili mi, ascendisti,* et cetera, de regno ac victoriis David intellegitur. Per verbum, spiritalis de Christo, sive ecclesia, sensus, cum idem sermo patriarchae de dominica passione ac resurrectione fideliter accipitur. Item allegoria facta, tropologicam, hoc est, moralem perfectionem designat, ut tunica talaris et

[98] An utterance taken from its own meaning and applied to a different similitude.

[99] Allegory is the trope in which something other is signified from what is said, as [John 4:35]: Lift up your eyes, and see the countries; for they are white already to harvest. That is, understand, for the people are ready to believe. There are many sorts of this trope, out of which seven are most important: Irony, antiphrasis (the use of a word in a sense opposite to its proper meaning), enigma, charientismos (jesting), paroemia (proverbs), sarcasm, asteismos (a refined mode of speech).

polymita quam Jacob patriarcha filio suo Joseph fecit, variarum virtutum gratiam, qua nos Deus pater usque ad terminum vitae nostrae semper indui praecepit et donat, insinuat. Allegoria verbi eamdem morum perfectionem significat, ut: *Sint lumbi vestri praecincti, et lucernae ardentes,* et caetera. Allegoria facti, anagogicum, hoc est, ad superiora ducentem sensum exprimit, ut: *Septimus ab Adam Enoch translatus est de mundo.* Sabbatum futurae beatitudinis, quae post opera bona saeculi hujus, quae sex aetatibus peragitur, electis in fine servatur, figurate praesignat. Allegoria verbi, eadem vitae caelestis gaudia demonstrat, ut: *Ubicumque fuerit corpus, illic congregabuntur et aquilae,* quia ubi mediator Dei et hominum est corpore, ibi nimirum et nunc sublevatae ad caelos animae, et, celebrata gloria resurrectionis, colligentur etiam corpora justorum. Nonnumquam in una eademque re, vel verbo, historia simul et mysticus de Christo vel ecclesia sensus, et tropologia, et anagoge, figuraliter intimatur, ut: templum domini, juxta historiam, domus quam aedificavit Salomon; juxta allegoriam, corpus dominicum, de quo ait, *Solvite templum hoc, et in tribus diebus excitabo illud,* sive ecclesia ejus, cui dicitur: *Templum enim Dei sanctum est, quod estis vos;* per tropologiam, quisque fidelium, quibus dicitur, *An nescitis quia corpora vestra templum est spiritus sancti, qui in vobis est?* per anagogen, superni gaudii mansiones, cui aspirabat qui ait: *Beati qui habitant in domo tua, domine, in saeculum saeculi laudabunt te.*[100]

[100] Asteismos is a multiplex trope, and of numerous powers: for whatever saying is lacking in rustic simplicity and is sufficiently polished with fine urbanity is reckoned to be asteismos, such as: I would they were even cut off, who trouble you [Gal. 5:12]. It is to be noted that allegory is sometimes made with events, sometimes with words. . . . Allegory of the word or of the deed figuratively declares sometimes the historical matter, sometimes the typical, sometimes the tropological, that is, the moral concern, sometimes the anagogical, that is, the sense that leads to higher things. For history is represented through history, when the creation of the first six or seven days is likened to just so many ages of the present world. History is represented through the word, when by this which the patriarch Jacob says, Judah is a lion's whelp; to the prey, my son, thou art gone up, etc. [Gen. 49:9], is understood as applying to the reign and victories of David. The spiritual sense is represented through the word regarding Christ or the Church, when the same discourse of the patriarch is taken faithfully as applying

Thus *asteismos* is "high style" not simply in the refinement of the literary surface, but in its content of higher meaning. Bede does not deny the value of polished rhetoric: he is deliberate in his use of Greek rhetorical terms, and he is at pains to demonstrate the excellence of scriptural language by rhetorical standards. But the criterion he insists on is the suitable reference of this polish to intellectual content, and he has little time for schemes and tropes as accomplishments in themselves.

---

to the passion and resurrection. In like manner an allegorical deed represents the tropological, that is the moral, perfection, as the long and many-colored tunic which the patriarch Jacob made for his son Joseph signifies the gift of various virtues, which God the Father teaches and gives us to clothe ourselves in always until the end of our lives [cf. Gen. 37:3]. Allegory of the word signifies the same perfection of virtues, as Let your loins be girt, and lamps burning, etc. [Luke 12:35]. Allegory of the deed represents the anagogical, that is the sense leading to higher things, as The seventh after Adam, Enoch was carried from the world [cf. Jude 14, Gen. 5:24, Ecclus. 44:16, Hebr. 11:5]. This signifies the sabbath of the blessedness to come, which after the good works of this world, which are accomplished in six ages, is reserved in the end for the elect. Allegory of the word represents the same joy of the heavenly life, as in: Wheresoever the body shall be, there shall the eagles also be gathered together [Matt. 24:28], for wherever the mediator of God and men is in the body, there certainly will be gathered together both now the souls lifted up to the heavens, and, when the glory of the resurrection has been celebrated, the bodies of the just. Sometimes in one and the same thing, or word, the history and the mystic sense about Christ or the Church, and the tropological, and the anagogical, are figuratively intimated, as in: the temple of God, according to the historical sense, is the house which Solomon built; according to the allegorical, the Lord's body, of which it is said, Destroy this temple, and in three days I will raise it up [John 2:19], or His Church, of which it was said, For the temple of God is holy, which you are [1 Cor. 3:17]; according to the tropological, it is each of the faithful, about whom it is said, Know you not that you are the temple of God, and that the spirit of God dwelleth in you? [1 Cor. 3:16]. According to the anagogical sense, it is the mansions of eternal joy, to which he aspired who said: Blessed are they that dwell in thy house, O Lord, they shall praise thee for ever and ever [Ps. 83:5].

[165]

Homilies (2.6)

Bede's description of his homilies, "homiliarum evangelii libros II,"[101] makes it clear that he thought of them as an organized collection, like the two series of vernacular homilies by Aelfric. The usefulness of the collection made it internationally popular, but its contents were soon reordered (Bede followed the Romano-Neapolitan use) and sometimes replaced (Paulus Diaconus, died ca. 800, substituted another for Bede's homily on Benedict Biscop, lest the number fifty be diminished by the removal of a homily "quae utique minime ad legendum nostris congruere videbatur officiis").[102] The freedom with which these changes could be made, and the frequent recopying of the collection, led to a thorough-going masking of Bede's work, and not until Morin's study in 1892 was the shape of the original identified.

The fifty homilies, much alike in length, follow Bede's claim that in these and other writings "in scripturam sanctam meae meorumque necessitati ex opusculis venerabilium patrum breviter annotare, sive etiam ad formam sensus et interpretationis eorum superadicere curavi."[103] His sources, often heavily depended on, are Augustine, Gregory, Jerome, Ambrose, Isidore, and others, the founders of the exegetical technique which Bede inherited and did so much to perpetuate. His *Homily* II.6 on Mark 7:31-37 is characteristic:

> Surdus ille et mutus quem mirabiliter curatum a domino modo cum evangelium legeretur audivimus genus designat humanum in his qui ab errore diabolicae deceptionis divina

[101] Two books of homilies on the evangels.

[102] Which certainly seems to conform very little to the reading of our offices.

[103] I have striven to annotate briefly the sacred Scripture for my own need and that of those about me, out of the works of the venerable fathers, or to add onto them according to the manner of their meaning and interpretation.

merentur gratia liberari. Obsurduit namque homo ab audiendo vitae verbo postquam mortifera serpentis verba contra Deum tumidus audivit; mutus a laude conditoris effectus est ex quo cum seductore colloquium habere praesumpsit.[104]

The homilies may not all have been composed at the same time, but the collection appears to come after the commentary on Mark (720 x 725?) and certainly before its mention in *HE* (731).

Verses (2.7)

In addition to the metrical life of St. Cuthbert, Bede mentions a "librum hymnorum diverso metro sive rhythmo" and a "librum epigrammatum heroico metro, sive elegiaco."[105] No rhythmic works of Bede appear to have survived (the edition of *opera rhythmica* by Fraipont has been criticized as containing only prose and metrical poetry), but other poetry does, which may include a portion of the "libri" to which he referred in *HE* v.24.

1. The sixteen hymns published by Dreves, *Analecta hymnica*, 50.96-116. One is the hymn on Queen Etheldryd (from *HE* IV.18) in 27 abecedarian elegiac couplets—thirteen in iambic dimeters, two (paraphrases of Ps. 41 and 112), in hexameters (Fraipont nos. 1-13, 16, 18).

2. A poem in 9 elegiac couplets, *VP*, ch. 42.

3. A poem in 11 elegiac couplets following the introduction to *Exp.* (*PL* 93.133-134).

---

[104] The deaf man and the mute whom we hear of being miraculously cured by the Lord when the Gospel is read, signify the human race in those people who have deserved to be freed from the error of diabolic deception by divine grace. For man became deaf to hearing the word of life when, swollen up against God, he listened to the words of the serpent; and he was made mute in the praise of his maker from that time when he presumed to have conversation with his seducer.

[105] Book of hymns in diverse meter or rhythm; book of epigrams in heroic or elegiac meter.

4. Three elegiac couplets at the end of ch. 3 of *De locis sanctis*.

5. Two elegiac couplets at the beginning of *DNR*.

6. A prayer based on Ps. 83 in 10 elegiac couplets (Fraipont no. 17).

7. A poem "O Deus aeternae . . . vitae" in 13 elegiac couplets (Fraipont no. 15).

8. Three epitaphs in elegiacs and one in hexameter in *HE*, some at least probably by Bede:

    a. II.I (Pope Gregory), 8 elegiacs.

    b. v.7 (King Cadwalla), 12 elegiacs.

    c. v.8 (Archbishop Theodore), opening and clos-
       ing 2 elegiacs.

    d. v.19 (Bishop Wilfrid), 20 hexameters.

9. *De die judicii* (163 hexameters; Fraipont no. 14). Attributed to Bede in many MSS, including some early ones, it closes with an address to Acca of Hexham, an authentic detail hardly likely to have been the work of a forger.

There are several other poems which may well be his:

10. Poem (*MGH*, Poetae IV.25, 1067) alone in one MS and before *Comm. in Cath. Epist.* in three others.

11. *Libellus precum* in MS Cologne Dombibliothek 106 (Fraipont no. 20).

12. Fragment in 3 hexameters (Fraipont no. 19).

There remains finally a large group of poems certainly not Bede's, but attributed to him at one time or another because they treated subjects about which he had writ-ten: they include the *Cuculus* that is probably Alcuin's, the metrical *Martyrology* attributed in early MSS to Sisebut, the *Passio Justini*, and the four poems *De ratione temporum, De xii signis zodiaci, De aetatibus, Dionysius de annis*. A MS mentioned item 88 in the catalogue of H. P. Kraus, *Fifty Mediaeval and Renaissance MSS*.

(New York, 1958), included an unedited poem "In absida basilicae" attributed to Bede.

History (2.8)

The *Historia ecclesiastica gentis anglorum* was finished in 731, as Bede makes clear in v.23, "Qui sit in praesenti status gentis Anglorum, vel Britanniae totius,"[106] but underwent at least some subsequent revision; another phrase in the same chapter refers to the battle of Tours, in which Charles Martel defeated the Saracens in 732. There are other signs of reworking: Plummer has pointed out that the description of Aldhelm's writings (v.18) seems out of place, and "cujus supra meminimus"[107] in the account of Benedict Biscop (IV.16) refers to nothing in *HE* (although it may refer to the *HAB*). All of I.34, the last chapter in the book, may be a later addition, for it breaks the continuity of the story of the Augustinian mission in Book I and the life of Gregory in Book II. But Bede had a clear outline when he set out: he can mention a subject and then put it aside for later discussion.

This structure is roughly chronological, extending from the invasion of Julius Caesar to 731, but sections within each book are devoted to subjects which may extend over several chapters. At the end of such a section it is necessary for Bede to skip back in time to pick up the beginning of his next topic. Thus in Book v, chs. 2-6 are devoted to the miracles of John, Bishop of Hexham. The subject is "chronologically" introduced by the last sentence in v.i, "Gesta vero sunt haec temporibus Aldfridi regis, qui post fratrem suum Ecgfridum genti Nordanhymbrorum decem et novem annis praefuit."[108]

[106] This is for the present the state of the nation of the English, or of all of Britain.
[107] Of whom I spoke above.
[108] These things were, truly, done in the time of King Aldfrith,

v.2 begins, "Cujus regni principio defuncto Eata episcopo, Joannes vir sanctus Hagustaldensis ecclesiae praesulatum suscepit. . . ."[109] Aldfrith reigned 685-705, Eata died 687; the time of the chronological subject is the mid-680's. Bede goes on to recount for many pages the life and miracles of John of Hexham, ending with his death in 721, the limit of his "topic" organization; he then goes back to the last point in his "time" organization and picks it up again, with the baptism of Cadwalla in Rome in 689. This pattern grows out of the kind of book Bede is writing, a mixture of the chronicle (of which he had by then written two, and would add a third as a summary to *HE*) with its purely temporal sequence, and the history—especially hagiography—with its subject organization. In the latter case the temporal sequence would usually be followed, for men live in time; but when the work is a collective hagiography like *HE*, the dissynchronization of dozens of lives and hundreds of events distorts the strict chronological order. As a result, perhaps, some questions even of date arise: Bede puts the conversion of Iona to the Roman Easter as 716 in v.22, but 715 in III.4, and the summary in v.23 may itself be a recognition that the mixture has produced some confusion.

In writing dates, Bede did not consistently employ one era or chronological system, though he used our present Christian Era possibly more than any other. There were at the time at least seven different eras commonly used in the West. An example of one, the indiction, is his report of the *concilium* at Hatfield (IV.15).

> In nomine domini nostri Jesu Christi salvatoris, imperantibus dominis piissimis nostris Ecgfrido rege Hymbronensium, anno x regni ejus, sub die xv Kalendas

---

who after his brother Ecgfrith ruled over the people of Northumbria for nineteen years.

[109] In the beginning of whose reign, Bishop Eata being dead, the holy man John took the bishopric of the church of Hexham.

Octobres, indictione VIII; et Aedilredo rege Mercinen-
sium, anno sexto regni ejus; et Aldwulfo rege Estranglorum,
anno XVII regni ejus; et Hlothario rege Cantuariorum,
regni ejus anno VII.[110]

Bede faced difficulties enough without taking the year of
the indiction, a fifteen-year cycle too brief for a work of
this scale; or of the reign of the king, or of a bishop, when
many kingdoms and dozens of dioceses were his subject,
and the occupants of thrones and sees enjoyed little se-
curity of tenure. Apparently Bede preferred to use whatever dates he found in his sources, without attempting to
adjust them to a single pattern. But since events recorded
on paschal tables (annals) were perforce attached to dates
in the Christian or Dionysiac Era, that system was
dominant. Because Bede was the first historian who had
such opportunity to employ the Dionysiac tables in this
fashion, he is credited, quite properly, to be sure, with
having introduced the Christian Era into historiography.

No single term will describe Bede's book. It includes a
great deal of material quoted from papal and episcopal
letters, *concilia*, epigraphic and verbal accounts; it ig-
nores, and thus condemns to oblivion, the greater part of
the history of the period with which it deals, yet it repeats
in detail the lives of monks who took no part in the public
affairs of their day; it devotes two chapters (v.16-17) to
excerpts from a book on the holy places of the Middle
East; it includes (v.12; III.11) snatches from Virgil of
no apparent relevance. Yet it is no commonplace book,
though no history either. Its purpose—increasingly ignored by subsequent historians as the values and his-

---

[110] In the name of our Lord and savior Jesus Christ, in the reigns
of our most holy lords Ecgfrith King of the Northumbrians, in the
tenth year of his reign, on the seventeenth day of September, in the
eighth indiction; and Aethilred King of the Mercians, in the sixth
year of his reign; and Aldwulf King of the East Anglians, in the
seventeenth year of his reign; and Hlothar King of the Kentish, in
the eighth year of his reign.

torical canons of Bede's days grew more and more distant
—is expressed in the prefatory letter to King Ceolwulf:

> Historiam gentis Anglorum ecclesiasticam, quam nuper
> edideram, libentissime tibi desideranti, rex, et prius ad
> legendum ac probandum transmisi, et nunc ad tran-
> scribendum ac plenius ex tempore meditandum retrans-
> mitto; satisque studium tuae sinceritatis amplector, quo non
> solum audiendis scripturae sanctae verbis aurem sedulus
> accommodas, verum etiam noscendis priorum gestis sive
> dictis, et maxime nostrae gentis virorum illustrium, curam
> vigilanter impendis. Sive enim historia de bonis bona
> referat, ad imitandum bonum auditor sollicitus instigatur;
> seu mala commemoret de pravis, nihilominus religiosus ac
> pius auditor sive lector devitando quod noxium est ac per-
> versum, ipse sollertius ad exsequenda ea, quae bona ac Deo
> digna esse cognoverit, accenditur.[111]

As an *ecclesiastical* history—and no event without ecclesiastical relevance is mentioned in the book—Bede's
work is an adjunct to scriptural study, that study which
he elsewhere (v.24) described as his life's occupation.
The New Testament contained the revelation; the Old
Testament, the prefiguration of it. For Bede, the history
of the Church in England was the sequel to the New Testament in revealing through historical fact the order of
divine intention. He makes this clear in two ways: his

---

[111] The ecclesiastical history of the nation of the English which
I had recently written, O King, I both most gladly sent to you at
your desire to read and examine formerly, and now send again to be
copied and thought over more fully at leisure; and I rejoice greatly
at the study of your zeal, in which you not only sedulously give ear
to the words which are to be heard in sacred Scripture, but also
vigilantly expend your study on the deeds or words of our fore-
fathers which are to be found out, and particularly those of the
famous men of our race. For either a history has to do with the
good things done by good men, so that the thoughtful reader is
moved to imitate the good; or it recalls the evil things done by bad
men, so that nonetheless the religious and pious hearer or reader,
by avoiding what is harmful and perverse, is inflamed to pursue
more carefully those things which he knows to be good and worthy
of God.

often-noted care for historical fact, and his now almost
totally disregarded concern for the spiritual pertinence of
historical fact. The evidence for the former is widespread.
He lists his authorities—his contemporaries, the glean-
ings from papal archives, earlier writers, his own experience—in the preface, and he takes care to mention a
source, to quote it verbatim if possible, to qualify his reliance in it:

> Hoc autem miraculum memoratus abbas non se praesente
> factum, sed ab his, qui praesentes fuere, sibi perhibet esse
> relatum.[112]   (*HE* v.5)

The famous passage about his own role in historiography
deserves to be quoted in full:

> Scripsi autem haec de persona et operibus viri praefati;
> nequaquam in eo laudans aut eligens hoc, quod de ob-
> servatione paschae minus perfecte sapiebat; immo hoc
> multum detestans, sicut in libro, quem de temporibus com-
> posui, manifestissime probavi; sed quasi verax historicus,
> simpliciter ea, quae de illo sive per illum sunt gesta,
> describens, et quae laude sunt digna in ejus actibus laudans,
> atque ad utilitatem legentium memoriae commendans.[113]
>
> (*HE* iii.17)

His only other reference to the business of historiography
in the book is in the preface:

> Lectoremque suppliciter obsecro, ut, siqua in his, quae
> scripsimus, aliter quam se veritas habet, posita reppererit,

[112] The aforesaid abbot says that this miracle was not done in his
presence, but was related to him by those who were present.
[113] I have written these things about the person and the works of
the aforesaid man; by no means praising it in him or making a
point of it that he had imperfect understanding about the observation of Easter; but rather hating that very greatly, as I gave ample
proof in the book about times which I composed; but as a truthful
historian, simply describing those things which were done of him
or through him, and praising those things in his deeds which are
worthy of praise, and commending them to the utility of readers'
memory.

non hoc nobis imputet, qui, quod vera lex historiae est, simpliciter ea, quae fama vulgante collegimus, ad instructionem posteritatis litteris mandare studuimus.[114]

Bede has no contempt for historical fact, but he does not cherish it because "it makes history"—the section (IV.7-10) on the plague at the nunnery of Barking is not history, however factual, but hagiography. Bede instead values history that serves the purpose he outlined in his preface:

> Erat autem Mellitus corporis quidem infirmitate, id est podagra, gravatus, sed mentis gressibus sanis alacriter terrena quaeque transiliens, atque ad caelestia semper amanda, petenda, et quaerenda pervolans. Erat carnis origine nobilis, sed culmine mentis nobilior.[115]   (*HE* II.7)

And after a miracle of extinguishing a fire,

> Et quia vir Dei igne divinae caritatis fortiter ardebat, quia tempestates potestatum aeriarum a sua suorumque lesione crebris orationibus vel exhortationibus repellere consuerat, merito ventis flammisque mundialibus praevalere, et, ne sibi suisque nocerent, obtinere poterat.[116]   (*HE* II.7)

The treatment parallels closely that of the similar miracle in the *VP* quoted above (2.3).

Bede is relatively free from his sources in *HE*, once he gets past the introductory chapters leading up to the

[114] And I humbly implore the reader that, if he finds set down anything in these things which I have written that is otherwise than the truth, he should not impute it to me, who, as is the true law of history, simply labored to write down those things I collected from common report, for the instruction of posterity.

[115] Mellitus was afflicted in the body with a certain ailment, that is gout, but he quickly passed over earthly things with healthful steps of the mind, always desiring the heavenly things that are to be loved, prayed for and sought for. He was noble in the origin of his flesh, but more noble by altitude of mind.

[116] And because the man of God burned fiercely with the flame of divine love, because he was wont to repel the tempests of the powers of the air from harming him or his by frequent prayers and exhortations, with merit he succeeded in prevailing against worldly winds and flames so that they should harm neither him nor his.

Augustinian mission. Up to that point he depends heavily on Orosius, Gildas, Eutropius, and somewhat less on Prosper and Marcellinus Comes, although some of the most notable passages are his own:

> Haec in praesenti, juxta numerum librorum, quibus lex divina scripta est, quinque gentium linguis, unam eandemque summae veritatis et verae sublimitatis scientiam scrutatur, et confitetur, Anglorum videlicet, Brittonum, Scotorum, Pictorum et Latinorum, quae meditatione scripturarum ceteris omnibus est facta communis.[117]
>
> (*HE* i.1)

> Hibernia autem et latitudine sui status, et salubritate ac serenitate aerum multum Britanniae praestat, ita ut raro ibi nix plus quam triduana remaneat; nemo propter hiemem aut faena secet aestate, aut stabula fabricet jumentis; nullum ibi reptile videri soleat, nullus vivere serpens valeat; nam saepe illo de Britannia allati serpentes, mox ut, proximante terris navigio, odore aeris illius attacti fuerint, intereunt; quin potius omnia pene, quae de eadem insula sunt, contra venenum valent. Denique vidimus, quibusdam a serpente percussis, rasa folia codicum, qui de Hibernia fuerant, et ipsam rasuram aquae immissam ac potui datam, talibus protinus totam vim veneni grassantis, totum inflati corporis absumpsisse ac sedasse tumorem.[118]   (*HE* i.1)

[117] At present the island studies and confesses one and the same wisdom of the highest truth and true blessedness, with the languages of five nations, that is the English, the British, the Irish, the Picts, and the Latins (which by the study of Scripture is made common to all the rest), according to the number of books in which the divine law is written.

[118] Now Ireland surpasses Britain greatly both in the extent of its width, and the wholesomeness and peacefulness of its air, so that it is rare for snow to lie there more than three days; no one on account of the winter either cuts hay in the summer, or builds a stable for his cattle; no reptile is wont to be seen there, for no serpent can live there; for often when serpents are brought there from Britain, as soon as the ship comes near to land, they are touched by the scent of its air, and they die forthwith; and even more, all the things of the island are efficacious against venom. Indeed I have seen it, that, when some men were bitten by a snake, the scrapings from the leaves of books that came from Ireland being put into water and given to the men to drink, immediately the force

He also uses Constantius' *Vita Germani episcopi Autissiodorensis* and an anonymous *Passio sancti Albani* in these introductory chapters, but this kind of hagiographical borrowing, as distinct from the chronological framework he took from Orosius and the others, is common to the entire work: cf. iii.19, taken from the Irish *Vita sancti Fursei*. His use of written documents as a part, rather than as a source, of his history is even more striking than his independence elsewhere. From the *Responsiones Gregorii* i.27 to the very long letter of Ceolfrid to the Picts v.21, he inserts the text of his materials again and again. In part he is anticipating the footnotes and appendices of the modern historian, but in part, too, he is recording the testimony of a Church in which tradition plays a commanding role. Not a few of these documents have to do with the Easter controversy, which Bede clearly regards as the most significant single aspect of the ecclesiastical history of his people: it afflicted Augustine's first contact with the British Church (1.25) and it is still a concern in the penultimate chapter: "Brittones, quamvis et maxima ex parte domestico sibi odio gentem Anglorum, et totius catholicae ecclesiae statum pascha minus recto, moribusque improbis impugnent. . . ."[119]

On the other hand Bede abandons documentary evidence, and even the evidence which living tradition can pretend to preserve accurately, in his frequent use of direct discourse. Other genres than history, among them particularly liturgy and its offshoots, liturgical paraphrase and hagiography, must have influenced him here: he is, in fact, following at one remove the narrative technique of the Bible to which he devoted so many years of his

---

of the spreading venom was arrested and the swelling of the bloated bodies went down.

[119] The Britons, although for the most part they hate both the nation of the English on account of their own spite, and wrongfully and with evil ways the appointed Easter of the whole Catholic Church. . . .

life. In this way the central document of medieval civilization has impinged again on the form of his work, just as
his theories of scriptural interpretation have influenced the
selection and organization of the historical narrative.

Levison has pointed out that Bede wrote in a dark age
of historiography; that through the *HE* itself, as well as
through the continuation of the chronicle in v.24 and the
eventual adoption of the year of the incarnation for historical dates, he determined the shape of much medieval
history after him; and that his subject and influence have
thereby largely conditioned the nature of modern studies
of medieval history. So much is true, despite the sometimes antihistorical attitudes which Bede held, and
despite the perhaps ungrateful observation that, owing to
the excellence of his work, much earlier material—not
entirely subsumed in it—has disappeared and is lost to
the modern historian. Every age has made the book its
own, however, apart from the narrative material it contains: the ninth century translated it as fit to join Boethius' *Consolatio* and Gregory's *Dialogi,* surely as a
moral no less than as an historical document; in the six-
teenth century, the English Catholic Stapleton translated
it again, to demonstrate the character of the early Church
and the points at which the reformed Church deviated
from it. Both translations, unlike many subsequent more
strictly academic applications, share the quality of *pietas*
with the original. If a king or a queen is to read this book
with profit, it must deal with matters of nationhood, and
yet in the extended stories of private sanctity we see little
of high national importance. The answer lies in Bede's
vision of the Church as the source of a kind of national
unity which no political organism can promise; thus the
life and death of Gregory, who never touched English
soil, occupy more space than those of any English king,
and thus too the problem of disunity over the Easter question commands more attention than any political dis-

ruption. The unity and continuity of the Church and of
the revelation of which it is the vessel are the subject as
well as the frame of the book, and every historical event
takes its importance, not from having happened, but from
participating in this chronological continuum:

> Qua arridente pace ac serenitate temporum, plures in
> gente Nordanhymbrorum, tam nobiles, quam privati, se
> suosque liberos, depositis armis, satagunt magis, accepta
> tonsura, monasterialibus ascribere votis, quam bellicis ex-
> ercere studiis. Quae res quem sit habitura finem, posterior
> aetas videbit.[120]   (*HE* v.23)

Historia abbatum

Bede's *HAB* is in part based on the anonymous *Historia abbatum* by a monk of Wearmouth (see 3.9), which
he had used in his *Chronicon* at the end of *DTR* in 725.
It is probable that he had not yet composed his own *HAB*
but, as it is mentioned in *HE*, and certainly preceded it,
the date is 725 x 731, more likely 726 x 730. The *HAB* is
in twenty-three chapters divided into two books, of which
almost all the first and the beginning of the second are
devoted to Benedict Biscop. In this Bede departs from
his source, which concentrates on Abbot Ceolfrid; it is
usually called *Vita sanctissimi Ceolfridi* in the MSS.

The work is full of the sense of spiritual meaning in
historical events:

> Nobili quidem stirpe gentis Anglorum progenitus, sed non
> minori nobilitate mentis ad promerenda semper angelorum
> consortia suspensus. Denique cum esset minister Oswiu
> regis, et possessionem terrae suo gradui competentem illo
> donante perciperet, annos natus circiter xxv fastidivit
> possessionem caducam, ut acquirere posset aeternam; despexit

[120] Now that there is the pleasantness of peace and serenity in our
times, many among the nation of the Northumbrians, as much
noblemen as private persons, putting aside their weapons, strive
more to receive on themselves and on their children the tonsure, to
enroll themselves in monastic vows, than to practice warlike ways.
And a later age shall see what outcome this matter shall have.

militiam cum corruptibili donativo terrestrem, ut vero regi militans, regnum in superna civitate mereretur habere perpetuum; reliquit domum, cognatos, et patriam propter Christum et propter evangelium, ut centuplum acciperet, et vitam aeternam possideret; respuit nuptiis servire carnalibus, ut sequi valeret agnum virginitatis gloria candidum in regnis caelestibus; abnuit liberos carne procreare mortales, praedestinatus a Christo ad educandos ei spiritali doctrina filios caelesti in vita perennes.[121]   (ch. 1)

The same sense obviously occupied the subject, Benedict, in his arrangement of the monastery:

Nam et tunc dominicae historiae picturas quibus totam beatae Dei genetricis, quam in monasterio majore fecerat, ecclesiam in gyro coronaret, attulit; imagines quoque, ad ornandum monasterium ecclesiamque beati Pauli apostoli de concordia veteris et novi testamenti summa ratione compositas exibuit; verbi gratia, Isaac ligna, quibus immolaretur portantem, et dominum crucem in qua pateretur aeque portantem, proxima super invicem regione, pictura conjunxit. Item serpenti in heremo a Moyse exaltato, filium hominis in cruce exaltatum comparavit.[122]   (ch. 9)

[121] He was born of a noble family of the race of the English, but was lifted up to the merited companionship of angels forever, being of no less nobility of mind. For when he was a minister of King Oswy, and received from that giver the possession of a plot of land suitable for his degree, when he was about twenty-five years old, he disdained perishable possessions, that he might acquire eternal ones; he despised earthly warfare with its corruptible gifts, so that he might fight for the true King, and deserve to have perpetual reign in the celestial city; he left his home, his family, and his homeland for Christ and for the Gospel, that he might receive a hundred fold, and possess eternal life; he refused to serve carnal marriage, so that he might be worthy to follow the Lamb, bright with the glory of virginity, in the heavenly kingdom; he declined to engender mortal children of the flesh, being predestined by Christ to rear for Him sons in spiritual teaching to be everlasting in the heavenly life.

[122] For also at this time he brought pictures of the Lord's history, with which he crowned round about the whole church of the blessed Mother of God, which he had built in the greater monastery; he also displayed paintings collected to show the concord in the highest sense of the Old and New Testaments, for the ornament of the monastery and church of blessed Paul the Apostle; for example,

But if *HAB* looks back to Bede's scriptural exegesis in this attitude, it looks forward to *HE* in others, including the dissynchronization in collective hagiography ("verum his de vita venerabilis Eosterwyni breviter praelibatis, redeamus ad ordinem narrandi," ch. 9);[123] the quotation verbatim and in extenso of a document (Hwaetberht's letter to Pope Gregory II, ch. 19); the occasional gratuitous Virgilianism (ch. 8); the forceful description:

> Neque enim facile quisquam lacrimas tenere potuit, videns comites ipsius partim patre amisso caeptum iter agere; partim mutata intentione, qua Romam ire desiderant, domum magis, qua hunc sepultum nuntiarent, reverti; partim ad tumbam defuncti inter eos, quorum nec linguam noverant, pro inextinguibili patris affectu residere,[124]

(the death of Ceolfrid in France, ch. 21). He has not yet settled on one way of expressing dates; indeed most of the dates, either of the kind

> Sedecim ut diximus annos monasterium rexit, primos octo per se sine alterius assumptione abbatis; reliquos totidem viris venerabilibus et sanctis Eosterwyni, Sigfrido et Ceolfrido abbatis se nomine, auctoritate, et officio juvantibus; primo quattuor annos, secundo tres, tertio unum,
>
> (ch. 14)

or

---

he juxtaposed in a picture Isaac carrying the faggots on which he was to be immolated, and in the next space above the Lord carrying the cross on which He was to suffer. Likewise he compared the Son of Man lifted up on the cross to the serpent lifted by Moses in the desert.

123 Now that these things have been mentioned as a foretaste about the life of the venerable Eosterwine, let us return to the sequence of the narration.

124 Nor was anyone easily able to hold back his tears, seeing some of the companions, having lost their father, take up the path they had begun; and some, having changed their intention, in which they wished to go to Rome, rather go back home, where they might report his burial; and some remain, for the imperishable love of their father, by the tomb of the dead man, among those people of whose very language they knew nothing.

Quod factum est, sicut et in prohemio memini, ad ostium
fluminis Wyri ad levam anno ab incarnatione domini
sexcentesimo septuagesimo quarto, indictione secunda, anno
autem quarto imperii Ecgfridi regis,[125]   (ch. 4)

are quoted from his source, and are among the most faithfully followed passages.

Letters (2.9)

Ad Ecgberhtum

Bede's *Epistola ad Ecgberhtum episcopum* is the nearest thing to a jeremiad that he wrote. It was composed
November 5, 734, according to the last line, which—although it is possibly not authentic—agrees well with
other allusions to date in chs. 10 and 13, and with the
omission of mention of the letter from *HE* v.24 (731).
Its recipient was consecrated Bishop of York 734, which
seems to be the occasion of Bede's letter; Bede has
pointed out that the instructions of Gregory to Augustine provided for twelve bishops, "in quibus Eboracensis
antistes, accepto a sede apostolica pallio, metropolitanus
esse deberet" (ch. 9),[126] and suggests that the monks
be allowed to select a bishop either from their number or
from their diocese, "Quod si hoc ita, ut suggerimus, domino adjuvante, perfeceris, facillime etiam, ut arbitramur,
hoc obtinebis, ut juxta decreta sedis apostolicae, Ebo-

[125] For sixteen years, as I have said, he ruled the monastery, for
the first eight by himself without the appointment of another abbot;
the remainder with the aid in the name, authority, and office of
abbot of the venerable and holy men Eosterwine, Sigfrith, and Ceolfrid, the first for four years, the second for three, the third for
one. . . . Which was made, as I mentioned also in the prologue, on
the left bank of the mouth of the river Wear in the 674th year since
the incarnation of the Lord, in the second indiction, in the fourth
year of the reign of King Ecgfrith.
[126] Among whom the Bishop of York, having received the apostolic pallium, was to be metropolitan.

racensis ecclesia metropolitanum possit habere pontificem"
(ch. 10).[127]

Bede's theme is the duties of a bishop:

> Quod non ita loquor, quasi te aliter facere sciam, sed quia
> de quibusdam episcopis fama vulgatum est, quod ita ipsi
> Christo serviant, ut nullos secum alicujus religionis aut
> continentiae viros habeant; sed potius illos, qui risui, jocis,
> fabulis, commessationibus et ebrietatibus, ceterisque vitae
> remissioris illecebris subigantur, et qui magis cottidie ven-
> trem dapibus, quam mentem sacrificiis caelestibus parent.[128]
>
> (ch. 4)

He describes episcopal duties in the diocese and in its
monasteries, and it is with the latter that his special concern lies. The charters which many of them depend on
were given for ungodly purposes, and even now some
are inhabited by laymen who have installed themselves as
abbots for their own glorification, without giving up
worldly ways:

> Tui, inquam, est officii procurare, ne in locis Deo con-
> secratis diabolus sibi regnum usurpet, ne pro pace discordia,
> pro pietate jurgia, pro sobrietate ebrietas, pro caritate
> et castitate fornicationes sibi et homicidia sedem vin-
> dicent. . . .[129]   (ch. 14)

[127] And if you do this with the aid of God, as we suggest, I believe
that you will achieve most easily that the church of York will be
able to have its metropolitan pontiff according to the decrees of the
apostolic see.

[128] I do not speak in this fashion, as though I knew you to be
doing otherwise, but because the reputation of some bishops is that
they serve Christ in such a manner, that they have no men of any
holiness of continence about them; but rather those, who are given
over to laughter, jests, fables, hilarity, and drunkenness, and the
other enticements of remiss living, and who rather provide for their
bellies with feasts daily, than for their minds with heavenly
sacrifices.

[129] It is for you, I say, to bring it about, lest the devil usurp the
rule for himself in places consecrated to God, lest discord instead
of peace, strife instead of piety, drunkenness instead of sobriety,
fornication and homicide instead of charity and chastity claim for
themselves the place.

[182]

Much of the letter is more moderate, but all of it makes considerable use of the tone of Gildas, and especially of his characteristic dependence on quotations from Scripture. In all, it gives a stirring picture of Bede in the last months of his life, established by *HE* as the doyen of ecclesiastical scholarship in the north, indeed in the world, instructing from his sickbed the new Bishop of York in terms of vigor and authority.

Bede also supplies a picture of the pastoral latinity of his region:

> Et quidem omnes, qui Latinam linguam lectionis usu didicerunt, etiam haec optime didicisse certissimum est; sed idiotas, hoc est, eos qui propriae tantum linguae notitiam habent, haec ipsa sua lingua discere, ac sedulo decantare facito. Quod non solum de laicis, id est, in populari adhuc vita constitutis, verum etiam de clericis sive monachis, qui Latinae sunt linguae expertes, fieri oportet.[130]

> (ch. 5)

Ad Albinum

This little letter was printed by Mabillon (*Vetera analecta*, 398) from a MS now lost. It accompanied a copy of *HE* sent to Albinus, abbot of the monastery of SS. Peter and Paul 709x710–732x734, who is described in *HE* (pref.) as "auctor ante omnes atque adjutor opusculi hujus,"[131] in return for some gifts sent by the Nothelm whom Bede mentions in the *Quaestiones in libros regum* and later in the preface as the London priest who reported to him the results of researches in the Vatican archives.

[130] And certainly all who have learned to read the Latin tongue have doubtless come to know these things; but see that the unlearned, that is, those who have knowledge only of their own language, come to know them in their tongue, and repeat them sedulously. And this should be done not only among the laity, that is, those still set in worldly life, but also among the clerics and monks who are ignorant of the Latin language.

[131] The principal author and assistant in this little work.

[183]

Doubtful and Spurious Works (2.10)

Even though he wrote his own bibliography late in his life, Bede's canon soon underwent at least two kinds of change. First, portions of his work were incorporated in the work of others, somewhat as he had himself borrowed from earlier writers. Second, and more frequent, works not his own were attributed to him in MSS. As a result, the problem of his canon has not yet been fully solved. The five works below under *dubia* probably belong, at least in part, in his canon, but modern editions have not yet appeared to make careful study possible. The list of prose works under *spuria* is not complete: it complements the poetry mentioned under that section, and gives the names only of those treatises most often falsely ascribed to Bede.

Dubia

1. *Aliquot quaestionum liber.* A little treatise in fifteen sections on various questions, of which nos. i-viii, on Scripture, appear to be by Bede, and nos. ix-xv, on doctrinal topics, do not. Date difficult; post 731? (*PL* 93.455-478; *CPL* 1364.)

2. *In proverbia Salomonis allegoricae interpretationis fragmenta* (*PL* 91.1051-1066; *CPL* 1352, "inter spuria reponit F. Stegmüller, deest apud Laistner").

3. *In epistolam ad Hebraeos* (*CPL* 1361).

4. *De titulis psalmorum.* A lengthy work in which each psalm is treated in an *argumentum, explanatio* and *commentarium.* The first two are compiled from Cassiodorus, and the compiler may well have been Bede; but the commentary, the longest part, is by Mangold of Lautenbach and must be a later addition. (*PL* 93.477f.; *CPL* 1384.)

5. *Capitula lectionum in Pentateuchum Moysi, Josue,*

Judicum (*PL* 93.233f.; *CPL* 1363a: "excerpta videntur ex Isidori quaestionibus").

    Capitula lectionum in Esdram et Nehemiam (*PL* 91.807-809; *CPL* 1363b).

    Capitula lectionum in Cantica canticorum (*PL* 91.1077-1084; *CPL* 1363c).

Spuria

EXEGESIS: *Collectaneum, Interpretationes nominum hebraicum, Interpretatio psalterii, In Matthaei evangelium commentarium, In psalmorum librum exegesis, Quaestiones in octoteuchum, Quaestiones V in acta apostolorum, In librum Job commentarium.*

HOMILIES, ETC.: *Poenitentiale Bedae, Psalterium Bedae, De trinitate, Liber tertius homiliarum, De musica theoria, De S. Scholastica, Scintillarum liber.*

CHRONOLOGICAL WORKS: *De tonitruis, De mundi constitutione, Liber calculi, Computus hibernicus.*

chapter three:

the age of bede

Aethilwald (3.1)

Almost nothing is known about the identity of Aethilwald. Jaffé's suggestion that he is the same as the Aethelbald who was King of Mercia 716-757 was accepted by Ehwald and others, but Brandl has shown it to be wrong. Aethilwald was a student of Aldhelm; there remains a letter from the pupil to the master, as well as a (later?) one from Aldhelm to Aethilwald (see 1.5). Aethilwald's works also include three or five surviving poems and at least one other which is lost, but the study of them must begin with the letter to Aldhelm. It is addressed "abbati Aldhelmo" in the sole extant MS (a collection of Boniface's letters, Vienna MS 751); the date must therefore be 675x705. Aethilwald begins:

> Aestivi igitur temporis cursu, quo immensis feralium passim congressionum expeditionibus haec miserrima patria lugubriter invidia vastatrice deformatur, tecum legendi studio conversatus demorabar. Tum mihi, licet indigno, tuae beatitudinis sacrosancta sagacitas omnibus, ut reor, propemodum panegyricis tam saecularium litterariae verbositatis facundia editorum quam etiam spiritalium ecclesiastici dogmatis stilo elucubratorum plenissime voluminum scriptis imbuta arcana liberalium litterarum studia, opacis dumtaxat mysteriorum secretis ignaris quibusque mentibus obstrusa abrepto propere spissae stoliditatis velamine patefaciens liquidissime propalarat.[1]

[1] During the course of the summer, in which this most wretched land was devasted by the ruinous hatred, the huge invasion of savage armies, time and again, I remained with you for the purpose of reading. Then the holy wisdom of your goodness divulged to me, although I was unworthy, the arcane studies which flow, I believe, in almost all the panegyrics written as much by the copiousness of

[186]

After a couple of paragraphs expressing his debt to Aldhelm for his tuition, he comes to the subject of the letter:

> Huic autem nostrae parvitatis epistolae trina cantati modulaminis carmina binis generibus digesta subdidimus, quorum primum dactylico heroici poematis hexametro ac pedestri, ut autumo, regula enucleate trutinatum et in LXX coaequantium versuum formulas, casu ita obtingente vel, ut verius dicam, supernae dispensationis nutu moderante, divisum; tertium quoque non pedum mensura elucubratum, sed octenis syllabis in uno quolibet versu compositis, una eademque littera comparis linearum tramitibus aptata cursim calamo perarante caraxatum, tibi, sagacissime sator, transmittens dicavi; medium vero meo tuoque clienti Wihtfrido de transmarini scilicet itineris peregrinatione simillimis itidem versuum et syllabarum lineis confectum repraesentans porrexi.[2]

The prose style, as the content suggests, shows the influence and even the imitation of Aldhelm's own.

There follow in the MS five poems, all octosyllabic; the hexameter mentioned in the letter is lost. Of the five, the fourth appears to be the "tertium" of the letter, and the

---

the literary verbosity of secular writers as by the ecclesiastical pen of dogma by writers of spiritual volumes most fully composed by lamplight, right up to those things hidden from certain ignorant minds in the opaque secrets of mysteries, which you made most clearly plain by quickly removing the veil of dense obtuseness.

[2] I have added hereunder to the letter of my unworthiness three poems written in two kinds of metrical composition, of which the first is measured in the dactylic hexameter of heroic poetry and, I believe, simply by the rule of metrical feet, and divided into seventy portions of equal verses, either just by chance or, as I might more truly say, with the intervening will of divine dispensation; the third is not laboriously worked out in the measure of metrical feet, but there being eight syllables put together in each verse, I have dedicated and sent it to you, most wise instructor, written with one and the same letter fitted by the rapidly writing pen to the equal paths of the lines; the middle one, about a trip across the sea, likewise composed in most similar lines of verses and syllables, I have sent to you by way of my protegé and yours, Wihtfrid, to show to you.

second the "medium." The third is much in the style of the second and fourth—it is not separated from the fourth in the MS—and most authorities attribute it to Aethilwald with them. The fifth, like the third and first not mentioned in the letter, nonetheless contains Aethilwald's name:

> Ave, Offa altissime,
> Olim sodes sanctissime,
> Salutatis supplicibus
> Aethilwaldi cum vocibus.[3]

These four poems, two of them apparently corresponding to two mentioned in the letter, constitute the probable surviving poetry of Aethilwald, and in the MS all are introduced "incipit carmen al" (probably "Aethilwaldi," although the first concludes "finit carmen Aldhelmi,"[4] almost certainly wrongly). The idea that Aethilwald was the later King of Mercia, however, discouraged critics from attributing the first poem to the author of the others, as the signs are that its poet was a cleric. As we have seen, the poet was not the king, and he may as easily have been a cleric as anything else. Two further clues are provided for the attribution of the first poem. One is the address in the opening lines,

> Lector, casses catholicae
> Atque obses athletice,
> Tuis pulsatus precibus
> Obnixe flagittantibus
> Hymnista carmen cecini
> Atque rem sponsam reddidi,
> Sicut pridem pepigeram.[5]

[3] Hail, most high Offa, in the future (if I may say so) most holy with the suppliant prayer of Aethilwald for your health.

[4] Here begins the poem of "al"; of Aethilwald; here ends the poem of Aldhelm.

[5] Reader, catholic helmet and athletic hostage, struck by your energetically pleading prayers I have as a hymnist composed this poem and given back the thing promised, as I earlier had agreed.

Some have read this as referring to Aldhelm, some to a hypothetical Helmgisl ("casses . . . atque obses"). The next lines,

> Quando profectus fueram
> Usque diram Domnoniam
> Per carentem Cornubiam
> Florulentis cespitibus
> Et foecundis graminibus,
> Elementa inormia
> Atque facta informia
> Quassantur sub aetherea
> Convexi caeli camera,
> Dum tremet mundi machina
> Sub ventorum monarchia,[6]

refer to Devon and Cornwall, both within the diocese of Sherborne which was Aldhelm's 705-709. The word "lector," sometimes emended to "rector" and sometimes regarded as referring to the ecclesiastical order, requires neither emendation nor such a narrow application. Even the cautious Ehwald has been led to resolve "carmen al" as "carmen [clerici cujusdam ignoti] Al[dhelmo datum],"[7] but no solution seems preferable to attributing all the poems to the author of the letter.

In the first poem, Aethilwald describes a storm and the refuge he took from it in a monastery. The first part of the poem ends at line 114, and the second part (lines 115-200) continues with a description of the monastic matins and the damage caused by the storm. Like the other poems, this one draws heavily on Aldhelm's poetry and somewhat less on Virgil and the *Hisperica famina* for its material and inspiration.

[6] When I journeyed as far as frightful Devon, through Cornwall lacking in flowering grasses and fruitful herbs, the immoderate elements and horrid things were shaken violently beneath the airy vault of the convex heaven, while the fabric of the world trembled under the monarchy of the winds.

[7] The poem of a certain cleric unknown given to Aldhelm.

The second poem is the one described by the letter as "de transmarini itineris peregrinatione" dedicated to Wynfrith (although Traube, noting that Aldhelm never seems to have met Wynfrith-Boniface, emended to Wihtfrid, to whom Aldhelm had written a letter). In 184 lines it tells the story of three men, two of them brothers, who went to Rome; there one of the brothers died, but the other two men, after two years, returned to Britain rich in spiritual and material gifts. The third poem is a brief (46-line) prayer which illustrates the link that all five form between the Irish rhythmical hymns and the later continental poetry of the Carolingian renaissance. The fourth poem, of 78 lines—the "tertium" of the letter—is in praise of Aldhelm:

> Ita Cassis per culmina
> Prisci candunt praefulgida
> Gloriosa per agmina
> Gemmifera ornamina,
> Rutulanti redimita
> Obryzo, velut limpida
> Astra convexi Olympi
> Orbi clarescunt viridi.
> Althelmum nam altissimum
> Cano atque clarissimum
> Alto nostratim nomine
> Nuncupatum et numine
> Pollentem per caelestia
> Potente et terrestria,
> Sic, sic sane sublimibus
> Satis ornatum cultibus,
> Caeli ceu per culmina
> Candunt exorta fulmina:
> Illis, illis in omnibus
> Aequalem dico actibus.[8]

[8] Thus do the gem-bearing ornaments of Aldhelm shine through the gleaming high, glorious in the host, wreathed about with ruddy gold, as the bright stars of the convex heaven shine on the green earth. For I sing of great and famous Aldhelm, called in our fashion by a high name and mighty in his majesty in both heavenly and earthly power, thus, thus indeed adorned with much sublime erudi-

The last poem, of the same length as the fourth, has been attributed by Traube, Jaffé and others to Aldhelm, as a grateful reply to the earlier poems; but the attribution requires two emendations to the lines quoted above, "Offa" to "Ave" and "Aethilwaldi" to "Aethilwalde." Ehwald points out that the same lines are echoed by a letter written by Lull about 740x747 to an unknown person, "vale semper, salutatus supplicibus tuorum amicorum cum vocibus,"[9] and that the Offa of the poem may be the same as the Obba or Offa of Felix's ch. 45 (see 3.13), whom Felix calls a retainer of King Aethelbald of Mercia. Assuming that the name gives weight to the attribution to the Mercian king of this and the other poems, Ehwald goes on to date the fifth poem from the time of his exile, when he was given refuge by Guthlac. But Offa is a common name, and the language of the poem does not suggest anything of a king addressing his *comes*; it is, instead, a salutation to an equal, an exercise in rhythmical verse more interesting for the cultural influences it reflects than for its technical or literary achievement.

Vita antiquissima sancti Gregorii (3.2)

In the *S. Gregorii magni vita* which he wrote 872x882, Joannes Diaconus referred to earlier lives which existed "apud Saxones, et apud Langobardorum . . . gentem."[10] The Lombard life is almost certainly the one written by Paulus Diaconus (ca. 725-ante 800); the Saxon life appears to be the one preserved in the unique MS St. Gall 567. The theory that Paulus also knew the anonymous Saxon life was based on some passages from it which

---

tion, just as the lightning comes forth and flashes through the heights of the sky: I say he is in all his deeds equal to such.

[9] Farewell forever, hailed by the prayerful voices of your friends.

[10] Among the Saxons, and the nation of the Lombards.

appear in his version, but Grisar has shown them to be later interpolations. The St. Gall life has been known for centuries, but many scholars thought it nothing more than an abbreviation of the version by Joannes. In 1604 Canisius wrote of it as "fabulis . . . scatentem" (*Antiquae lectiones*, VI.460).[11] The discovery of the real contents of the MS was by Ewald, who described it and published extracts in 1886. A complete edition by Gasquet appeared in 1904; a modern edition by Colgrave is awaited.

Aside from the connections with the lives by Joannes and Paulus, there is the problem of the relationship with Bede's account of Gregory in *HE* II.1. Recent opinion has held that neither author knew the work of the other, but that both employed somewhat similar sources, among them Gregory's own writings. Generally, Bede knows these better than the anonymous author does, but he leaves out information which the other includes, and at some points—such as the ordination of Mellitus and Laurentius—the two versions conflict. But the anonymous author similarly omits some information which Bede includes, and the early popularity of *HE* suggests that the anonymous life must have been written before it. Jones argues that the neglect of the hagiographical models of Sulpicius Severus and Evagrius, which became popular in England in the early eighth century, implies a very early date for the *anonyma*. In any case it describes the translation of the relics of King Edwin when Aelffled (see 3.5) was Abbess of Whitby, so it must be after 680.

The author was a monk of Whitby; he speaks of it (ch. 19) as "nostrum coenobium." He says in the *Prohemium* that he wishes to write about Gregory because other doctors of the Church are memorialized in writing, but his sources are fewer than he wants:

[11] Abounding in fables.

De quo librum scribere cupientes cum pauca ejus de gestis
audivimus signorum, nec fastidium sit legentibus precamur,
si aliquid de laude tanti viri loquamur uberius. Multi igitur
a miraculis vitam quidem sanctorum solent considerare,
atque a signis sancta illorum merita metiri; et hoc nec
immerito.   (ch. 3)

De nostro igitur magistro beato Gregorio ea quae nobiscum
ab antiquis fama sanctitatis ejus a diversis notavit, refera-
mus. In quibus etiam per pauca de multis nos audisse
credimus, in eis tantum de hoc clarissimae famae ejusdem
signa sanctitatis qui requirunt, his possunt agnoscere satis
evidenter indiciis.   (ch. 5)

His igitur omnibus almi hujus viri signis, utcumque de
gestis eorum in Christo obsecramus lectorem, si quid melius
scire possit in illis, ne vituperationis suae dente nostrae
arrodet opus diligentiae tanti viri dilectione magis quam
scientia extorsum.[12]   (ch. 30)

He makes reference to the *Moralia* and *Dialogi* of Gregory, and to his homilies nos. 27 and 34, as well as to
Jerome's *Epist.* 66 and Augustine's *City of God*. His latinity is good, but the text has fared badly in transmission—
the MS is ca. 900, almost two hundred years younger
than the *Vita* itself, and even the chapter numbers are an
editorial addition.

[12] Wishing to write a book about him, although I have heard
only a few things about his deeds of wonder-working, I pray that
it will not be distasteful to my readers if I tell anything at length
in praise of such a man. For many people have the practice of
considering the lives of saints from the standpoint of miracles, and
of judging their holy merits by signs; nor is this practice unworthy.

I shall relate those things about our blessed master Gregory
from diverse old sources which have informed us of the fame of
his holiness. Among which I believe we have heard but few out of
many things, yet in them those who seek signs of holiness regarding
this man of most widespread fame, will be able to discover them
sufficiently evident in the records.

All these being the signs of that generous man, we ask the reader
in Christ of these deeds that, if he knows anything better regarding
them, he should not bite with the fang of his vituperation this work,
diligently composed more with the love of such a man than with
learning.

The author begins by describing Gregory's birth and
entry into monastic life, and his missions to Constanti-
nople; these two chapters are largely quoted from the
Dialogi. He speaks of England's special debt to Gregory,
and goes on to tell the famous story of the English boys
in the Roman market, which he returns to again in ch. 13
(see below). He then tells of the saint's unwilling election to the papacy and his formation of the Augustinian
mission. The middle third of the book (chs. 12-19) follows the history of the mission rather than the life of
Gregory, including events in the seventh century long
after his death in 604. Here the author expatiates on the
wordplay he introduced earlier:

> O quam pulchre quamque haec omnia decenter sibi con-
> veniunt praefata! Ergo nomen Anglorum, si una *e* littera
> addetur, Angelorum sonat; pro certo vocabulum quorum
> proprium est semper omnipotentem Deum in caelis laudare,
> et non deficere, quia non lassescunt in laude. Quos beatus
> Joannes, in Apocalypsin testatur voce exercitus caelestis
> vidisse et audisse, *tamquam vocem aquarum multarum, et
> tamquam vocem validorum tonitruorum dicentium Alleluia.*
> . . . Cujus expositio, duorum habet interpretationem ver-
> borum: hoc est *laus Dei.* Et *Aelli* duabus compositum est
> syllabis, quarum in priori cum *e* littera absumitur; et in
> sequenti pro *i* ponitur *e*, *Alle* vocatur, quod in nostra
> lingua omnes absolute indicat. Et hoc est, quod ait dominus
> noster: *Venite ad me omnes qui laboratis et onerati estis,*
> et reliqua. Sicut regem quoque significat *alle* patrem, *lu*
> filium, *ia* spiritum sanctum. . . . Edwinus, cujus nomen
> tribus syllabis constans, recte sibi designat sanctae mysterium
> trinitatis.[13]   (chs. 13-14)

[13] O how beautifully and how fittingly all these predicted things
came together in him! For the name of the Angles, if one letter, *e*,
is added, sounds like Angels; certainly a name for those whose
occupation it is always to praise the omnipotent God in the heavens,
and not to cease, for they never tire in praise. Whom the blessed
John, in the Apocalypse, testifies to have seen and heard as the
voice of a celestial army, "as the voice of many waters, and as the
voice of great thunders, saying, Alleluia" [Apoc. 19:6]. . . . The
exposition of this [i.e., Alleluia] is in its interpretation as two

In the final third of the book, the author returns to Gregory in Rome: he recounts four miracles of the saint, and concludes with several chapters on his writings. He then treats the *Moralia* and *Dialogi*. He intersperses two further miracles and a chapter on hagiography:

Inde etiam scimus sanctorum esse omnia per caritatem corporis Christi, cujus sunt membra communia. Unde si quid horum quae scripsimus de hoc viro non fuit, quae etiam non ab illis qui viderunt et audierunt per ore didicimus, vulgata tantum habemus, de illo ejus etiam esse in magno dubitamus minime, quod jam hic sanctus vir, in sua praefata sapientia, satis evidenter docet, ut amantium semper in alterutrum fiat quod cernitur in aliis.[14]   (ch. 30)

Last of all he treats the *Cura pastoralis* and the death of Gregory. The *Vita* is a serious and self-conscious effort at Christian biography, made almost entirely without the aid of models; the professions of humility and literary inadequacy are not yet formulae. But the result seems, despite Joannes' apparent reference to it, not to have had wide acceptance. To be sure, it was still being copied after Bede, Paulus, and Joannes wrote their versions, but the unique MS probably shows that the three better-

---

words, that is "God's praise." And *Aelli* is composed of two syllables, from which let the *e* be removed from the first; and let *e* be put for *i* in the second, and it becomes *Alle*, which in our language means "absolutely all." And this is what our Lord said, "Come to me, all you that labor and are burdened," etc. [Matt. 11:28]. Just as it signifies the king [Aelli of the Deiri], so *alle* also signifies the Father, *lu* the Son, *ia* the Holy Ghost. . . . Edwinus, whose name consists of three syllables, rightly represents the mystery of the Holy Trinity.

[14] Whence we know all things of the saints to be through the love of the body of Christ, whose common members they are. Hence if anything of which I have written was not of this man, which indeed I learned by word of mouth not from those who had actually seen and heard them, but rather from common report, I should yet little doubt that it too should be in such a great one, which indeed the holy man, in his predestined wisdom, so clearly teaches, that whatever is noted in some of those bound by love, will be also in the others.

known authors commanded the largest audience for a life of Pope Gregory.

Vita anonyma sancti Cuthberti (3.3)

The author of the anonymous *Vita sancti Cuthberti* was a monk of Lindisfarne, where the saint (ca. 634-687) was for two years bishop; the author writes not only of Aidan as "episcopus noster" but of the island, church, and monastery of Lindisfarne as "noster." Bede, for whom the *VA* was the principal source of both his *VP* and his *VM*, spoke of it in the preface to *HE* as "a fratribus ecclesiae Lindisfarnensis scripta,"[15] as though he knew of no name for the author, and possibly as though he thought of the book as a composite work. The preface to the *VA* itself, on the other hand, uses the first person throughout; and though it is almost entirely quoted from the epistle which accompanied the Victorian paschal treatise and from the preface to the Evagrian *Vita sancti Antonii*, one of the dozen or so original words in the *VA* preface is "mihi"; Bede's "fratribus"[16] may well indicate the anonymity, not the plurality, of the author.

The work is first of the several outstanding examples of Latin hagiography in eighth-century England. It was written, on its own evidence, after the translation of Cuthbert's body (698), and it mentions King Aldfrith of Northumbria as "qui nunc regnat pacifice."[17] Aldfrith died in 705, so the work is 699x705.

Dependent as it is on earlier hagiography and chronology—the sources also include Sulpicius Severus, the *Actus Silvestri*, Ambrose, Isidore of Seville, and a web of quotations from the Bible—the work nevertheless reveals more about the England of its subject and its author than do many of the hagiographies that followed it. The

[15] Written by the brothers of the church at Lindisfarne.
[16] To me; by the brothers.
[17] Who now reigns peacefully.

author is careful about geography, charting the course of the saint's travels and giving the names of the places through which he passed. Significantly, Bede—probably because he wanted to engage in a more spiritual and universalized eulogy—left much of this material out of his *VP*, and it is similarly lacking in the Whitby *Vita sancti Gregorii* and Felix's *Vita sancti Guthlaci*, although the other member of this group, Eddius' *Vita Wilfridi*, is again more detailed. This feature of the hagiographical convention is present, it seems, chiefly when the author is himself situated within the geographical environment of the legend, and when he can expect his audience to have some personal associations with the detail. It is not, then, historical in the sense that such material might be in a later work, but a kind of pious propaganda, more analogous to vivid detail in fictive writing than to the minutiae of scrupulous historiography; although the author takes information from eyewitnesses and, in some chapters, verbatim accounts, the generalized assurance (1.2) of fidelity is a commonplace of the form.

Consistent with this aspect of the *Vita* is the constant association of Cuthbert's feats with those of earlier saints and, particularly, with the holy men of the Bible. Such a technique is common in earlier writing in this genre, including the sources of this book, but it is equally at home in a work written perhaps no more than fifteen years after the death of the man it describes and by a member of his own community. A characteristic chapter from the second of the *Vita*'s four books, which are divided into his youth, his life in the monastery, his life as a hermit, and his episcopate and death, is the third, quoted in part above, pp. 136-37.

Waldhere of London (3.4)

Waldhere was the fifth Bishop of London, in succession to Erconwald; he probably occupied his see in 693, and may have been consecrated by Archbishop Berhtwald. He must have died before 716, when his successor Ingwald, the sixth Bishop, was present at the Council of Clovesho. His name appears in a charter of Swaebraed dated 704, and in an almost certainly forged grant by Ethelred. Bede (*HE* IV.11) mentions that he was present at the death of King Sebbi of the East Saxons: "venit ad antistitem Lundoniae civitatis, vocabulo Waldheri, qui Erconwaldo successerat."[18]

The only documentary survival of Waldhere's episcopate is a letter (MS Cotton Aug. ii.18) he wrote sometime between the accession of Kenred of Mercia (704) and the division of the bishopric of Wessex (705). In it he asks Berhtwald to advise him what to do at the forthcoming meeting between King Ina of Wessex and the rulers of the East Saxons on a number of disputes.

> Quaerere etenim tuae sanctitatis consilium prospere rebus succedentibus, tuisque sapientissimis jussionibus famulari animus devotus mihi semper inerat; quanto magis in adversis et in difficilibus rerum eventibus tuae providae considerationis industriam consulari voluntaria necessitas meam insciolam parvitatem perurget. Inde ergo nunc instante necessitatum causa, quid agi debeat tuae benevolentiae ingenium flagitando inquirere operae pretium reor.[19]

The style becomes less self-consciously formal and ornamental toward the end of the letter, dispensing with the comparison *quanto magis* and the alliteration.

> Inde per omnipotentem rerum conditorem tuae sanctitatis privilegium obsecro ut mihi innotescere digneris quid de

[18] He came to the bishop of the city of London, Waldhere by name, who had succeeded Erconwald.

[19] I have always had a devout mind, ready to seek the advice of your holiness and to attend to your most wise commands, when things were going well; how much more in the adverse and difficult way of things does voluntary necessity urge my unwise littleness to consult the industry of your thoughtful consideration. Whence, therefore, I think it worthwhile to inquire with prayer of the wisdom of your benevolence what I should do, now that there is immediate pressing cause.

[198]

hac re agere debeam, quia nullo modo possum inter illos
reconciliare et quasi obses pacis fieri, nisi maximum com-
munionis consortium inter nos misceatur, quod nec volo
nec ausus sum agere nisi tuae licentiae voluntas annuerit;
quia memor sum quomodo in praeteriti anni synodo statutum est illis non communicandum, si non tuum judicium
in ordinatione episcoporum implere festinarent, quod adhuc
neglectum habentes non perficiebant.[20]

Indeed, the clausal structure here has become a kind of un-
premeditated string, the subordinate elements following one
another without correlation or apposition. Letter-writing as
a form, which had so influenced Aldhelm and his circle,
is scarcely in evidence here.

Aelffled of Whitby (3.5)

Aelffled was a sister of King Aldfrith and daughter of
King Oswy; the sources for her life are *HE* III.24 and IV.24;
Eddius' *Vita Wilfridi*, chs. 43, 59, and 60; the Whitby
Vita sancti Gregorii, ch. 18; *VA* III.6, IV.10; and Bede's
VP, chs. 23 and 24. She was born in 654 and dedicated to
religion as an infant; first at Hartlepool, later at Whitby,
where she was a nun under Abbess Hilde, whom she succeeded at her death in 680. Eddius, whose admiration she
may have aroused by her assistance to Wilfrid's cause,
called her "abbatissa et sapientissima virgo";[21] her association with the Cuthbert legend likewise helped to preserve
her memory after her death in 713.

[20] Hence by the Almighty Creator of things I implore the
authority of your holiness that you deign to inform me what I
should do in this matter, for I can bring no manner of reconciliation
between them, and I am made as it were a hostage of peace, unless
the greatest reciprocal relationship grows up among us, which I
neither want nor dare to bring about unless the wish of your
permission grants it; for I recall how in the synod of last year it
was decided that we should have no communication with them if
they did not hasten to carry out your decree on the ordination of
bishops, which up to now they have neglected and have not
fulfilled.

[21] An abbess and a most wise virgin.

Sometime before her death, but probably after 700, she wrote a letter to Adola, Abbess of Pfalsel near Trier, commending to her care an English abbess who was traveling that way on a pilgrimage to Rome. The style of the first paragraph—almost half the letter—is competent, even learned, but self-consciously elaborate in the Aldhelmian manner :

> Ex quo famam vestrae sanctitatis ab adventantibus ex illis partibus rumore celebri referente cognovimus, fateor in primis nos vestrum visceraliter juxta praeceptum dominicum ex intimo pectore amorem caepisse domino dicente: *Hoc est praeceptum meum, ut diligatis invicem.* Quapropter precibus subnixis suppliciter poscimus, ut sacrosanctis flammigerisque oraculis vestris nos apud almipotentem dominum defendere dignemini; siquidem vobis vicem reddere nostra humilitas minime pigebit apostolo Jacobo hoc ipsum praecipiente ac dicente: *Orate pro invicem, ut salvemini.*[22]

The mixture of extravagant compliment with "hard" words on one hand, scriptural tags on the other, reflects the influence of the epistolary tradition that Waldhere and Berhtwald seem hardly to have felt.

Berhtwald of Canterbury (3.6)

Berhtwald is described by Bede (*HE* v.8) on the occasion of his elevation to the see of Canterbury in succession to Theodore in 692.

[22] From that which we have learned of the fame of your holiness from those who have returned from those places, bringing back the famous report, I confess that we have taken a great inward love of you in our heart of hearts from the first, according to the holy precept of the Lord, Who said, This is my commandment, that you love one another [John 15:12]. Therefore we beg you with trusting prayers, that you deign to intercede for us with the mightily gracious Lord in your holy and burning orisons; indeed our humility disdains not at all to exchange this with you, as the Apostle James himself taught and said it: Pray one for another, that you may be saved [James 5:16].

Successit autem Theodoro in episcopatum Berhtwald, qui
erat abbas in monasterio, quod juxta ostium aquilonale
fluminis Genladae positum, Racuulfe nuncupatur; vir et
ipse scientia scripturarum imbutus, sed et ecclesiasticis
simul ac monasterialibus disciplinis summe instructus,
tametsi praedecessori suo minime comparandus. . . .[23]

He died in 731. (For other documents relating to his archi-
episcopate, see *H&S* III.228-310, and *Gesta pontificum, RS*
52, pp. 52-55, 376.) He wrote a letter to Forthere, Bishop
of Sherborne 709-738, in which he mentions Beorwald,
Abbot of Glastonbury, who was dead by 712; the letter is
therefore 709x712. The letter deals with the ransom money
for a girl named Eppa, whose release Berhtwald is seeking
to obtain. It is short, but reveals sound latinity and attention to style:

> Per quas obsecro, ut ipse omnino obtineas a praedicto abbate,
> quatenus pro eadem puella trecentos accipiat solidos de
> manu praesentium geruli et ei tradat illam huc usque
> perducendam, quo possit reliquum vitae suae spatium cum
> consanguineis suis non in servitutis tristitia, sed in libertatis
> transigere laetitia.[24]

Berhtwald is aware of variation ("a praedicto abbate . . . pro
eadem puella") and parallelism ("in servitutis tristitia . . .
in libertatis . . . laetitia"), but he does not seem to seek, as
Aldhelm had done, to reinforce the matter of his argument
with the manner of his composition.

[23] Now Berhtwald succeeded Theodore in the bishopric, who
was abbot in a monastery called Reculver, situated at the north
mouth of the river Yenlade; a man who was himself learned in the
study of Scriptures, and also fully instructed in ecclesiastical and
monastic disciplines as well, but still hardly to be compared to his
predecessor. . . .
[24] By these letters I implore, that you obtain by all means from
the aforesaid abbot himself, that he accept 300 shillings for the
same girl from the hand of the bearer of these presents and turn
her over to him to be brought here, where she may spend the remaining space of her life with her relatives, not in the sadness of
servitude, but in the joy of liberty.

Acca of Hexham (3.7)

Bede gives most of the information about Acca in *HE* V.20:

Suscepit vero pro Wilfrido episcopatum Hagustaldensis ecclesiae Acca presbyter ejus, vir et ipse strenuissimus, et
coram Deo et hominibus magnificus; qui et ipsius ecclesiae
suae, quae in beati Andreae apostoli honorem consecrata est,
aedificium multifario decore ac mirificis ampliavit operibus.
Dedit namque operam, quod et hodie facit, ut acquisitis
undecumque reliquiis beatorum apostolorum et martyrum
Christi, in venerationem illorum poneret altaria, distinctis
porticibus in hoc ipsum intra muros ejusdem ecclesiae; sed
et historias passionis eorum, una cum ceteris ecclesiasticis
voluminibus, summa industria congregans, amplissimam ibi
ac nobilissimam bibliothecam fecit, nec non et vasa sancta,
et luminaria, aliaque hujusmodi, quae ad ornatum domus
Dei pertinent, studiosissime paravit. Cantatorem quoque
egregium, vocabulo Maban, qui a successoribus discipulorum
beati papae Gregorii in Cantia fuerat cantandi sonos
edoctus, ad se suosque instituendos accersiit, ac per annos
xii tenuit; quatinus et, quae illi non noverant, carmina
ecclesiastica doceret; et ea, quae quondam cognita longo
usu vel neglegentia inveterare coeperunt, hujus doctrina
priscum renovarentur in statum. Nam et ipse episcopus Acca
cantator erat peritissimus, quomodo etiam in litteris sanctis
doctissimus, et in catholicae fidei confessione castissimus, in
ecclesiasticae quoque institutionis regulis solertissimus ex-
stiterat; et usquedum praemia piae devotionis accipiat,
existere non desistit; utpote qui a pueritia in clero sanctissimi ac Deo dilecti Bosa Eboracensis episcopi nutritus atque
eruditus est; deinde ad Wilfridum episcopum spe melioris
propositi adveniens, omnem in ejus obsequio usque ad
obitum illius explevit aetatem; cum quo etiam Romam
veniens multa illic, quae in patria nequiverat, ecclesiae
sanctae institutis utilia didicit.[25]

[25] But Acca, his priest, in the place of Wilfrid took over the
bishopric of Hexham, a man most courageous himself, and distinguished before God and men; who likewise enlarged the building of his own church, which was consecrated in honor of blessed
Andrew the Apostle, by means of sundry decorations and marvelous

In *HE* v.23 he refers to Acca as still in the see of Hexham, but in the year *HE* was completed or thereabouts Acca was expelled from the see under unexplained circumstances. He died in 740. He was the dedicatee of many of Bede's exegetical works, and—with Abbot Tatberht of Ripon—of Eddius' *Vita Wilfridi* as well. He is the authority for *HE* III.13 and IV.13. The language of Bede's dedications to him suggests that the two men were often in communication and enjoyed each other's confidence, but only one letter from Acca—as a prologue to Bede's commentary on Luke —survives. In it, Acca seeks to encourage Bede to write an exposition of Luke, even though Ambrose has already done so; as Bede himself did, he quotes Augustine, "necesse est plures a pluribus fieri libros diverso stilo sed non diversa

---

works. For he set himself the task, as he does even today, that, having acquired from everywhere the relics of the blessed Apostles and martyrs of Christ, he would set up altars in their honor, each by itself in separate side chapels within the walls of the same church; and also, bringing together with the greatest industry the histories of their sufferings, along with other ecclesiastical books, he made there a most great and grand library, and he most studiously prepared in addition sacred vessels, and lamps, and other things of the same sort, which are suitable to ornament the house of God. And he also summoned a famous singer by the name of Maban, who was educated in the manner of singing by the successors of the disciples of blessed Pope Gregory in Kent, for the instruction of himself and his clergy, and for twelve years he kept him there, so that he might teach them the ecclesiastical songs which they did not know; and those, which having once been known had begun to become decayed through long use of negligence, were restored to their original state by his teaching. For Bishop Acca was himself a very learned singer, just as he was outstanding also in holy writ by his learning, in confession of the Catholic faith by his chastity, and in the rules of the ecclesiastical institution by his scrupulousness; and so he shall not cease to be until he receives the rewards of his pious devotion; for he was raised and taught from his childhood among the clergy of the most holy and beloved of God Bishop Bosa of York; and afterward coming to Bishop Wilfrid in hope of a better position, he lived out his years in his service up to his death; with whom journeying to Rome, he learned many things there useful in the regulation of the holy Church, which he had not known in his homeland.

fide" (*De trinitate*)[26] and Terence, "nihil sit dictum quod non sit dictum prius" (*Eunuchus*).[27] He brings up one point in particular for Bede to consider: "Intimandum sane tuae sanctitati credidi quia movet quosdam quare in expositione apocalypsis ubi ad IV animalia ventum est nova interpretatione Matthaeum in leone Marcum in homine designatum dixeris cum nonnulli contra Matthaeum homini quia quasi de domino scribere incipiat Marcum leoni in quo *vox in deserto rugientis audiatur* assignent rogoque in hoc opere plenius quid tibi de his verius videatur insinues."[28]

As influential as he was in the intellectual development of Northumbria, Acca did not have widespread fame in the later middle ages. In several MSS of Bede's *De templo Salomonis*, for example, the dedication is described as "ad Nothelmum" (or "Nothelinum") and in others the vocative "Acca" is transcribed "et te" with damage to the syntax. In many MSS of the *De die judicii*, Bede's concluding lines addressed to Acca have been replaced with others by Eugenius.

Ceolfrid of Jarrow (3.8)

Ceolfrid, afterwards Abbot of Wearmouth-Jarrow, was born in 642 of noble parents, according to the two principal sources for his life, Bede's *Historia abbatum* (see 2.8) and the anonymous *Historia abbatum* or *Vita sanctissimi Ceolfridi abbatis* (see 3.9). He became a monk of the monastery

[26] It is needful that many books be made by many writers, in sundry styles but in a single faith.

[27] Nothing is said that has not been said before.

[28] I have believed that it was surely to be mentioned to your holiness that it disturbed some people that in your exposition of the Apocalypse it comes about that you have by a new interpretation said that Matthew was symbolized by a lion and Mark by a man, whereas many others on the contrary say that Matthew was symbolized by a man, for they assign Mark to the lion, since he sets about writing about the Lord "A voice is heard of one roaring in the desert" [Mark 3:3]; and I beg of you that you say something more fully about how the truth of this appears to you.

at Gilling in 660, at the age of eighteen, where his cousin Tunberht was later abbot. He removed to Ripon with Tunberht at the invitation of Wilfrid in 669, when he was 27. From there he visited Canterbury, perhaps to study with the newly arrived Theodore and Hadrian, and then East Anglia. Upon his return to Ripon "nemo per id temporis . . . doctior illo posset inveniri"[29] in the laws of the Church (*HAA,* ch. 4). Upon the foundation of Wearmouth in 674, he joined Benedict Biscop there; he returned to Ripon briefly, but he was with Benedict Biscop when he traveled to Rome in 678. Jarrow was founded in 682, and Ceolfrid became its abbot. In 688 or 689 he became Abbot of Wearmouth as well. During his abbacy, "bibliothecam, quam de Roma vel ipse, vel Benedictus attulerat, nobiliter ampliavit ita ut inter alia tres pandectes faceret describi, quorum duo per totidem sua monasteria posuit in ecclesiis, ut cunctis qui aliquod capitulum de utrolibet testamento legere voluissent, in promptu esset in venire quod cuperent; tertium autem Romam profecturus donum beato Petro apostolorum principi offerre decrevit" (*HAA,* ch. 20).[30] He resigned as abbot in June 716, in order to make another visit to Rome before his death, but he died on the way at Langres on September 25, 716, aged seventy-four. One letter and one poem remain.

Two texts of the poem are extant: the one quoted in *HAA,* ch. 37,

> In quibus videlicet muneribus erat pandectes, ut diximus, interpretatione beati Hieronymi presbyteri ex Hebraeo et Graeco fonte transfusus, habens in capite scriptos hujusmodi versiculos:

[29] No one in those days could be found more learned than he.

[30] He nobly increased the library which he and Benedict brought from Rome, so that among other things he caused three Bibles to be transcribed, of which he placed two in the churches of his two monasteries, so that for all who wished to read any chapter of either Testament, it would be easy to find what they wanted; and the third he decided when he was about to go to Rome to offer as a gift to blessed Peter, prince of the Apostles.

Corpus ad eximii merito venerabile Petri,
    Dedicat ecclesiae quem caput alta fides,
Ceolfridus, Anglorum extremis de finibus abbas,
    Devoti affectus pignora mitto mei.
Meque meosque optans tanti inter gaudia patris
    In caelis memorem semper habere locum,[31]

and the somewhat altered text on the first folio of the Codex Amiatinus, one of the pandects mentioned above. This MS, probably of native Jarrow manufacture (although sometimes said to be the work of Italian scribes writing in England), was first associated with Ceolfrid by de Rossi, and his theory was later confirmed on the basis of the verses in *HAA*. The composition of the verses must be about the date of the Rome trip, 716.

The letter is quoted verbatim in *HE* v.21, and Plummer thought, on the basis of verbal resemblances, it was the work of Bede himself; but C. W. Jones has pointed out that the verbal resemblances are of the sort common in chronological literature, and that Bede's attribution of it to Ceolfrid is not to be doubted. Bede dates it "eo tempore," i.e., 709-710. It comprises a lengthy reply to the request of the Pictish King Naiton for guidance on the paschal and tonsorial controversies. Ceolfrid includes a reference to Plato's *Republic*:

> Nam et vere omnino dixit quidam saecularium scriptorum, quia felicissimo mundus statu ageretur, si vel reges philosopharentur, vel regnarent philosophi,[32]

too commonplace to prove any direct knowledge of Plato in eighth-century England (e.g., Boethius *De consolatione*

---

[31] Among which gifts there was the Bible, as I have said, translated from the Hebrew and Greek sources in the interpretation of the blessed priest Jerome, having at the beginning verses written as follows: I, Ceolfrid, abbot from the furthest borders of the English, send vows of my devoted love to the body of Peter, excellent in venerable merit, whom the high faith of the Church declares its head.

[32] For truly indeed a certain secular writer said that the world would be in a most happy state, if either the kings took up philosophy, or the philosophers ruled.

philosophiae I, pr. 4). He goes on to give three basic rules for the observation of Easter.

> Praecepit enim lex, ut pascha primo mense anni et tertia ejusdem mensis septimana, id est a xv die usque ad xxi, fieri deberet; additum est per institutionem apostolicam ex evangelio, ut in ipsa tertia septimana diem dominicam expectare, atque in ea temporis paschalis initium tenere debeamus,[33]

which he elaborates at length including a typical as well as a chronological justification for the regulations:

> Quod si mysticam quoque vos in his rationem audire delectat, primo mense anni, qui etiam mensis novorum dictus est, pascha facere jubemur; quia renovato ad amorem caelestium spiritu mentis nostrae, sacramenta dominicae resurrectionis et ereptionis nostrae celebrare debemus, tertia ejusdem mensis septimana facere praecipimur; quia ante legem et sub lege promissus, tertio tempore saeculi cum gratia venit ipse, qui pascha nostrum immolaretur Christus; quia tertia post immolationem suae passionis die resurgens a mortuis, hanc dominicam vocari, et in ea nos annuatim paschalia ejusdem resurrectionis voluit festa celebrare; quia nos quoque ita solum veraciter ejus sollemnia celebramus, si per fidem, spem et caritatem pascha, id est transitum, de hoc mundo ad patrem, cum illo facere curamus. Post aequinoctium veris plenilunium mensis praecipimur observare paschalis; ut videlicet primo sol longiorem nocte faciat diem, deinde luna plenum suae lucis orbem mundo praesentet; quia primo quidem sol justitiae, in cujus pennis est sanitas, id est dominus Jesus, per resurrectionis suae triumphum cunctas mortis tenebras superavit; ac sic ascendens in caelos, misso desuper spiritu, ecclesiam suam, quae saepe lunae vocabulo designatur, internae gratiae luce replevit. Quem videlicet ordinem nostrae salutis propheta contemplatus aiebat: *Elevatus est sol, et luna stetit in ordine suo.*[34]

---

[33] For the law commanded that the passover should be held in the first month of the year, and the third week of the same month, that is, from the fifteenth to the twenty-first day; it was added by apostolic institution from the Gospel, that in the same third week we should wait for the Lord's day, and on it observe the beginning of the paschal period.

[34] If you would like to hear the mystical reason why, in the first

Ceolfrid next deals with the question of the tonsure; he regards it as a matter of suitability rather than a matter of
necessity, unlike paschal reckoning, that the whole Church
should observe the same practice. He associates the crown-
shaped tonsure with Peter and provides symbolic and scriptural justification, while he regards the Celtic tonsure (the
head shaved forward of a line from ear to ear) as that of
Simon Magus.

Bede's comments on the reception of the letter at Naiton's court provide an insight into the state of Celtic latinity:

> Haec epistola cum praesente rege Naitono multisque viris
> doctioribus esset lecta, ac diligenter ab his, qui intellegere
> poterant, in linguam ejus propriam interpretata, multum
> de ejus exhortatione gavisus esse perhibetur.[35]

---

month of the year, which is called the month of new things, we
are commanded to observe Easter; it is because the spirit of our
mind being renewed in celestial love, we should celebrate the mysteries of the Lord's resurrection and our own deliverance; and we
are bidden to do so on the third week of the same month because
Christ, Who was promised before the law and under the law, came
Himself in the third age of the world with grace, to be immolated
as our paschal lamb; because rising from the dead on the third day
after the immolation of His passion, He desired it to be called the
Lord's day, and us to celebrate the paschal feast of His resurrection the same day every year; because we also only truly observe
its solemnities, if we desire to make the passover, that is the
journey from this world to the Father, with Him in faith, hope, and
charity. We are taught to observe the full moon of the paschal
month after the spring equinox; so that the sun may first make the
day longer than the night, then the moon may present to the world
the full orb of her light; because first the sun of justice, in whose
wings is salvation, that is, the Lord Jesus, overcame by the triumph of His resurrection all the shadows of death; and so ascend-
ing into heaven, having sent the Holy Ghost from above, He filled
His Church, which is often called by the name of a moon, with
the light of interior grace. The prophet, contemplating this order
of our salvation, said: The sun was lifted up, and the moon stood
in her order [cf. Habb. 3:11].

[35] When this letter was read in the presence of King Naiton
and many learned men, and carefully translated into his own tongue
by those who could understand it, it is reported that many rejoiced
at his exhortation.

Historia abbatum anonyma (3.9)

The anonymous *Vita sanctissimi Ceolfridi* (*HAA*) must have been written after Ceolfrid's death in 716, and before 725, when Bede made use of it in his *DTR*. Its author refers again and again to Wearmouth-Jarrow as "noster," but there is nothing else to identify him; the tradition that Hwaetberht, Wintbert, or someone else of similar name wrote the book is unfounded. The narrative concentrates on Ceolfrid's life at Wearmouth-Jarrow, supplying at the same time a good deal of material about Benedict Biscop, Eosterwine, Sigfrith, and Hwaetberht, which Bede incorporated into his *HAB*. In one anecdote which Bede does not include, that of the little boy who helped Ceolfrid at divine office during a visitation of the plague, has been seen a reference to Bede himself, but the interpretation is unsound. The author does include the dedicatory verses by Ceolfrid which are inscribed on the Codex Amiatinus (see 3.8), a letter from Hwaetberht to Pope Gregory II (see 3.12), also in Bede, and the Pope's reply, which Bede omits. The longest episode is one which has less to do with the history of Ceolfrid's regime at the monastery than with the effect of his character upon it, the circumstances surrounding his resignation and departure and the grief of the bereft community.

> Completa allocutione, rursus assumpta antiphona cum psalmo memorato egrediuntur ad fluvium, lugubre carmine patrem utpote jam decessurum deducentes, itidemque singulis osculum pacis dat, intercepto saepius cantu prae lacrimis, et dicta in litore oratione, ascendit navem, residet in prora, sederunt juxta diacones, unus crucem, quam fecerat, auream, alter cereas tenens ardentes,[36] (ch. 26)

[36] When the address is completed, and the antiphon resumed with the above-mentioned psalm, they go out to the river, leading forth their father with a sad song as one already about to die, and in like manner he gives to each of them the kiss of peace, the song being interrupted most frequently by tears, and having said a prayer on the shore, he goes into the boat and seats himself in the prow, while the deacons sit beside him, one holding a golden cross which he had made, and the other holding lighted candles.

[209]

which Bede adapted:

> Veniunt ad litus; rursum osculo pacis inter lacrimas omni-
> bus dato, genua flectunt; dat orationem, ascendit navem
> cum comitibus. Ascendunt et diacones ecclesiae cereas
> ardentes et crucem ferentes auream, transiit flumen, adorat
> crucem, ascendit equum, et abiit, relictis in monasteriis suis
> fratribus numero ferme sexcentorum.[37]   (ch. 17)

Nothing of miracles during his life, and very little (in the
short final chapter) of those after his death is said; the *Vita*
is as much a piece of local historiography as hagiography,
and it shares little with the other saints' lives of its time in
the way of elaborate language or large-scale borrowings
from earlier hagiographical classics.

Eddius Stephanus (3.10)

Eddius' *Vita Wilfridi* was written after Wilfrid's death
in 709 and it refers to Acca, who was deposed in 731, as
bishop. The modern editor of the *Vita* thinks that it is probably 710x720. The attribution to Eddius Stephanus is traditional, based on notes in the two MSS (of the eleventh
and twelfth centuries), William of Malmesbury's *Gesta
pontificum* III (Prol.), and the mention (in ch. 14 and
HE IV.2) of an Aedde who accompanied Wilfrid. He must
have been a monk of Ripon, to judge by the description of
Wilfrid's gifts to Ripon in ch. 17, "quae omnia et alia
nonnulla in testimonium beatae memoriae ejus in ecclesia
nostra usque hodie reconduntur, ubi reliquiae illius
requiescunt. . . ."[38]

---

[37] They come to the shore; and having exchanged the kiss of
peace with them all amidst tears, they fall on their knees; he prays,
and goes into the boat with his companions. The deacons of the
Church also go carrying burning candles and a golden cross, and he
goes across the river, prays to the cross, mounts a horse, and
departs, leaving behind some six hundred brothers in his monasteries.

[38] All of which things and not a few others are preserved in our
church where his relics repose until this day in testimony of his
blessed memory. . . .

The life was written, according to the preface, by order
of Acca and Abbot Tatberht; the preface goes on to make
the conventional protestations of unworthiness and assur-
ances that eyewitnesses are the authority, but in words almost entirely borrowed from the anonymous *Vita sancti
Cuthberti* (itself largely derived from the Evagrian *Vita
sancti Antonii*), the *Epistola Victorii ad Hilarium* and the
Vita Martini Turonensis by Sulpicius Severus. Eddius
also borrows from the *VA* in ch. 11 when he catalogues
Wilfrid's virtues, but most of his material—excepting the
many scriptural citations and the several letters and other
documents—is in his own words. His style is loose and
somewhat strangled by other-than-narrative requirements:

Navigantibus quoque eis de Gallia Britannicum mare cum
beatae memoriae Wilfrido episcopo, canentibus clericis et
psallentibus laudem Dei pro celeumate in choro, in medio
mari validissima tempestas exorta est, et venti contrarii,
sicut discipulis Jesu in mare Galileae erant. Flante namque
vento euroaustro dure, albescentia undarum culmina in
regionem Australium Saxonum, quam non noverant, pro-
jecerunt eos. Mare quoque navem et homines relinquens,
terras fugiens, litoraque detegens, et in abyssi matricem
recessit. Gentiles autem cum ingenti exercitu venientes,
navem arripere, praedam sibi pecuniae dividere, captivos
subjugatos deducere resistentesque gladio occidere in-
cunctanter proposuerunt. Quibus sanctus pontifex noster
copiosam pecuniam promittens, animas redimere cupiens
leniter pacificeque loquebatur. Illi vero feroces et indurato
corde cum Pharaone populum Dei dimittere nolentes et
dicentes superbe, sua esse omnia quasi propria, quae mare
ad terras projecit. Stans quoque princeps sacerdotum
idolatriae coram paganis in tumulo excelso, sicut Balaam,
maledicere populum Dei et suis magicis artibus manus
eorum alligare nitebatur. Tunc vero unus ex sodalibus pontificis nostri lapidem ab omni populo Dei benedictum more
Davidico de funda emittens, fronte perforata usque ad
cerebrum magi exprobrantis illisit; quem, retrorsum exani-
mato cadavere cadente, sicut Goliath in harenosis locis mors
incerta praevenit. Ad bellum ergo se praeparantes pagani,
aciem frustra in populum Dei direxerunt. Dominus enim

[211]

pro paucis pugnavit; sicut jam Gedeon domini jussu cum
ccc viris bellatorum Madianitum cxx milia uno impetu occi-
dit, ita et isti sodales sancti pontificis nostri bene armati, viriles
animo, pauci numero—erant enim cxx viri in numero
Mosaicae aetatis—inito consilio et pacto, ut nullus ab alio
in fugam terga verteret, sed aut mortem cum laude aut
vitam cum triumpho, quod Deo utrumque facile est, habere
mererentur.[39]   (ch. 13)

Colgrave has listed a number of instances of false concord
and wrong or unusual forms, cases, and tenses in the work,
and it is clearly true that Eddius had little familiarity with

[39] Also when they were navigating the British sea on their way
from Gaul with Bishop Wilfrid of blessed memory, and the priests
were singing the praise of God and reciting psalms to keep the
oarsmen in time, a violent storm arose in mid-ocean, and the winds
were contrary, as they were to the disciples of Jesus in the sea of
Galilee. With the wind blowing hard from the southeast, the foamy
crests of the waves cast them into the region of the South Saxons,
which they knew not. The sea receded into the depth of the abyss,
leaving the ship and men, fleeing the land, and wiping clean the
shores. Then approaching pagans with a huge army threatened to
take the ship, to divide the spoils among themselves, to lead away
the captives they took and to put those who resisted to the sword
without delay. To whom our holy bishop spoke softly and peaceably
promising them much money, wishing to save their lives. Those,
however, were fierce and hard-hearted like Pharaoh, not wishing
to let the people of God go free and saying proudly, that all that
was theirs, which the sea cast up on the land. Also the chief of
the priests of idolatry, standing before the pagans on a large
mound, like Balaam, sought to curse the people of God and to bind
their hands by his magic arts. Then, however, one of the companions of our bishop, throwing a stone blessed by all the people
of God, in the manner of David, with a sling, it pierced into the
brain of the mocking wizard, having broken through his forehead;
whom unexpected death overcame, his lifeless body falling backward, like Goliath, in the sandy place. Therefore the pagans, pre-
paring themselves for combat, set up their line of battle against
the people of God in vain. For the Lord fought for the few; just as
before Gideon at the command of the Lord slew in one rush 120,-
000 of the Midianite warriors with his 300 men, likewise also the
companions of our holy bishop, well armed, strong in spirit, few
in number—there were 120 men, the age of Moses—took counsel
and agreed at the outset, that none would turn his back on another
in flight, but that they would strive to have either death with honor
or life with triumph, both of which are easy for God to bring about.

the hagiographical models whose latinity was a virtuoso technical display. Some phrases are favorites:

> . . . inter saecularesque undas fluctuantes moderate navem ecclesiae gubernat. Sicut enim eum unda convivii non demersit, ita et abstinentiae in superbiam non projecit. . . .[40]
>
> (ch. 21)

> Nam antiquae inimicitiae suasores, quasi de sopore somni excitati, mare hujus saeculi in gaudio serenum, procella flante turbinis invidiae folliculo, ad triste naufragium moventes, et facem dissensionis extinctam resuscitavere,[41]
>
> (ch. 45)

even when they result in a mixture of metaphors.

Yet even though Wilfrid's life was a famous one in the eighth century, and even though Eddius wrote about it from a biased point of view, he remains the sole source of many of the facts and impressions we have about the bishop. The *Vita* is unlike many of the hagiographies of the age in that the author was a companion of the subject, and that the subject was a controversial public figure. The result of this partisan commitment is that much of the story concerns only the controversy; the miracles themselves are often adduced in justification of Wilfrid, and little that does not bear on the issues of his two great crises so much as makes an appearance. Some of the most interesting matter, as a consequence, is to be found in incidents that are not in the focus of the controversy, when such incidents occur. One is the presentation of the papal letters to the second synod convened by Berhtwald:

> Post lectionem, cunctis tacentibus, Berhtfridus, secundus a rege princeps, ad archiepiscopum dixit: "Nos, qui in-

[40] He steered the ship of the Church carefully amid the tossing waves of the world. Thus the billow of feasting did not submerge him, and likewise that of abstinence did not cast him into pride. . . .

[41] But the agitators of the old enmity, as though aroused from sleep, having blown up a storm with the bellows of envy on the sea of this world, then serene in peace, brought again to life the extinct torch of dissension.

terpretatione indigemus, quid apostolica auctoritas dicat, audire delectat." Et respondit ei archiepiscopus, dicens: "Judicia apostolicae sedis longo circuitu et ambagibus verborum, unum tamen intellectum de eadem re utrique libri ostendentes, quorum in brevi sermone sensum tantum explicabo."[42]   (ch. 60)

Eddius' concern and his limitations are both clear from his preface, where in the few words that are his own he begs his readers to study his work, not simply because—and here he differs from the usual formula—the subject is a great and manifold one, but because popular report may have said otherwise:

> Obsecro itaque eos qui lecturi sunt, ut fidem dictis adhibeant, relinquentes antiqui hostis millenos invidiae stimulos et recolentes, quod eloquentia pertonabat. Semper enim in propatulo fortitudo emulos habet: feriuntque summos fulgora montes.[43]   (Pref.)

The partisan obligation not only draws Eddius into the business of biography, for which, unlike Bede and Felix, he was not particularly well fitted, but it also influences the outcome of his labor. That the outcome was nonetheless a success is shown by the 1,200 years of popular admiration of Wilfrid since Eddius took up his pen, admiration which the plain facts of the bishop's life could hardly have sustained.

[42] After the reading, when all were silent, Berhtfrith, chief second only to the king, said to the archbishop: "We who need a translation, would be glad to hear what the apostolic authority says." And the archbishop answered him, saying, "The judgment of the apostolic see expresses in roundabout manner and enigmatic form of words one meaning about the same subject in both books, of which I shall explain the basic sense in a brief discourse."

[43] So I beg those who are about to read this, that they rely on what I say, ignoring the thousand goads of the envy of the old enemy, and remembering that which eloquence declares. For fortitude always has its rivals in the open: and the lightnings strike the tallest mountains.

Tatwine of Canterbury (3.11)

The chief source for our knowledge of Tatwine is *HE* v.23, "pro quo [sc. Berhtwald] anno eodem [sc. 731] factus est archiepiscopus, vocabulo Tatwini, de provincia Merciorum, cum fuisset presbyter in monasterio quod vocatur Briudun . . . vir religione et prudentia insignis, sacris quoque litteris nobiliter instructus."[44] He died, according to the *Bedae continuatio*, in 734. He left a collection of forty riddles surviving in two MSS and a grammar surviving in four. According to William of Malmesbury, he went to Rome to receive the pallium in 733, but the tradition is doubtful, and the letter concerning it attributed to Pope Gregory III (*Gesta pontificum, RS* 52, p.55) is certainly spurious.

The initial letters of the forty riddles read "Sub deno quater haec diverse aenigmata torquens," and the final letter of the first line of each, beginning with the fortieth and reading backwards, give "Stamine metrorum exstructor conserta retexit."[45] The two lines form the first two of an introductory riddle, and an appended poem explains the principle:

> Versibus intextis vatem nunc jure salutat,
> Litterulas summa capitum hortans jungere primas
> Versibus extremas hisdem ex minio coloratas,
> Conversus gradiens rursum perscandat ab imo.[46]

[44] In the same year [731] a man by the name of Tatwine was made archbishop in place of him [i.e., Berhtwald]; he was of the province of the Mercians, and had been a priest in the monastery called Bredon . . . a man outstanding in his religion and wisdom, and nobly learned in holy writ as well.

[45] Turning forty times under these riddles differently, the maker reveals the hidden things in the thread of meters.

[46] Now let the reader rightly salute the poet in the interwoven lines, calling on the first letters of the line-beginnings to join from the top and also those in the same lines furthest from the initials colored with red lead; let him contrariwise climbing back raise himself up from the bottom.

A foreword—which appears at the end of the riddles in the London manuscript—suggests that Tatwine was not yet archbishop when he wrote them:

> Sublimitatis vestrae oboediens praecepto, quo nostrae medio-
> critati injunxistis ut aliquid dignum scriberem vestrae
> serenitati, misi ad vestram excellentiam hoc monitorium
> opus ut inter reipublicae curas vestra excellentia salubritatis
> praecepta ad mentem revocans habeatis ubi honestatis et
> salutis possitis invenire speciem,[47]

although Ebert thinks they are not Tatwine's at all, but merely a scribe's.

Just as the acrostic technique recalls Aldhelm's collection, so does the appearance in both MSS of the solutions as title to the riddles, and of frequent scholia to gloss hard words or interpret difficult allusions. Formally, however, the riddles are more conservative than Aldhelm's, and they cover a different range of subjects. The first, "Philosophia," is the longest, with twelve lines; the next three are of seven, six, and five lines respectively; nos. 5-10, of six lines; nos. 11-30, of five; nos. 31-39, of four; and the last one, of five. While this is more flexible than the rigid three-line system of Symphosius, it still reflects a consciousness of length as a formal feature of the riddle, which Aldhelm had largely disregarded. In subject, "Philosophia" would hardly have appealed to Aldhelm, who was generally more interested in the material world, but it is characteristic of at least part of Tatwine's collection, which includes other abstractions like "Faith, Hope, and Charity," "Charity," "Evil," "Humility," "Pride," and "The Five Senses." Another class of Tatwine's riddles does involve material objects—scissors,

---

[47] Obeying the precept of your sublimity, in which you called upon my mediocrity that I should write something to your serenity, I have sent to your excellency this instructive work so that your excellency, recalling the precepts of salvation to mind amid the cares of public affairs, might have something in which you might be able to find a model of honesty and wholesomeness.

anvil, sword and sheath, and so forth—and still another, of which "Philosophia" is also an example, considers aspects of the learned world: the four levels of meaning, the letters of the alphabet, the vellum book (which has an analogue in the OE riddles of the Exeter Book), the pen, the trivium and quadrivium:

> De historia et sensu et morali et allegoria
>
> Bis binas statuit sua nos vigiles dominatrix
> Thesauri cellaria conservare sorores,
> Diversis quae intus fulgent ornata metallis,
> Omnigena et florum dulcedine serta virescunt:
> Gaudentes nostris haec mox reseramus amicis,
> Ingratisque aditum sed jure negamus apertum,[48]

where the Cambridge MS has the gloss on *dominatrix*, "i.e. trinitas," and on *ingratis*, "i.e., malis lectoribus."[49]

The riddles are reasonably independent of earlier ones, although some verbal recollections have been noted by Manitius and Hahn, especially of Aldhelm, and the choice of subjects by a priest, perhaps already archbishop, must have been merely traditional in at least some instances (spear, quiver, winnowing-fork, one-eyed person). They are moreover less metrically perfect as hexameters than Aldhelm's, without his flashes of insight, and they overwork a few simple tropes, especially numerical paradox and the metaphorical child-parent relationship: "Una tres natae sumus olim ex matre sagaci"[50] (Faith, Hope, and Charity), where the glossator interprets *matre*, "i.e., trinitate."

---

[48] The literal, figurative, moral, and allegorical meanings. Our lady created us two times two watchful sisters to preserve her storehouses of treasure, which adorned shine within with diverse metals, and garlanded flourish with every sort of the sweetness of flowers. Joyful we preserve them presently for our friends, but we rightly refuse free access to the ungrateful.

[49] Our lady, that is, the Trinity [the noun is feminine in Latin]; ungrateful ones, i.e., evil readers.

[50] We three were born erstwhile from a single wise mother.

The *Riddles* and the *Grammar* are linked in several ways. The riddling description of "Philosophia,"[51] "Nulla manus poterit, nec me contingere visus," may recall the *Grammar*'s illustration of the difference between corporeal and incorporeal objects, "incorporale vero quod nec tangi, nec videri valet ut 'sapientia'." More genrally characteristic are the compound forms like *solifero, dulcifero, frugifero*; the word play *Caesar/Caesus* (no. 7), *alta re/altare* (no. 8), the overtly classical references to Phoebus (no. 1), and Mars (nos. 17, 32).

Two ninth-century catalogues record MSS of Tatwine's grammar, St. Riquier and Lorsch, and the Lorsch MS has survived as Vatican MS Palatine 1746. There are also two Paris MSS (7560 and 17959), and two fragments of a Reichenau MS; the lost item 31 of Bodleian MS Laud Misc. 126 was yet another copy. The *Ars Tatwini* is a reworking of Consentius, with some reference to Priscian and a little to Donatus; a few other sources, including Servius, Pompeius, Hieronymus, Eutyches, Asper, Martianus Capella, Isidore of Seville, and the *Ars anonyma Bernensis*, have been traced. The result is more an expansion than a compilation, and it would serve the beginner less well than the more compact Donatus, the advanced student less well than the more coherent Consentius. Tatwine follows Donatus' framework in discussing noun, pronoun, verb, adverb, participle, conjunction, preposition, and interjection. His citations of pagan authors—Cicero, Virgil, Terence—seem to stem from the citations in other grammars, as do his etymologies for the parts of speech which he adduces as one aspect of the logical basis of grammar: "verbum a verberatione aeris," "modus a moderando."[52] One feature, the Latin chapter headings transliterated into Greek, probably does not go back to Tatwine, but to a copyist.

[51] No hand and no vision can touch me; something incorporeal like "wisdom" can be neither touched nor seen.

[52] "Verb" comes from the reverberation of the air; "mode" from moderating.

Hwaetberht of Jarrow (3.12)

Bede's commentaries on Acts and Apocalypse both mention a "frater noster Eusebius" in the preface, and the preface to *DTR* mentions "dilectissimus abbas meus Hwaetberhtus"; the preface to the fourth book of his commentary on Samuel makes it probable that this is the same man: "Hwaetberhtum juvenum, cui amor studiumque pietatis jam olim Eusebii cognomen indidit, ad regendas sacerdotio ducatuque spiritali fidelium animas, abbatis vice substituit"[53] at the resignation of Ceolfrid in 716. The riddles by Eusebius that follow those by Tatwine in both MSS are usually regarded as being by the same Hwaetberht; the letter which constitutes ch. 19 of *HAB* and ch. 30 of *HAA* is certainly by him, and the letters to him from Gregory II in *HAA* ch. 39 and from Boniface (Tangl, no. 76, pp. 158-159) are probably also genuine. His name, however, is often corrupted or confused in the MSS, sometimes with those of other people: common corruptions are Hucberct, Hwetberegtus, and confusions with Withmerus and Withbert.

The chief sources for our knowledge of Hwaetberht are *HAB*, chs. 18-20 and Bede's source, *HAA* 28-30, and 39. Bede wrote:

> Eligitur itaque abbas Hwaetberhtus qui a primis pueritiae temporibus eodem in monasterio non solum regularis observantia disciplinae institutus, sed et scribendi, cantandi, legendi ac docendi fuerat non parva exercitatus industria. Romam quoque temporibus beatae memoriae Sergii papae accurrens, et non parvo ibidem temporis spatio demoratus, quaeque sibi necessaria judicabat, didicit, descripsit, retulit; insuper et duodecim ante haec annos presbyterii est functus officio. Hic igitur electus abbas ab omnibus utriusque

---

[53] Our brother Eusebius; my most beloved Abbot Hwaetberht; he appointed in place of the abbot young Hwaetberht, whom the love and study of piety had previously given the cognomen of Eusebius, to rule the souls of the faithful in the priesthood and spiritual leadership.

praefati monasterii fratribus, statim assumptis secum aliqui-
bus fratrum, venit ad abbatem Ceolfridum cursum navis
qua oceanum transiret expectantem; quem elegerant abbatem nuntiant: Deo gratias, respondit, electionem con-
firmat, et commendatoriam ab eo epistolam apostolico papae
Gregorio deferendam suscepit; cujus, memoriae causa,
putavimus etiam in hoc opere versus aliquot esse ponendos.[54]

He left no works aside from the riddles and the letter to
Pope Gregory; the *HAA* and *VA*, most recently attributed to him in *CPL*, p. 301, can hardly be his. The language of *HAA* ch. 29, "ecclesiastica simul ac monasteriali
scientia imbutus,"[55] is not autobiographical, and the attribution of the *VA* arises out of Hahn's supposition that one
Herefrith was the author, and that Eusebius was Herefrith.
Bede specifically says that the *VA* is the work of Lindisfarne
monks; had it, or the *HAA* which he also used as a source,
been the work of his friend Hwaetberht, he would hardly
have hidden the fact. (Hahn later associated "Hwantbercht"
with Eusebius, and added Bede's sermon on Benedict
Biscop to his canon!)

The two copies of the letter are substantially the same.
Both are incomplete: *HAA* calls the excerpt the "exordium," and Bede, giving the same material, concludes "et

[54] So Abbot Hwaetberht was elected, who from the earliest days
of his youth was not only instructed in the same monastery in the
observance of monastic discipline, but also practiced by not a little
industry writing, singing, reading, and teaching. Betaking himself
to Rome also in the days of Pope Sergius of blessed memory, and
remaining there for not a small period of time, those things which
he judged needful to himself he learned, he copied, and he brought
back; he was, moreover, discharging the office of priest twelve
years before these things happened. Therefore, when he was elected
abbot by all the brothers of both the aforesaid monasteries, immediately taking with him some of the brothers he came to Abbot
Ceolfrid, awaiting the boat on which he was to journey over the
ocean; they announced whom they had elected abbot; thanks be
to God, he responded, confirmed the election, and took from him a
commendatory letter to be carried to the apostolic Pope Gregory;
of which, for the sake of memory, I think some lines should be
inserted in this work.

[55] Learned in ecclesiastical and monastic wisdom alike.

cetera, quae epistolae sequentia continent."[56] As far as it
goes, the letter is Hwaetberht's commendation of the wel-
fare of Ceolfrid to the Pope. He salutes the pontiff and re-
joices in his universal government, and continues

> Commendamus autem tuae sanctae benignitati, dilectissime
> in Christo pater et domine, venerabiles patris nostri di-
> lectissimi canos, Ceolfridi videlicet abbatis, ac nutritoris
> tutorisque nostrae spiritalis in monastica quiete libertatis et
> pacis. Et primum quidem gratias agimus sanctae et in-
> dividuae trinitati, quod ipse, etsi non sine maximo nostro
> dolore, gemitu, luctu, ac prosecutione lacrimarum a nobis
> abiit; ad suae tamen diu desideratae quietis gaudia sancta
> pervenit; dum ea, quae juvenem se adisse, vidisse, atque
> adorasse semper recordans exultabat, etiam senio defessus
> beatorum apostolorum devotus limina repetiit. Et post
> longos amplius quadraginta annorum labores curasque con-
> tinuas, quibus monasteriis regendis abbatis jure praefuit, in-
> comparabili virtutis amore, quasi nuper ad conversationem
> vitae caelestis accitus, ultima confectus aetate, et prope jam
> moriturus, rursus incipit peregrinari pro Christo, quo li-
> berius prisca sollicitudinum saecularium spineta, camino spi-
> ritali fervens compunctionis ignis absumat.[57]

[56] The beginning; and the rest, which the remainder of the letter
contains.

[57] We commend to your holy benignity, O most beloved father
and lord in Christ, the venerable grey hairs of our beloved father,
that is Ceolfrid the abbot, our nourisher and spiritual guardian in
the monastic repose of liberty and peace. And first, indeed, we give
thanks to the holy and indivisible Trinity, that even though it was
not without our greatest sorrow, groans, weeping, and accompani-
ment of tears that he went from us; nonetheless he has come to the
holy joys of his long-desired rest; while those things which he,
recollecting, always rejoiced to have visited, seen, and adored as
a young man, now worn out in old age, he has devotedly visited
anew the thresholds of the blessed Apostles. And after the long
labors and continual cares of more than forty years, in which he
ruled over his monasteries with the authority of abbot, and with the
incomparable love of virtue, as if recently called to the company
of the heavenly life, worn out with extreme age, and nearly ready
to die, he begins again to be an exile for Christ, whereby the earlier
thorns of secular cares may be more freely consumed by the flames
of repentance in the spiritual forge.

[221]

Aside from the historically interesting use of "Saxonia" to describe Britain (or perhaps only Northumbria) in the salutation, there is nothing very arresting about the letter. The latinity is straightforward in the Jarrow tradition, clear, free from Hisperic mannerisms, even in a formal letter with little factual content.

Hwaetberht's sixty riddles follow Tatwine's forty in both MSS, and are usually assumed to have been added to make up the traditional hundred (even though some—like "De cruce Christi"—duplicated some of Tatwine's). Forty-six are of four lines; the last ten are five to thirteen lines, and there are four others of five to nine lines. Hwaetberht is equally traditional in the choice of many of his subjects, some of which, along with not a little of his language, goes back to Aldhelm, although his tendency—like Tatwine's— is to favor abstract and religious subjects: the first ten are God, angel, demon, man, sky, earth, the alphabet, wind and fire, the letter A, and the sun.

De litteris

Innumerae sumus et simul omnes quaeque sonamus,
Una loqui nequit; nos tetrae ludimus albis;
Et licet alta loquamur, non sonus auribus instat;
Praeteritum loquimur, praesens et multa futura.[58]

Of such are all up to no. 39; numbers 40 to 60, with the exception of no. 48, "De die et nocte," are of the bestiary sort:

De die et nocte

Non sumus aequales, quamvis ambaeque sorores,
Tetrica nam facie et una stans, altera pulchra,
Horrida sed requiem confert, et grata laborem.
Non simul et semper sumus, at secernimur ipsi.[59]

[58] "The Alphabet." We are countless, and although we all have sound, not one of us can speak; black, we play on the white; and though we speak loudly, no sound strikes the ears; we say that which is past, present, and much to come.

[59] "Day and Night." We are not equals, although both sisters, for one has a dark face, and the other a lovely one, but the ugly

De panthere

Foedera multigenis reddens animantibus orbis,
Trux ego valde draconi: sic erit emulus ipse.
Me genitrix gestans alium generare nequibit,
Et genitor dicor, si littera tertia cedat.[60]

Indebted in part to Isidore's *Etymologies*, Bk. 12, "De
dracone" offers interesting parallels to portions of *Beowulf*,
and "De panthere" to the OE "Panther" in the Exeter Book.
Especially ingenious are the several riddles on letters of the
alphabet, such as

De X littera

Post alias reliquas augustus me creat auctor;
Utor in alterius, nam non specialis imago
Concessa est mihi, cum pro denis sola videbor,
Unaque sum forma, sed vim retinebo duarum.[61]

This seems to have been rather too ingenious: the glossator
has commented on *reliquas* ("i.e., litteras"), *alterius*
("scilicet, potestate") and *duarum* ("i.e., *cs* uel *gs*"). The
similar treatment of *J* and *V* may show acquaintance with
Donatus' *De arte grammatica*.

Felix (3.13)

Felix identifies himself by name in the introduction to
his only known work, but tells us nothing of his monastery or life; he was not, in any case, a monk of Croyland, as
often claimed. His *Vita sancti Guthlaci* is dedicated to King

---

one gives rest, and the lovely one gives labor. We are not at the
same time but we are forever, and we are distinguished by that.

[60] "The Panther." Although I keep a pact with many sorts of
creature in the world, I am most fierce toward the dragon: thus
he will be my rival. My mother, when she bore me, was unable
to bring forth any other, and I should be called a parent, if the
third letter were gone [*panther/pat(h)er*].

[61] "The letter X." My noble author created me after all the
others. I am used in the role of another, for no particular notion
is associated with me, since by myself I stand for ten, and I have a
single form, but I have the meaning of two.

Aelfwald of East Anglia, who requested it; the work must fall during Aelfwald's reign, ca. 713-749. No mention of Guthlac (who is said to have died in 714) appears in Bede's *HE*, although Bede does mention the King Aethelbald who figures importantly in the Guthlac legend. It is reasonable therefore to put the date of the *Vita* between 731 or 735 and 749 (*pace* Duckett).

The work is highly derivative; though Bede did not know Felix, Felix knew and used Bede's *VP*, often verbatim (with only the saint's name changed) and at length. But Bede's style was less influential than Aldhelm's, and tags and longer quotations from the *De metris, De laudibus virginitatis*, as well as a general Aldhelmian coloring of the prose, betray the debt. For this reason, the work was several times revised and recast after the Norman Conquest, by Ordericus Vitalis, Petrus Blesensis, and Henricus Abrincensis, although it was popular even in its original form: it was translated into OE prose, taken as the source for an OE poem, copied in many MSS of which thirteen survive, and employed directly or (through the revisions) indirectly as the basis for their entries about Guthlac by the chroniclers Matthew Paris, pseudo-John of Wallingford, pseudo-Ingulph of Croyland, Alexander of Ashby, and perhaps the author of the Middle English *Guthlac* poems in the South English Legendary.

The historical value of the narrative is difficult to estimate; incidents, as well as much of the language, are taken directly from earlier saint's lives on the model of Evagrius' translation of the Athanasian *Vita sancti Antonii,* and the motives of religious and East Anglian propaganda (even though Guthlac was a Mercian saint and his hermitage was in Mercia) have shaped the *Vita* to a great degree. But the literary contribution is easier to identify. The very features which link the *Vita* so suspiciously with Bede and other popular hagiography of the time are those which place it among the most important examples of the flourishing hagiographical genre in eighth-century England: the eloquent prose, the vivid description, the expansive treatment (55 pages in the standard edition) of episodic material within a firm narrative framework. One of the short early chapters illustrates Felix's style and the nature of his attitude toward his subject:

Igitur decursis bis quaternis dierum voluminibus, cum ad salutaris lavacri sacratas undulas propinquasset, ex appellatione illius tribus, quam dicunt Guthlacingas, proprietatis vocabulum velut ex caelesti consilio Guthlac percepit, quia ex qualitatis compositione assequentibus meritis conveniebat. Nam ut illius gentis gnari perhibent, Anglorum lingua hoc nomen ex duobus integris constare videtur, hoc est "Guth" et "lac," quod Romani sermonis nitore personat "belli munus," quia ille cum vitiis bellando munera aeternae beatitudinis cum triumphali infula perennis vitae percepisset, secundum apostolum dicentem: *Beatus vir qui suffert temptationem, quoniam cum probatus fuerit, accipiet coronam vitae, quam repromisit Deus diligentibus se.*[62]

(ch. 10)

The disclaimer in his prologue

Sed si fortisan alius animositatis nostrae fastibus hoc opus nos arripere imputat, dum alii plurimi Anglorum librarii coram ingeniositatis fluenta inter flores rhetoricae per virecta litteraturae pure, liquide lucideque rivantur, qui melius luculentiusve componere valuerunt, sciat nos hoc

[62] So after the space of twice four days had gone by, when he was brought near to the holy waters of the bath of salvation, he received his personal name from the name of that tribe which is called the Guthlacingas, as though by heavenly counsel, for it suited his virtues to come by the quality of its composition. For as those who are familiar with that tribe tell, that name in the language of the English is shown to consist of two elements, that is "Guth" and "lac," which represents in the elegance of Latin speech "battle gift," for by battling against vice he received the gift of eternal blessedness with the triumphal insignia of everlasting life, as the Apostle said, Blessed is the man that endureth temptation; for when he hath been proved, he shall receive the crown of life which God hath promised to them that love Him [James 1:12].

[225]

opusculum non tam volentiae quam oboedientiae gratia incepisse. Propterea laboris mei votis, o lector, quisquis es, faveas; sin autem, ut assolet, more obtrectatoris successeris, cave, ut ubi lucem putaveris, ne a tenebris obcaeceris, id est, ne cum rata reprehenderis, ignorantiae tenebris fusceris. Moris enim caecorum est, cum in luce perambulant, tunc in tenebris errare putant. Lucem enim nesciunt, sed in tenebris semper oberrant. Caecitas enim in scripturis ignorantia est, ut ait apostolus: *Caecitas ex parte contigit in Israel, donec plenitudo gentium subintraret.* Origo quidem totius mali ab ignorantia venit. Quapropter te admoneo, lector, ut aliena non reprehendas, ne ab aliis quasi alienus reprehendaris. Sed ne sensus legentium prolixae sententiae molesta defensio obnubilet, pestiferis obtrectantium incantationibus aures obturantes, velut transvadato vasti gurgitis aequore, ad vitam sancti Guthlaci stilum flectendo quasi ad portum vitae pergemus,[63]

is inherited and formulaic, and its very style belies its sense. Whoever Felix may have been, the appearance of his ap-

[63] But if perhaps someone else may impute my taking up this work to my pride of boldness, while many other writers among the English are led to the streams of invention among the flowers of rhetoric through the glades of literature, purely, clearly, and lucidly, who could compose better and more splendidly, let him know that I began this little work not so much on account of my wish as of obedience. Therefore, O reader, whoever you are, be favorable to me in my labors; but if, as is usual, you approach in the manner of a detractor, beware, that where you think there is light, you are not blinded by the shadows, that is, lest when you reprehend certainties, you are not darkened by the shadows of ignorance. For it is the way of the blind, when they walk in the light, then to believe they wander in the dark. They know not the light, but always wander in the shadows. For blindness, in the Scriptures, is ignorance, as the Apostle says: Blindness in part has happened in Israel, until the fullness of the Gentiles should come in [Romans 11:25]. Indeed the origin of all evil comes from ignorance. Therefore I warn you, reader, that you reprehend not strange things, lest by others you are reprehended as a stranger. But lest the tedious defense of my prolix discourse shroud the understanding of my readers, let us proceed to the life of St. Guthlac by changing our course as though to the haven of life, stopping up our ears against the pestiferous incantations of our detractors as though by traversing the water of a vast whirlpool.

parently unique work, like that of its close relatives, the *Vita Wilfridi* by Eddius Stephanus and the anonymous *Vitae* of St. Gregory and St. Cuthbert, is astounding: four such proficient productions by authors who wrote, it would seem, nothing else, argue a highly assimilated, widely disseminated, and most viable genre at this period, assisted by frequent and fruitful communication between centers of learning.

biBLiography

GENERAL

Asterisked items have not been examined by the author.

Allison, T. *Pioneers of English Learning*. Oxford 1932.
————. *English Religious Life in the Eighth Century*. London 1929.
Baxter, J. H., C. Johnson, and J. F. Willard. "An Index of British Latin Writers, A.D. 400-1520," *ALMA*, 7 (1932), 110-219. (Also published separately, Paris 1932.)
Blatt, F., ed. *Novum glossarium mediae latinitatis ab anno DCCC usque ad annum MCC*. Copenhagen 1957———— (in progress).
Campbell, A. "Some Linguistic Features of Early Anglo-Latin Verse and its Use of Classical Models," *Trans. Philological Soc.* (1953), 1-20.
Colgrave, B. "The Earliest Saints' Lives Written in England," *PBA*, 44 (1958), 35-60.
Drane, A. T. *Christian Schools and Scholars* (repr. of 2d edn., 1881). New York 1910.
Duckett, E. S. *Anglo-Saxon Saints and Scholars*. New York 1947.
Erhardt-Siebold, E. von. *D. lateinischen Rätsel d. Angelsachsen*. Anglistische Forschungen 61. Heidelberg 1925.
Farmer, H. "The Studies of Anglo-Saxon Monks, A.D. 600-800," *Los Monjes y los Estudios*. Poblet 1963, 87-103.
Hahn, H. *Bonifaz und Lul*. Leipzig 1883.
*Hanning, R. W. *The Vision of History in Early Britain*. New York 1966.
*Jacob, E. F. "Some Aspects of Classical Influence in Mediaeval England," *Vorträge d. Bibliothek Warburg* (1930-1931), 1.

[229]

Jaffé, P. *Monumenta moguntina.* Berlin 1866.

Jones, C. W. *Saints' Lives and Chronicles in Early England.* Ithaca 1947.

Kenney, J. F. *The Sources for the Early History of Ireland.* New York 1929.

Laistner, M. L. W. *Thought and Letters in Western Europe, A.D. 500 to 900* (rev. edn.). London 1957.

Langosch, K., ed. "Überlieferungsgeschichte d. mittellateinischen Literatur," *Geschichte d. Textüberlieferung d. antiken und mittelalterlichen Literatur.* Zürich 1964, II, 9-185.

Latham, R. E. *A Revised Medieval Latin Word-List from British and Irish Sources.* London 1965.

Leach, A. F. *The Schools of Medieval England.* London 1915.

Levison, W. *England and the Continent in the Eighth Century.* Oxford 1946.

Lightfoot, J. *Leaders in the Northern Church* (2d edn.). London 1907.

Manitius, M. "Geschichtliches aus alten Bibliothekskatalogen," *NA*, 48 (1929), 148-156.

―――. *Handschriften antiker Autoren in mittelalterlichen Bibliothekskatalogen* (Zentralblatt f. Bibliothekswesen, Beiheft 67; Leipzig 1935).

―――. *Philologisches aus alten Bibliothekskatalogen.* Frankfurt/M. 1892.

*McGuire, M. R. P. *Introduction to Mediaeval Latin Studies.* Washington 1964.

Meyer, W. "D. Verskunst d. Iren in rythmischen lateinischen Gedichten," *Gött. Nachrichten,* Phil.-Hist. Kl. (1916), 605-644.

Miles, G. *The Bishops of Lindisfarne, Hexham, Chester-le-Street, and Durham.* London 1898.

Ogilvy, J. D. A. *Books Known to Anglo-Latin Writers from Aldhelm to Alcuin (670-804).* Cambridge, Mass. 1936.

Pelzer, A. *Abréviations latines médiévales.* Louvain-Paris 1964.

Petrie, H. and J. Sharpe. *Monumenta historica Britannica.* London 1848.

Prinz, O., J. Schneider, *et al.*, eds. *Mittellateinisches Wörterbuch bis zum ausgehenden XIII. Jrht.* Munich 1959——(in progress).

Roger, M. *L'enseignement d. lettres classiques d'Ausone à Alcuin.* Paris 1905.

Schoell, C. W. *De ecclesiasticae Britonum Scotorumque historiae fontibus.* Berlin 1851.

Schröbler, I. "Zu d. Carmina rhythmica . . . oder über d. Stabreim in d. lateinischen Poesie d. Angelsachsen," *Beiträge zur Geschichte d. deutschen Sprache und Literatur,* 79 (1957), 1-42.

Theopold, L. *Kritische Untersuchungen über d. Quellen d. angelsächsischen Geschichte d. achten Jrhts.* Lemgo 1872.

Thomson, J. A. K. *The Classical Background of English Literature.* London 1948.

Traube, L. *Karolingische Dichtungen.* Berlin 1888.

*Wallace-Hadrill, J. M. "Rome and the Early English Church: Some Questions of Transmission," *Settimane di studi del Centro Italiano di Studi sull' alto medioevo VII: Le chiese nei regni dell'Europa occidentale e i loro rapporti con Roma sino all'800.* Spoleto 1960, II.519ff.

Whitelock, D. *English Historical Documents, c. 500-1042.* Cambridge 1954.

INTRODUCTION: British Latin before 597

0.1. The Roman Occupation

This selective bibliography includes only works on the literary and linguistic aspects of the Roman Occupation.

Burn, A. R. *The Romans in Britain: An Anthology of Inscriptions.* Oxford 1932.

Charlesworth, M. P., ed. *The Heritage of Early Britain.* London 1952.

Haverfield, F. J. "The Romanization of Roman Britain," *PBA*, 2 (1905-1906), 185-217.

———. *The Romanization of Roman Britain* (4th edn.). Oxford 1923.

Hübner, E. *Inscriptiones britanniae christianae.* Berlin 1876.

Jackson, K. *Language and History in Early Britain.* Edinburgh 1953.

———. "On the Vulgar Latin of Roman Britain," *Medieval Studies in Honor of J. D. M. Ford* (eds. U. T. Holmes and A. J. Denomy). Cambridge, Mass. 1948.

———. "What was the Language of Roman Britain?" *Report of the Annual Meeting of the British Assoc. for the Advancement of Science* (1935), 425.

Lewis, H. *Yr Elfen Ladin yn yr Iaith Gymraeg.* Cardiff 1943.

Loth, J. *Les mots latins dans les langues brittoniques.* Paris 1892.

Macalister, R. A. S. *Corpus inscriptionum insularum celticarum.* Dublin 1949, Vol. II.

Momigliano, A. "*Panegyricus Messallae* and 'Panegyricus Vespasiani,'" *JRS*, 40 (1950), 39-42.

Moore, R. W. *The Romans in Britain.* London 1938.

Pogatscher, A. *Zur Lautlehre der griechischen, lateinischen, und romanischen Lehnworte im Altenglischen.* Strassburg 1888.

Zachrisson, R. E. *Romans, Kelts, and Saxons in Ancient Britain.* Uppsala 1927.

0.3. Vinisius

Nicholson, E. W. B. *"Vinisius to Nigra": a Fourth-Century Christian Letter.* London 1904.

[232]

0.4. Pelagius

This list omits works already included in the bibliography by J. Ferguson, *Pelagius*. Cambridge 1956.

*Anon. "Genius and Character of Pelagius," *Literary and Theological Rev.*, 4 (1837), 469.

Anon. "Pelagius and Celestius," *Christian Remembrancer*, N.S., 53 (1867), 290-327.

Antin, P. "Rufin et Pélage dans Jérôme, Prol. I *In Hieremiam*," *Latomus*, 22 (1963), 792-794.

Armstrong, C. B. "St. Augustine and Pelagius as Religious Types," *CQR*, 162 (1961), 150-164.

*Barbero, G. *Il pensiero politico cristiano, dai Vangeli a Pelagio*. Turin 1962.

Bardy, G. "Grecs et latins dans les premières controverses pélagiennes," *Bull. de littérature ecclésiastique*, 49 (1948), 3-20.

Birch, A. H. "A Fifth-Century Apostle of Free Will," *Hibbert Jnl.*, 46 (1947-1948), 56-62.

Bohlin, T. *D. Theologie d. Pelagius und ihre Genesis* (trans. from Swedish by H. Buch). Uppsala 1957.

*Buonaiuti, E. "Pelagio e l'Ambrosiastro," *Ricerche religiose*, 4 (1928), 1-17.

Chapman, H. J. "Pélage et le texte de S. Paul," *RHE*, 18 (1922), 469-481; 19 (1923), 25-42.

*Charlier, C. "Cassiodore, Pélage et les origines de la Vulgate paulinienne," *Studiorum Paulinorum congressus internationalis catholicus*, 2 (Rome 1963), 461-470.

Chéné, J. "Les origines de la controverse semi-pélagienne," *L'année théologique augustinienne*, 13 (1953), 56-109.

Coméliau, J. "A propos de la prière de Pélage," *RHE*, 31 (1935), 77-89.

*Dempsey, J. J. *Pelagius's Commentary on St. Paul*. Rome 1937.

Disdier, M. T. "Le pélagianisme au concile d'Ephèse," *Echos d'Orient*, 30 (1931), 314-333.

*Ernst, J. "Pelagianische Studien II," *D. Katholik*, 65 (1885), 241-269.

Evans, R. F. "Pelagius, Fastidius and the Pseudo-Augustinian *De vita christiana*," *JTS*, N.S. 13 (1962), 72-98.

———. "Pelagius' Veracity at the Synod of Diospolis," *Studies in Medieval Culture*. Western Michigan Univ. 1964, 21-30.

*Florkowski, E. *Soteriologia Pelagiusza*. Studium history-czno-dogmatyczne. Rozprawy Wydzialu theologicz-nego Uniw. Jagiellonskiego 1.3 (1949).

Frede, H. J. *Pelagius, d. irische Paulustext, Sedulius Scottus*. Freiburg/B. 1961.

———. "Eine neue HS d. Pauluskommentars von Pelagius," *RB*, 73 (1963), 307-331.

Grosjean, P. "S. Jérôme, Pélage et Gildas," *AB*, 75 (1957), 206-211.

Guzzo, A. *Agostino contro Pelagio*. Turin 1958.

Hellmann, S. *Sedulius Scottus*. Munich 1906.

Koopmans, J. H. "Augustine's First Contact with Pelagius and the Dating of the Condemnation of Caelestius at Carthage," *Vigiliae christianae*, 8 (1954), 149-153.

*Krabbe, M. K. C. *Epistula ad Demetriadem de vera humilitate*. Catholic University of America Patristic Studies XCVII. Washington 1965.

Liebeschütz, W. "Did the Pelagian Movement Have Social Aims?" *Historia*, 12 (1963), 227-241.

Martini, G. C. "Sei frammenti del *De fide trinitatis* di Pelagio," *Ricerche religiose*, 20 (1949), 35-64.

Michalski, M. "Nauka Chrystologiczna Pelagjusza," *Collectanea theologica*, 17 (1936), 143-164.

*Mönnich, C. W. "Het 'Pelagianisme' van de Neologie," *Nieuw Theologisch Tijdschrift*, 32 (1943), 25-54.

Morin, G. "Le *De uita christiana* de l'évêque breton

Fastidius et le livre de Pélage *Ad uiduam,*" *RB*, 15 (1898), 481-493.

———. "Pélage ou Fastidius?" *RHE*, 5 (1904), 258-264.

———. "Un traité Pélagien inédit du commencement du cinquième siècle," *RB*, 26 (1909), 162-188.

Morris, J. "Pelagian Literature," *JTS*, N.S. 16 (1965), 26-60.

Müller, K. "Pelagius Heimat," *Gött. Nachrichten*, Phil.-Hist. Kl. (1931), 113-116.

Myres, J. N. L. "Pelagius and the End of Roman Rule in Britain," *JRS*, 50 (1960), 21-36.

Piault, B. "Autour de la controverse pélagienne," *RSR*, 44 (1956), 481-514.

*Pirenne, R. *La morale de Pélage*. Rome 1961.

de Plinval, G. "Pélage et le mouvement pélagien," *Histoire de l'église* (eds. A. Fliche and V. Martin). Paris 1937, IV, 79-128.

———. "Pélage et les premiers aspects du pélagianisme," *Rev. d. sciences philosophiques et théologiques*, 25 (1936), 429-458.

———. "Points de vues récents sur la théologie de Pélage," *RSR*, 46 (1958), 227-236.

———. "Le problème des versions pélagiennes du texte de s. Paul," *RHE*, 59 (1964), 845-853.

———. "Vue d'ensemble de la littérature pélagienne," *Rev. d. études latines*, 29 (1951), 284-294.

*Prete, S. *Pelagio e il pelagianismo*. Brescia 1961.

———. "Lo scritto pelagiano 'De castitate' è di Pelagio?" *Aevum*, 35 (1961), 315-322.

*Reiter, S. "Eine unedierte Schrift d. Pelagius," *Serta Hartel* (1896), 134.

*Riggenbach, E. *Neue Jahrbücher f. deutsche Theologie*, 1 (1892), 592; 3 (1894), 350.

Rivière, J. "Hétérodoxie d. Pélagiens en fait de rédemption?" *RHE*, 41 (1946), 5-43.

*Schäfer, K. T. "D. Paulustext d. Pelagius," *Studiorum Paulinorum congressus internationalis catholicus*, 2 (Rome 1963), 453-460.

Smith, A. J. "Pelagius and Augustine," *JTS*, 31 (1929), 21-35.

*Smits, C. "Ephese en het pelagianisme," *Katholiek*, 7 (1931), 446-456.

Souter, A. *The Earliest Latin Commentaries on the Epistles of St. Paul.* Cambridge 1927.

*Tinnefeld, F. H. *Untersuchungen zur altlateinischen Überlieferung d. I Timotheusbriefs. D. latein. Paulustext . . . in d. Kommentaren . . . d. Pelagius.* Wiesbaden 1963.

Turmel, J. "Pélage et le pélagianisme dans les églises Celtiques," *Annales de Bretagne*, 17 (1902), 309-322.

Ulbrich, H. "Augustins Briefe zur entscheidenden Phase d. Pelagianischen Streites," *Rev. d. études augustiniennes*, 9 (1963), 235-258.

Williams, H. "Zimmer on the History of the Celtic Church," *ZCP*, 4 (1903), 527-574.

0.5. Fastidius and Faustus

FASTIDIUS

Baer, J. *De operibus Fastidii britannorum episcopi.* Nuremberg 1902.

Caspari, C. P. *Briefe, Abhandlungen und Predigten aus d. zwei letzten Jrhten. d. kirchlichen Alterthums und d. Anfang d. Mittelalters.* Christiania 1890.

Evans, R. F. "Pelagius, Fastidius and the Pseudo-Augustinian *De vita christiana*," *JTS*, N.S. 13 (1962), 72-98.

Haslehurst, R. S. T. *The Works of Fastidius.* London 1927.

Kirmer, A. D. *Eigentum d. Fastidius im pelagianischen Schrifttum.* St. Ottelier 1938.

BIBLIOGRAPHY

Künstle, K. "D. Schriften d. britischen Bischofs Fastidius,"
  TQ, 82 (1900), 193-204.
Morin, G. "Le *De uita christiana* de l'évêque breton Fasti-
  dius et le livre de Pélage *Ad uiduam*," *RB*, 15 (1898),
  481-493.
——. "Fastidius ad Fatalem?" *RB*, 46 (1934), 3-17.
——. "Un ms inconnu et complet de trois d. opuscules
  de l'évêque breton Fastidius," *Basler Zt.*, 26 (1927),
  234-241.
——. "Pélage ou Fastidius?" *RHE*, 5 (1904), 258-264.
——. "La prétendu 'epistula Fastidii ad Fatalem,'"
  RB, 13 (1896), 339-340.
Morris, R. "The Theology of the Early British Church,
  with Special Reference to Fastidius," *Trans. of the
  Hon. Soc. of Cymmrodorion* (1914-1915), 43-67.
Pitra, J. B. "Epistola Fastidii ad Fatalem," *Analecta sacra
  et classica*. Paris 1888, v.1, 134-36.

FAUSTUS

*Baümer, S. "Ueber drei verloren geglaubte Schriften d.
  Faustus von Riez," *D. Katholik*, 67 (1887), 386.
Bergmann, W. *Studien zu einer kritischen Sichtung d.
  südgallischen Predigtliteratur d. fünften und sechsten
  Jrhts*. Studien zur Geschichte d. Theologie und d.
  Kirche, Leipzig 1898, 1.4.
Cappuyns, M. "Fragments-tests de Fauste de Riez et de
  Lactance dans un ms d'Averbode (cod. 44 E xiv),"
  RB, 74 (1964), 36-43.
Chadwick, N. K. "Intellectual Contacts between Britain
  and Gaul in the Fifth Century. A Note on Faustus
  and Riocatus," *Studies in Early British History*.
  Cambridge 1954, 189-263.
Elg, A. G. "De usu datavi comparationis apud Faustum
  Reiensem," *Eranos*, 45 (1947), 78-80.
——. *Epistula Fausti Reiensis tertia*. Uppsala 1946.

Elg, A. G. *In epistulam Fausti Reiensis tertiam adnotationes.* Lund 1945.

——. "In Faustum Reiensem adversaria," *Eranos,* 42 (1944), 24-46.

——. *In Faustum Reiensem studia.* Uppsala 1937.

Engelbrecht, A. "Beiträge zur Kritik und Erklärung d. Briefe d. Apollinaris Sidonius, Faustus und Ruricus," *Zt. f. österreichischen Gymnasien,* 41 (1890), 677-699.

——. *Fausti Reiensis . . . opera. CSEL,* XXI, Vienna 1891.

——. "Kritische Untersuchungen über wirkliche und angebliche Schriften d. Faustus Reiensis," *Zt. f. österreichischen Gymnasien,* 41 (1890), 289-301.

——. *Studien über d. Schriften d. Bischofes von Reii Faustus.* Vienna 1889.

——. "Zur Kritik d. Predigten d. Faustus," *Zt. f. österreichischen Gymnasien,* 43 (1892), 961-976.

Griffe, E. "Les sermons de Fauste de Riez. La 'collectio gallicana' du Pseudo-Eusèbe," *Bull. d. littérature ecclésiastique,* 61 (1960), 27-38.

Huhn, J. "*De ratione fidei* als ein Werk d. Faustus von Reji," *TQ,* 103 (1950), 176-183.

Koch, A. "D. anthropologische Lehrebegriff d. Bischofs Faustus von Riez," *TQ,* 71 (1889), 287-317, 578-648.

Koch, A. D. hl. Faustus, Bischof von Riez. Stuttgart 1895.

Krusch, B. *Fausti aliorumque epistulae ad Ruricium aliosque. MGH,* Auct. ant. VIII, Berlin 1887.

Leeming, B. "The False Decretals, Faustus of Riez and the Pseudo-Eusebius," *Studia patristica,* 2 (1957), 122-140.

Morin, G. "La collection gallicane dite d'Eusèbe d'Emèse et les problèmes qui s'y rattachent," *Zt. f. d. neutestamentliche Wissenschaft,* 34 (1935), 92-115.

——. "Critique d. sermons attribués à Fauste de Riez," *RB,* 9 (1892), 49-61.

[238]

————. "Hiérarchie et liturgie dans l'église gallicane au ve siècle, d'après un écrit restitué à Fauste de Riez," *RB*, 8 (1891), 97-104.

Rehling, B. *De Fausti Reiensis epistula tertia*. Münster 1898.

*Simon, E. *Etude sur St. Fauste*. Toulon 1879.

Souter, A. "Observations on the Pseudo-Eusebian Collections of Gallican Sermons," *JTS*, 41 (1940), 47-57.

*Weigel, G. *Faustus of Riez: An Historical Introduction*. Philadelphia 1938.

Wörter, P. "Zur Dogmengeschichte d. Semipelagianismus, II : D. Lehre d. Faustus von Riez," *Kirchengeschichtlichen Studien*, 5 (1899), 45-103.

0.6. Patrick

This list omits works already included in the bibliography by W. Bonser, *Anglo-Saxon and Celtic Bibliography (450-1087)*, Oxford 1957, Vol. I, items 4541-4760, and works published before 1905.

Anscombe, A. "Professor Zimmer and the Deaconship of Palladius," *Eriu*, 4 (1910), 233-234.

————. "St. Victricius of Rouen and St. Patrick," *Eriu*, 7 (1913), 13-17.

Bieler, L. "D. Bibletext d. hl. Patrick," *Biblica*, 28 (1947), 31-58, 236-263.

————. "Codices patriciani latini. Addenda et corrigenda," *AB*, 63 (1945), 242-256.

————. "The 'Creeds' of St. Victorinus and St. Patrick," *Theological Studies*, 9 (1948), 121-124.

————. "Exagellia," *American Jnl. of Philology*, 69 (1948), 309-312.

————. "A Linguist's View of St. Patrick," *Eigse*, 10 (1962), 149-154.

————. "The Mission of Palladius," *Traditio*, 6 (1948), 1-32.

Bieler, L. "Patrician Studies in the *IER*," *IER*, 102 (1964), 359-366.

―――. " 'Patrick and the Kings.' Apropos a new Chronology of St. Patrick," *IER*, 85 (1956), 171-189.

―――. "Patrick's Synod: A Revision," *Mélanges offerts à Mlle. Christine Mohrmann*. Utrecht 1963, 96-102.

―――. "The Place of St. Patrick in Latin Language and Literature," *Vigiliae christianae*, 6 (1952), 65-98.

―――. "St. Patrick and the Irish People," *Rev. of Politics*, 10 (1948), 290-309.

―――. "Vindiciae patricianae. Remarks on the Present State of Patrician Studies," *IER*, 79 (1953), 161-185.

―――. "Was Palladius Surnamed Patricius?" *Studies*, 32 (1943), 323-326.

Binchy, D. A. "Patrick and His Biographers, Ancient and Modern," *Studia hibernica*, 2 (1962), 7-173.

Carney, J. "Patrick and the Kings," *Studies in Irish Literature and History*. Dublin 1955.

―――. *The Problem of St. Patrick*. Dublin 1961.

―――. "St Patrick's *Confessio*," *IER*, 97 (1962), 148-154.

Chamberlain, G. A. *St. Patrick, His Life and Work*. Dublin 1932.

Cogan, L. S. "The Home of St. Patrick," *IER*, 75 (1951), 193-204.

*Delamare, E. *Conquérant de l'Irlande. S. Patrick*. Paris 1964.

Delius, W. "D. Einführung d. Christentums in Irland," *Theologische Studien und Kritiken*, 106 (1934-1935), 356-375.

*Dewar, M. W. "Was St. Patrick a Protestant?" *Christianity Today*, 1 (1957), 3.

Esposito, M. "Notes on Latin Learning and Literature in Mediaeval Ireland," *Hermathena*, 20 (1930), 225-260.

———. "The Patrician Problem and a Possible Solution," *Irish Historical Studies,* 10 (1956), 131-155.

———. "Pseudopatriciana," *Hermathena,* 47 (1932), 253-271.

———. "St. Patrick's *Confessio* and the *Book of Armagh*," *Irish Historical Studies,* 9 (1954), 1-12.

Gallico, P. *The Steadfast Man; A Biography of St. Patrick.* New York 1958.

Gogan, L. S. "The Martin-Patrick Relationship," *IER,* 96 (1961), 283-289.

Grosjean, P. "Dominicati rethorici," *ALMA,* 25 (1955), 41-46.

———. "Notes chronologiques sur le séjour de S. Patrice en Gaule," *AB,* 63 (1945), 73-93.

———. "Palladius episcopus . . . qui Patricius," *AB,* 70 (1952), 317-326.

———. "La patrie de S. Patrice," *AB,* 63 (1945), 65-72.

———. "Les périodes de 30 ans dans la chronologie de S. Patrice," *AB,* 63 (1945), 93-94.

———. "Les pictes apostats dans l'Epître de S. Patrice," *AB,* 76 (1958), 354-378.

———. "Quand fut composée la Confession de S. Patrice?" *AB,* 63 (1945), 100-111.

———. "S. Patrice à Auxerre sous S. Germain. Le témoignage d. noms gaulois," *AB,* 75 (1957), 158-174.

———. "S. Patrice et S. Victrice," *AB,* 63 (1945), 94-99.

Gwynn, A. "St. Patrick and Rome," *IER,* 95 (1961), 217-222.

Hamilton, G. F. *St. Patrick and His Age.* Dublin 1932.

Hitchcock, F. R. M. "The Confessio and Epistola of Patrick of Ireland and their Literary Affinities in Irenaeus, Cyprian, and Orientius," *Hermathena,* 47 (1932), 202-238.

———. "The Creeds of SS. Irenaeus and Patrick," *Hermathena,* 14 (1907), 168-182.

———. "The Latinity of St. Patrick Compared with the

Latin Translation of Irenaeus's Treatise," *Hermathena*, 54 (1939), 93-109.

*Kenney, J. F. "St. Patrick and the Patrick Legend," *Thought* (1933), 18.

Kinsella, N. "St. Patrick's Way to Sanctity," *IER*, 95 (1961), 146-159.

Letts, W. M. *St. Patrick, The Travelling Man*. London 1932.

MacNeill, E. "The Other Patrick," *Studies*, 32 (1943), 308-314.

Marsh, A. *St. Patrick's Writings. A Modern Translation.* Dundalk 1961.

McGoldrick, P. J. and J. F. O'Doherty. "The Place of St. Patrick's Captivity," *IER*, 51 (1938), 314-315, 430-431; 54 (1939), 420-430.

*McKeown, L. "The Wood of Foclut," *Down and Connor Historical Soc. Jnl.*, 4 (1931), 40.

*McNally, R. E. "St. Patrick, 461-1961," *Church Historical Rev.*, 47 (1961-1962), 305-324.

Mohrmann, C. *The Latin of St. Patrick*. Dublin 1961.

*Morris, H. "The Wood of Fochluth," *Down and Connor Historical Soc. Jnl.*, 8 (1937), 5.

Mras, K. "St. Patricius als Lateiner," *Anzeiger d. oesterreichischen Akad. d. Wiss.*, Phil.-Hist. Kl., 90 (1954), 99-113.

Mulchrone, K. "The Mission of Patricius Secundus episcopus Scottorum," *IER*, 85 (1956), 155-170.

O'Brien, M. A. "On the Expression '*sugere mammellas*' in the Confessio Patricii," *Etudes celtiques*, 3 (1938), 372-373.

*ÓDomhnaill, P. "St. Patrick's Captivity," *Down and Connor Historical Soc. Jnl.*, 6 (1934), 23.

ÓFiaich, T., *et al. The Patrician Year* (*Seanchas Ardmhacha* 1961-1962). Includes: F. Shaw, "St. Patrick, Man of God"; L. Bieler, "Patriciology"; R. Louis, "St. Patrick's Sojourn in Auxerre"; T. ÓRaifeartaigh, "Padraic agus na Seniores"; G. Memser, "The Cult of St. Patrick in the Vicinity of Drackenstein"; J. Hennig, "Ulster Place-Names in the Continental Tradition of St. Patrick"; M. de Paor, "Relics of St. Patrick"; R. Bauerreis, "D. Kleeblatt d. hl. Patrick"; T. ÓFiaich, "Cerbh é Ninin Eigeas"; Anon., "The Veneration of St. Patrick in Italy and Spain."

——. "St. Patrick and Armagh: A Symposion," *Seanchas Ardmhacha*, 2 (1956), 1-31. Includes: E. ÓDoibhlinn, "Forgers All?"; S. MacAirt, "The Chronology of St. Patrick"; T. ÓRaifeartaigh, "Na Teorici Nua"; L. Bieler, "St. Secundinus and Armagh"; M. MacDermott, "Prof. Carney's Arguments."

ÓFiaich, T. "St. Patrick and Armagh," *IER*, 89 (1958), 153-170.

O'Meara, J. J. "The *Confession* of St. Patrick and the *Confessions* of St. Augustine," *IER*, 85 (1956), 190-197.

*Pádraig, Giolla (pseud.). "The Identification of Fochlut," *Catholic Bull.*, 7 (1917), 159.

Pringle, K. D. "The Home of St. Patrick," *Trans. Hon. Soc. of Cymmrodorion* (1955), 23-35.

Russell, J. C. "The Problem of St. Patrick the Missionary," *Traditio*, 12 (1956), 393-398.

Ryan, J., *et al. Patrick* (Thomas Davis Lectures). Dublin 1958.

Shaw, F. "The Linguistic Argument for two Patricks," *Studies*, 32 (1943), 315-322.

Tierney, M. "The European Background of St. Patrick's Mission," *Studies*, 21 (1932), 199-212.

Thurston, H. "Did St. Patrick Keep Saturday Holy Instead of Sunday?" *Month*, 173 (1939), 451-453.

Tolstoy, N. "Who was Coroticus?" *IER*, 97 (1962), 138-147.

*Veale, J. "St. Patrick and the *Kyrie eleison," American Ecclesiastical Rev.*, 90 (1934), 265-279.

———. "Some Key-Passages in St. Patrick's *Confession* Misinterpreted," *Ecclesiastical Rev.*, 100 (1939), 194-207.

*Waller, B. C. *Patrick the Man*. Dublin 1932.

Walsh, P. "Recent Studies on the Patrician Documents," *IER*, 39 (1932), 232-242.

Zimmer, H. "Über direkte Handelsverbindungen West-galliens mit Irland," *Sitzungsb. d. k. preuss. Akad. d. Wiss.* (1909), 363-400, 430-476, 543-613; (1910), 1031-1119.

0.7. Gildas

Anderson, A. O. "The Dating Passage in Gildas's Excidium," *Scottish Historical Rev.*, 25 (1928), 384-385.

———. "Gildas and Arthur," *Celtic Rev.*, 8 (1912), 149-165.

———. "Varia. 1. The Dating Passage in Gildas's Excidium. 2. Gildas and Arthur," *ZCP*, 17 (1928), 403-406.

Anscombe, A. "The Bearing of Two Passages in the Book 'De excidio Britanniae' upon its Ascription to St. Gildas of Ruys," *Academy* (September–November 1895), 206.

———. "The Date of the 'De excidio,'" *Academy* (September–November 1895), 411-413.

———. "King Arthur in Gildas," *Academy* (September–November 1895), 318-319.

———. "King Arthur in Gildas," *N&Q*, 155 (1928), 115.

———. "The Location in Britain of the Writer of the Book 'De excidio Britanniae,'" *Academy* (September–November 1895), 251-252.

————. *St. Gildas of Ruys and the Irish Regal Chronology of the Sixth Century*. London 1893.

Blair, P. H. "The Origins of Northumbria," *Arch. Ael.*, 4th Ser. 25 (1947), 1-51.

Borderie, A. de la. "La date de la naissance de Gildas," *Rev. celtique*, 6 (1883), 1-13.

*————. "St. Gildas l'historien d. Bretons," *Etudes historiques bretonnes*. Paris 1884.

*Briel, A. *S. Gildas Abbé de Rhuys*. Vannes 1908.

Burkitt, F. C. "The Bible of Gildas," *RB*, 46 (1934), 206-215.

Chadwick, O. "Gildas and the Monastic Order," *JTS*, N.S. 5 (1954), 78-80.

Clark, J. "St. Gildas," *Glastonbury Antiquarian Soc. Proc.* 2 (1904), 35-48.

Davies, W. H. "Gildas: Some Textual Notes and Corrections," *Papers of the British School at Rome*, N.S. 2 (1939), 42-48.

Deanesly, M. and P. Grosjean. "The Implications of the Term *sapiens* as Applied to Gildas," *Fritz Saxl Memorial Essays* (ed. D. J. Gordon). London 1957, 53-76.

Ernault, E. "Sur le nom breton de Gildas," *Rev. celtique*, 48 (1931), 130-136.

Evans, J. "The Arthurian Campaign," *Arch. Cant.*, 78 (1963), 83-95.

Fonssagrives, J. *St. Gildas de Ruis et la société bretonne au VIe siècle*. Paris 1908.

Grosjean, P. "La Bible de 'Gildas,'" *AB*, 75 (1957), 203-211.

————. "Le 'De excidio' à Malmesbury à la fin du VIIe siècle," *AB*, 75 (1957), 212-222.

————. "Le 'De excidio' chez Bède et chez Alcuin," *AB*, 75 (1957), 222-226.

————. "Emendations au texte du 'De excidio,'" *AB*, 75 (1957), 194-202.

Grosjean, P. "Quelques citations dans le 'De excidio," *AB*, 75 (1957), 189-194.

――――. "Remarques sur le *De excidio* attribué à Gildas," *ALMA*, 25 (1955), 155-187.

――――. "'Romana stigmata' chez Gildas," *Hommages à Max Niedermann* (Collection Latomus 23). Brussels 1956, 128-139.

――――. "S. Jérôme, Pélage, et Gildas," *AB*, 75 (1957), 206-211.

――――. "La tradition manuscrite du 'De excidio' attribué à Gildas," *AB*, 75 (1957), 185-189.

Hughes, M. W. "The End of Roman Rule in Britain: A Defence of Gildas," *Trans. Hon. Soc. of Cymmrodorion* (1946-1947), 150-187.

Johnstone, P. K. "Dual Personality of St. Gildas," *Antiquity*, 20 (1946), 211-213.

Lot, F. "Bretons et anglais au ve et vie siècles," *PBA*, 16 (1930), 327-344.

――――. "De la valeur historique de De Excidio et Conquestu Britanniae de Gildas," *Mediaeval Studies in Memory of Gertrude S. Loomis*. Paris 1927, 229-264.

Loth, J. "Le nom de Gildas dans l'île de Bretagne, en Irlande et en Armorique," *Rev. celtique*, 46 (1929), 1-15.

*Luco. *Histoire de S. Gildas de Rhuys*. Vannes 1870.

Lynn, W. T. "Gildas and the Battle of Mons Badonicus," *N&Q*, 6th Ser. 12 (1885), 461-462; 7th Ser. 4 (1887), 372-373; 8th Ser. 8 (1895), 406, 452.

Meyer, W. "Gildae oratio rythmica," *Gött. Nachrichten*, Phil.-Hist. Kl. (1912), 48-108.

Mommsen, T. *De excidio et conquestu Britanniae. MGH*, Auct. ant. XIII.I, Berlin 1894.

Nicholson, E. W. B. "King Arthur in Gildas," *Academy* (September–November 1895), 297-298.

――――. "Gildas Vindicatus," *Academy* (September–November 1895), 364-365.

———. "The Ruin of History," *Celtic Rev.*, 2 (1906), 369-380.

*Oheix, A. *Notes sur la vie de S. Gildas.* Nantes 1913.

Roberts, B. F. "Cyfieithiad Samuel Williams o *De excidio Brittaniae* Gildas," *National Library of Wales Jnl.*, 13 (1964), 269-277.

Roberts, P. *The Chronicle of the Kings of Britain . . . Original Dissertations on the History and Epistle Attributed to Gildas. . . .* London 1811.

*Sepet. *S. Gildas de Ruis.* Paris 1900.

Stevens, C. E. "Gildas and the Civitates of Britain," *EHR*, 52 (1937), 193-203.

———. "Gildas Sapiens," *EHR*, 56 (1941), 353-373.

Stevenson, W. H. "The Date of Gildas's 'De excidio britanniae,' " *Academy* (September–November 1895), 340-342.

Thurneysen, R. "Zum Geburtsjahr d. Gildas," *ZCP*, 14 (1923), 13-15.

Tregelles, S. P. "Gildas," *N&Q*, 4th Ser. 1 (1868), 271-272, 511-512.

Varin, P. "Etudes relatives à l'état politique et religieux d. îles britanniques au moment de l'invasion saxonne," *Mémoires présentés par divers savants à l'Académie d. inscriptions et belles-lettres*, 1st Ser. 5.1 (1857), 1-270.

Wade-Evans, A. W. "The Chronology of Arthur," *Y Cymmrodor*, 22 (1910), 125-149.

———. "Further Remarks on the *De excidio*," *Archaeologia Cambrensis*, 98 (1944), 113-128.

———. "Gildas and Modern Professors," *Y Cymmrodor*, 31 (1921), 60-80.

———. "Notes on the *Excidium Britanniae*," *Celtic Rev.*, 1 (1905), 289-295.

———. "The 'Picti' and 'Scotti' in the *Excidium Brittaniae*," *Celtic Rev.*, 9 (1914), 314-323.

Wade-Evans, A. W. "The Romani in the *Excidium Brit-taniae*," *Celtic Rev.*, 9 (1913), 35-41.

———. "The Ruin of *Britannia*," *Celtic Rev.*, 2 (1905), 46-58, 126-135.

———. "The Saxones in the *Excidium Britanniae*," *Arch. Cambrensis*, 6th Ser. 11 (1911), 170-183.

———. "The *Saxones* in the *Excidium Brittaniae*," *Celtic Rev.*, 10 (1915), 215-227, 322-333.

———. "The Scotti and Picti in the *Excidium Britanniae*," *Arch. Cambrensis*, 6th Ser. 10 (1910), 449-456.

———. "Some Insular Sources of the 'Excidium Britanniae,'" *Y Cymmrodor*, 27 (1917), 37-69.

———. *Welsh Christian Origins*. Oxford 1934.

———. "The Year of the Reception of the Saxones," *Y Cymmrodor*, 27 (1917), 26-36.

Wheeler, G. H. "Gildas *De excidio Britanniae*, Ch. 26," *EHR*, 41 (1926), 497-503.

Williams, H. *Gildas: The Ruin of Britain*. (Cymmrodorion Record Ser. 3.) London 1899, 1901.

0.8 Columba and Columban

Bieler, L. *Ireland, Harbinger of the Middle Ages*. London 1963.

Hillgarth, J. N. "Visigothic Spain and Early Christian Ireland," *Proc. Royal Irish Academy*, 62 (1962), 167-194.

Hughes, K. "Irish Monks and Learning," *Los Monjes y los Estudios*. Poblet 1963, 61-86.

Meyer, K. *Learning in Ireland in the Fifth Century and the Transmission of Letters*. Dublin 1913.

Ryan, J., ed. *Irish Monks of the Golden Age*. Dublin 1963.

COLUMBA

Anderson, A. O. and M. O. *Adomnan's Life of Columba*. Edinburgh 1961.

Anon. "An Irish Saint," *Catholic World*, 5 (1867), 664.

Anon. "St. Columba," *Dublin University Magazine*, 50 (1857), 255.

Anon. "St. Columba," *Good Words*, 1 (1860), 385, 401.

Anscombe, A. *The Date of the Obit of St. Columba.* Tottenham 1893.

————. "The Obit of St. Columba and the Chronology of the Early Kings of Alban," *EHR*, 7 (1892), 510-531.

Branford, V. *St. Columba.* Edinburgh 1913.

Bullough, D. A. "Columba, Adamnan and the Achievement of Iona," *Scottish Historical Rev.*, 43 (1964), 111-130; 44 (1965), 17-33.

Bute, John, Marquis of. *The Altus of St. Columba.* Edinburgh 1882.

Coffey, P. *Columcille.* Dublin 1926.

Colum, P. *The Legend of St. Columba.* London 1936.

Cooke, E. A. *St. Columba.* Edinburgh 1893.

Cuissard, C. "La prose de S. Columba," *Rev. celtique*, 5 (1882), 205-212. Cf. A. Boucherie, *Rev. d. langues romanes*, 3rd Ser. 8 (1882), 293-297.

Curtayne, A. *St. Columba.* Dublin 1934.

Duke, J. A. *The Columban Church.* Oxford 1932.

Ferguson, A. B. O. *St. Columba.* Dublin 1920.

*Geddes, P. *Songs and Tales of St. Columba.* 1909.

Gwynn, D. R. *St. Columba.* London 1928.

Hyde, D. *Songs of St. Columcille.* Dublin 1942.

Iona (pseud.). *The Story of St. Columba.* Dublin 1928.

Kelly, J. J. "The Columbian Monasteries and Rule," *IER*, 3d Ser. 2 (1881), 467-478; 3 (1882), 25-35.

Keyworth, S. *St. Columba.* London 1895.

Lindsay, W. M. "Columba's *Altus* and the *Abstrusa* Glossary," *CQ*, 26 (1923), 198-199.

Ludwig, G. *D. Leben d. hl. Columba.* Bern 1861.

Lynch, P. *Life of Columba.* Dublin 1914.

MacCarthy, B., *et al.* "The Obit of St. Columba," *Academy*, 42 (1892), 215-216, 460, 509, 542, 592.

MacGregor, D. *St. Columba.* Aberdeen 1897.

*Mac Nish, N. "St. Columba or Colum Cille," *Trans. Canadian Institute,* 3 (1892), 131.

Macphail, J. C. *Columba.* Edinburgh 1882.

Menzies, L. *St. Columba of Iona.* London 1920, Glasgow 1950.

Morrison, G. H. *St. Columba.* Edinburgh 1903.

Mould, D. D. C. P. "Naomh Colmcille," *IER,* 99 (1963), 381-391.

Muir, W. *The Life of St. Columba.* Iona 1889.

Mulcahy, C. "The Irish Latin Hymns," *IER,* 5th Ser. 57 (1941), 385-405.

Olden, T. *St. Columba.* London 1897.

O'Mahony, M. *St. Columba.* Liverpool 1926.

*Parlin, H. "Dates of St. Columba's Birth, Exile and Death," *County Louth Archaeological Jnl.,* 6 (1925), 3.

Piercy, W. C. *St. Columba.* London 1925.

Ψ (pseud.). "St. Columba," *Ulster Jnl. of Archaeology,* 6 (1858), 1-26.

Reeves, W. *The Life of St. Columba* (rev. edn.). Dublin 1874.

Richomme, F. *Histoire de S. Columb.* Paris 1861.

Ryan, J. "A Vindication of St. Columba of Iona," *Month,* 150 (1927), 312-320.

Ryan, J. "St. Columba of Derry and Iona," *Studies,* 52 (1963), 37-51.

Scott, A. B. "St. Columba . . . the Gaidheal," *Trans. Gaelic Soc. of Inverness,* 28 (1912-1914), 15-66.

Simpson, W. D. *The Historical St. Columba.* Aberdeen 1927.

Thomson, W. "St. Columba's Birthplace," *Scottish N&Q,* 4 (1890), 59, 77.

Troup, G. E. *St. Columba.* Edinburgh 1913.

*Villaret, J. "St. Columba et les destinées de l'Angleterre," *Science sociale,* 2 (1887), 1.

Walker, H. T. *St. Columba.* Paisley 1923.
Watt, L. M. "Columba: Saint, Statesman, and Poet," *Hibbert Jnl.,* 20 (1922), 236-250.

COLUMBAN

This list omits works already included in the bibliography by G. S. M. Walker, *Sancti Columbani opera* (Scriptores latini hiberniae, II, Dublin 1957) and those published before 1885.

Albers, B. "S. Colombano, sue fondazioni e sua regola," *Rivista storica benedettina,* 10 (1915), 33-49.
*Bellenger, L. "Note sur Orientius et Columban," *Rev. de Gascogne,* N.S. 4 (1904), 171.
Bieler, L. "Editing St. Columbanus. A Reply," *Classica et mediaevalia,* 22 (1961), 139-150.
*Blanke, F. "Columban am Bodensee," *Volkshochschule* (Zürich 1938), 170.
———. "Columban und d. Slaven," *Theologische Blätter,* 18 (1939), 304-308.
———. "Zur Erklärung von Jonas, Vita Columbani I.27," *Theologische Blätter,* 15 (1936), 159.
Dubois, M. M. *St. Columban: A Pioneer of Western Civilization* (trans. J. O'Carroll). Dublin 1961.
Esposito, M. "On the New Edition of the *Opera Sancti Columbani,*" *Classica et mediaevalia,* 21 (1960), 184-203.
*Kendige, P. F. *The Poems of St. Columban Translated into English Verse.* Philadelphia 1949.
*Kilger, L. "Columban in Tuggen," *Neue Zt. f. Missionswissenschaft,* 6 (1950), 241-245.
Laporte, J. "Etude d'authenticité d. oeuvres attribuées à S. Colomban," *Rev. Mabillon,* 45 (1955), 1-28; 46 (1956), 1-14; 51 (1961), 35-46.
———. *Le pénitentiel de s. Columban.* Tournai 1958.
Lawlor, J. *The MSS of St. Columban.* Dublin 1903.

Leclercq, J. "Un recueil d'hagiographie columbanienne,"
    AB, 73 (1955), 193-196.
Lugnano, P. "S. Gregorio Magno e S. Colombano nella
    storia della cultura latina," *Rivista storica benedettina*,
    10 (1915), 161-182.
MacManus, F. *St. Columban.* New York 1962.
Manitius, M. "Zur lateinischen Sprichwörterlitteratur,"
    Philologus, 55 (1896), 573-575.
*Massani, M. "S. Columbano di Bobbio nella storia, nella
    letterature, nell'arte," *Didaskaleion*, 6 (1928), 81.
McGann, M. J. "The Distribution of Cadences in the *De
    Mundi Transitu* of St. Columban," *ALMA*, 31
    (1961), 147-149.
*Metlake, G. *The Life and Works of St. Columban.* Phila-
    delphia 1914.
Mitchell, G. "St. Columbanus on Penance," *Irish Theo-
    logical Quarterly*, 18 (1951), 43-54.
Mohrmann, C. "The Earliest Continental Irish Latin,"
    Vigiliae christianae, 16 (1962), 216-233.
*Morin, G. "Deux pièces inédites du disciple de Fauste
    de Riez auteur d. soi-disant Instructiones Colum-
    bani," *Rev. Charlemagne* (1911), 161.
———. "Le 'Liber S. Columbani in Psalmos' et le ms
    Ambros. C. 301 Inf.," *RB*, 38 (1926), 164-177.
Mould, D. D. C. P. "St. Columban and the Mass," *IER*,
    97 (1962), 296-303.
O'Carroll, J. "The Chronology of St. Columban," *Irish
    Theological Quarterly*, 24 (1957), 76-95.
———. "The Luxeuil Congress in Honour of the Four-
    teenth Centenary of St. Columban," *IER*, 75 (1951),
    490-498; 76 (1951), 37-43.
Ramsay, R. L. "Theodore of Mopsuestia and St. Colum-
    ban on the Psalms," *ZCP*, 8 (1912), 421-451.
*Rossi, G. F. "Il commento di S. Colombano ai Salmi
    ritrovato a Bobbio in un codice della fine del sec. xii,"
    Divus Thomas, 67 (1964), 89-93.

Seebass, O. "Ein Beitrag zur Rekonstruktion d. Regel Columbas d. jüngeren [i.e., Columbanus]," *Zt. f. Kirchengeschichte*, 40 (1922), 132-137.

Vaccari, P., *et al. San Colombano e la sua opera*. Convegno storico colombiano (Bobbio, 1-2 Sett. 1951). Bobbio 1953. Includes: P. Vaccari, "L'opera di S. Colombano nel rinnovamento religioso"; R. Olmi, "L'iconografia di S. Colombano"; R. D. Cella, "S. Colombano poeta"; A. Maestri, "La primitiva ufficiatura di S. Colombano"; J. Duft, "S. Colombano e S. Gallo"; G. Cugnier, "Vers la découverte du fameux 'Comm. sur les Psaumes'"; N. G. Follini, "Le tradizioni popolari bobbiesi di S. Colombano"; C. G. Mor, "La fondazione di Bobbio"; E. N. Rocca, "Bobbio da 'borgo' monastico a 'città' vescovile"; A. G. Bergamaschi, "Le partecipazione di Bobbio all'attività di compilazione delle collezioni canoniche"; T. Leccisotti, "Il monastero di S. Colombano alla metà del sec. XVII"; G. Monaco, "I cimeli archeologici del Museo di S. Colombano"; M. Giuliani, "La chiesa di S. Colombano di Pontremoli"; M. Chialvo, "L'antico monastero di Pagno."

Wilson, J. *Life of St. Columban*. Dublin 1953.

0.9. *Hisperica famina*

Bieler, L. "Hibernian Latin," *Studies*, 43 (1954), 92-95.

Bradshaw, H. Appendix to *Collected Papers*. Cambridge 1889, 453-488, esp. 462-470.

Damon, P. W. "The Meaning of the *Hisperica famina*," *American Jnl. of Philology*, 74 (1953), 398-406.

Ellis, R. "On the Hisperica famina," *Jnl. of Philology*, 28 (1903), 209-221.

———. "Notes on MSS of Catullus and Hisperica famina," *Hermathena*, 12 (1902), 17-24.

Geyer, P. "D. Hisperica Famina," *Archiv f. lateinische Lexikographie*, 2 (1885), 255-266.

Grosjean, P. "Confusa caligo. Remarques sur les 'Hisperica famina,'" *Celtica*, 3 (1956), 35-85.

Jenkinson, F. J. H. *The Hisperica famina*. Cambridge 1908.

Macalister, R. A. S. *The Secret Languages of Ireland*. Cambridge 1937.

Mone, F. J. D. *gallische Sprache*. Karlsruhe 1851, 74-85. Cf. *Publ. de la section historique de l'Institut de Luxembourg*, 24 (1869), 311-315.

Niedermann, M. "Les dérivés latins en -*ōsus* dans les Hisperica famina," *ALMA*, 23 (1953), 75-101.

———. "Sur les Hisperica famina," *Essais d'étymologie et de critique verbale latines*. Neuchatel 1918, 62-87.

Rand, E. K. "The Irish Flavor of Hisperica famina," *Studien zur lateinischen Dichtung d. Mittelalters: Ehrengabe f. K. Strecker* (eds. W. Stach and H. Walther). Dresden 1931, 134-142.

Rhys, J. "The Luxembourg Folio," *Rev. celtique*, 1 (1872), 346-347; 13 (1892), 248-251.

*Stowasser, J. M. "Incerti auctoris Hisperica famina," *Jahresbericht über d. Franz-Joseph-Gymnasium in Wien*, 13 (1887).

———. "D. kommatische Teilung d. Hisperica famina," *Wiener Studien*, 31 (1909), 293-298.

*———. "D. Luxemburger-Pergamen," *Zt. f. classische Philologie*, 9 (1887), 116, 309.

———. "Zu d. Hisperica famina," *Archiv f. lateinische Lexikographie*, 3 (1886), 168-176.

*———. "De quarto . . . specimine," *Jahresbericht über d. Franz-Joseph-Gymnasium in Wien*, 15 (1889).

Strong, H. A. "Zu d. Hisperica famina," *Archiv f. lateinische Lexikographie*, 14 (1906), 508.

Thurneysen, R. "Zu d. Hisperica famina," *Archiv f. lateinische Lexikographie*, 3 (1886), 546-548.

Zimmer, H. "Neue Fragmente von *Hisperica famina*," *Gött. Nachrichten*, Phil.-Hist. Kl. (1895), 117-165.

[254]

CHAPTER ONE: The Seventh Century

1.1. Augustine of Canterbury

(This list omits the geographical, e.g. his route, the site of the oak, etc.)

A., P. "Le xiiie centenaire de l'arrivée de St. Augustin en Angleterre," *RB*, 14 (1897), 359-369.

Anon. "Was St. Augustine of Canterbury a Benedictine?" *Downside Rev.*, 3 (1884), 45, 223-240.

Ashworth, H. "Did St. Augustine Bring the *Gregorianum* to England?" *EphL*, 72 (1958), 39-43.

*Bassenge, F. E. *D. Sendung Augustins zur Bekehrung d. Angelsachsen, A.D. 596-604.* Leipzig 1890.

*Beeching, H. C. *Augustine of Canterbury.* 1895.

Bing, H. F. "St. Augustine of Canterbury and the Saxon Church in Kent," *Arch. Cant.*, 62 (1949), 108-129.

Brechter, H. S. *D. Quellen zur Angelsachsenmission Gregors d. Grossen.* Münster 1941.

Brou, A. *St. Augustine of Canterbury and his Companions.* London 1897.

Browne, G. F. *Augustine and His Companions* (2d edn.). London 1906.

Collins, W. E. *The Beginnings of English Christianity, with Special Reference to the Coming of St. Augustine.* London 1898.

Cutts, E. L. *St. Augustine.* London 1881.

Deanesly, M. *Augustine of Canterbury.* London 1964.

———. "The Capitular Text of the Responsiones of Pope Gregory I to St. Augustine," *JEH*, 12 (1961), 231-234.

——— and P. Grosjean. "The Canterbury Edition of the Answers of Pope Gregory I to St. Augustine," *JEH*, 10 (1959), 1-49.

Farmer, H. "St. Gregory's Answers to St. Augustine of

Canterbury," *Studia monastica*, 1 (1959), 419-422.

Foreville, R. "Deux apôtres de la foi romaine en Angleterre: Augustin de Canterbury et S. Wilfrid d'York," *Rev. d'histoire de la philosophie et d'histoire générale de la civilisation* (1946), 175-182.

Gasquet, F. A. *The Mission of Augustine and Other Addresses*. London 1924. (Also *Tablet*, May 8 and 15, 1897.)

*———. "St. Gregory's responsiones ad interrogationes B. Augustini," *Miscellanea Amelli*. Montecassino 1920.

———. "St. Gregory's Responsions to St. Augustine," *Downside Rev.*, 23 (1904), 2-14.

Howorth, H. *Saint Augustine of Canterbury*. London 1913.

Jones, P. F. "The Gregorian Mission and English Education," *Speculum*, 3 (1928), 335-348.

*Kahl, H. D. "Papst Gregor d. Grosse und d. christliche Terminologie d. Angelsachsen," *Zt. f. Missionswissenschaft*, 40 (1956), 93, 190.

*Lévêque, L. "Le centenaire de St. Augustin de Canterbury," *Etudes de la Compagnie de Jésus*, 73 (1897), 182.

———. "St. Augustin de Cantorbéry," *Rev. d. questions historiques*, 65 (1899), 353-423.

Machielsen, L. "Fragments patristiques non-identifiés du ms. Vat. Pal. 577," *Sacris erudiri*, 12 (1961), 488-539.

Markus, R. A. "The Chronology of the Gregorian Mission to England: Bede's Narrative and Gregory's Correspondence," *JEH*, 14 (1963), 16-30.

*Martin, S. "Anglo-Saxon Christianity and Augustine of Canterbury," *Exeter Hall Lectures*, 17 (1862), 45.

Mason, A. J. *The Mission of St. Augustine to England According to the Original Documents*. Cambridge 1897.

Meyvaert, P. "Les *Responsiones* de S. Grégoire le Grand
à S. Augustine de Cantorbéry," *RHE*, 54 (1959),
879-894.

Müller, M. "Zur Frage nach d. Echtheit und Abfassungs-
zeit d. Responsum b. Gregorii ad Augustinum episcopum," *TQ*, 113 (1932), 94-118.

Oakeley, F. *The Life of St. Augustine.* London 1901.

O'Hare, C. M. "St. Augustine and the Conversion of
England," *IER*, 5th Ser. 38 (1931), 124-141, 285-
299.

Saxton, A. J. *St. Augustine, Apostle of the English.* London 1890.

Stanley, A. P. *Historical Memorials of Canterbury* (5th
edn.). London 1883.

Surtees, F. R. "St. Augustine, and Augustine the Monk
and Archbishop," *Jnl. British Archaeological Assn.*,
40 (1884), 295-296.

1.2. Theodore of Canterbury

*Binterim, A. J. *De capitulis Theodori Cantuariensis haud
genuinis.* Düsseldorf 1811.

Browne, G. F. *Theodore and Wilfrith.* London 1897.

Cook, A. S. "Hadrian of Africa, Italy, and England," *PQ*,
2 (1923), 241-258.

————. "Theodore of Tarsus and Gislenus of Athens,"
PQ, 2 (1923), 1-25.

Finsterwalder, P. W. *D. Canones Theodori Cantuariensis
und ihre Ueberlieferungsformen.* Weimar 1929.

Fournier, P. "Les *Capitula* du Pseudo-Théodore et le
Décret de Burchard de Worms," *Florilegium . . . à
M. le marquis Melchior de Vogüé.* Paris 1909, 241-
255.

Le Bras, G. "Notes pour servir à l'histoire d. collections
canoniques, V : *Judicia Theodori,*" *Rev. historique de
droit français et étranger*, Ser. 4 (1931), 95-115.

Liebermann, F. "Zur Herstellung d. Canones Theodori Cantuariensis," *Zt. d. Savigny-Stiftung f. Rechtsgeschichte*, 43 (1922), 387-409.

Poole, R.L. "Monasterium Niridanum," *EHR*, 36 (1921), 540-545.

Reany, W. *St. Theodore of Canterbury*. St. Louis 1944.

Schmitz, H. J. "D. sog. Theodor'sche Bussbuch in d. Hamilton'schen Hssammlung d. kgl. Bibliothek zur Berlin," *Archiv f. katholisches Kirchenrecht*, 48 (1885), 381-411.

Seckel, E. "Zu d. Acten d. Triburer Synode 895," *NA*, 20 (1894), 291-353.

van Zuylen, G. "L'épanouissement de la culture intellectuelle en Angleterre aux viie et viiie siècles," *Rev. ecclésiastique de Liège*, 32 (1945), 276-282.

1.3. Benedict Biscop

Allison, T. "Benedict Biscop," *CQR*, 107 (1928), 57-79.

Hepple, R. B. "Early Northumbrian Libraries," *Arch. Ael.*, 3d Ser. 14 (1917), 92-106.

———. "The Monastery School of Jarrow," *History*, 7 (1922), 92-102.

Pfeilstücker, S. *Spätantikes und germanisches Kunstgut in d. frühangelsächsischen Kunst*. Berlin 1936, 92-98.

Savage, H. E. "Jarrow Church and Monastery," *Arch. Ael.*, 2d Ser. 22 (1900), 30-60.

*Zettinger, J. "Weremouth-Jarrow und Rom im 7. Jrht.," *D. Katholik*, 81 (1901), 193.

1.4. Wilfrid of York

Bailey, A. C. "St. Wilfred of Sussex," *Sussex County Mag.*, 18 (1944), 278-280.

Browne, G. F. *Theodore and Wilfrith*. London 1897.

Dallow, W. *St. Wilfrid*. London 1897.

Dann, M. E. "St. Wilfrid in Sussex," *Buckfast Abbey Chron.*, 7 (1937), 244-252.

Faber, F. W. "St. Wilfrid, Bishop of York," *Lives of the English Saints* (2d edn.). London 1901.

Fletcher, J. S. *The Life and Work of St. Wilfrid of Ripon.* Chichester 1925.

de Fontette, E. "Vie de S. Wilfrid," *Le correspondant*, 26 (1850), 408-423, 523-541.

Foreville, R. "Deux apôtres de la foi romaine en Angleterre: Augustin de Canterbury et S. Wilfrid d'York," *Rev. d'histoire de la philosophie et d'histoire générale de la civilisation* (1946), 175-182.

Horgan, M. P. *The Life and Labours of St. Wilfrid, Bishop of York.* Louth 1889.

Housman, H. *St. Wilfrid and the 'Conversion of Sussex.* Chichester 1889.

Hutton, W. H. "St. Wilfrid," *York Minster Historical Tract*, 5 (1927).

I'Anson, J. "St. Wilfrid," *Jnl. British Archaeological Assn.*, 43 (1887), 275-290.

Levison, W. L. "D. Akten d. römischen Synode von 679," *Zt. d. Savigny-Stiftung f. Rechtsgeschichte*, 33 (kanonische Abt. 2, 1912), 249-282.

Mitchell, G. "St. Wilfred's Chapel," *Sussex County Mag.*, 22 (1948), 108-109.

Obser, K. *Wilfrid d. ältere, Bischof von York.* Karlsruhe 1884.

Poole, R. L. "St. Wilfrid and the See of Ripon," *EHR*, 34 (1919), 1-24.

Raine, A. "St. Wilfrid," *York Minster Historical Tracts 627-1927* (ed. A. H. Thompson). London 1927.

Sawyer, F. E. "St. Wilfrith's Life in Sussex," *Sussex Archaeological Collections*, 33 (1883), 101-128.

Streeter, A. *St. Wilfrid.* London 1897.

van Tromp, H. "St. Wilfrid in Sussex," *Sussex County Mag.*, 6 (1932), 812-816.

Two Sisters of Notre Dame of Namur. *St. Wilfrid, 633-709.* London 1928.

*W., S. *Life of St. Wilfrid.* London n.d.

Walbran, J. R. "On St. Wilfrid, and the Saxon Church of Ripon," *Associated Architectural Societies' Reports,* 5 (1859), 63-96.

Whiting, C. E. "The Anglian Bishops of Hexham," *Arch. Ael.,* 4th Ser. 24 (1946), 119-156.

———. "St. Wilfrid of York," *Durham Univ. Jnl.,* 25 (1927), 242-257.

Wilkinson, A. M. *Wilfrid of Ripon.* Ripon 1955.

1.5. Aldhelm

Editions and studies of vernacular glosses on, and translations of, Aldhelm's works, are not included.

LIFE AND GENERAL WORKS

Alexander, J. J. "Sherborne and its First Bishop," *Devon [and Cornwall] N&Q,* 16 (1930), 26-31.

Anon. "St. Aldhelm," *Downside Rev.,* 5 (1886), 244-251.

Barnes, W. "Ealdhelm, First Bishop of Sherborne. . . ," *Proc. Somersetshire Archaeological and Natural History Soc.,* 20 (1874), 85-97.

Bönhoff, L. *Aldhelm von Malmesbury.* Dresden 1894.

Boger, C. G. "King Ina in Somerset," *Watford's Antiquarian (Antiquarian Mag. and Bibliographer),* 8 (1885), 256-260; 9 (1886), 21-26.

Boyer, B. B. "Insular Contribution to Medieval Literary Tradition on the Continent," *CP,* 42 (1947), 209-222.

Browne, G. F. "The Aldhelm Crosses of Somerset and Wilts.," *Proc. Clifton Antiquarian Club,* 6 (1904-1908), 121-127.

———. *St. Aldhelm.* London 1903.

Cook, A. S. "Aldhelm at the Hands of Sharon Turner," *Speculum*, 2 (1927), 201-203.

———. "Aldhelm's Legal Studies," *JEGP*, 23 (1924), 105-113.

———. "Sources for the Biography of Aldhelm," *Trans. of the Connecticut Acad. of Arts and Sciences*, 28 (1927), 273-293.

Dolan, J. G., and E. Horne. "St. Aldhelm," *Catholic Biographies* (reiss. London 1912; also published separately).

Ehwald, R. *Aldhelmi opera. MGH*, Auct. ant. xv.3, Berlin 1919.

———. "Aldhelm von Malmesbury," *Jrb. d. kgl. Akad. gemeinnütz. Wiss. zu Erfurt*, N.F. 33 (1907), 91-116.

Fowler, J. *Medieval Sherborne*. Dorchester, Dorset 1951.

———. *St. Aldhelm*. Sherborne 1947.

Furst, C. *A Group of Old Authors*. Philadelphia 1899.

Godwin, H. "Notes on the West Saxon Bishoprics, More Particularly that of Sherborne," *Jnl. British Archaeological Assn.*, 28 (1872), 313-327.

James, M. R. *Two Ancient English Scholars.* Glasgow 1931.

Jones, W. H. R. "The Life and Times of Aldhelm," *Wilts. Archaeological Mag.*, 8 (1864), 62-81. (Also published separately, London 1874.)

Lindsay, W. M. *The Corpus, Epinal, Erfurt and Leyden Glossaries*. London 1921 (esp. 97-105).

*Mády, Z. "An Eighth-century Aldhelm Fragment in Hungary," *Acta antiqua academiae scientiarum Hungaricae*, 13 (1965), 441-453.

Magoun, F. P., Jr. "Aldhelm's Diocese of Sherborne *bewestan wuda*," *Harvard Theological Rev.*, 32 (1939), 103-114.

Manitius, M. "Zu Aldhelm und Beda," *Vienna SB*, Phil.-Hist. Kl. 112 (1886), 535-634.

BIBLIOGRAPHY

Manser, A. "Le témoignage d'Aldhelm de Sherborne sur une particularité du canon grégorien de la messe romaine," *RB*, 28 (1911), 90-95.

Mazzoni, D. "Aldhelmiana: Studio critico letterario su Aldhelmo di Sherborne," *Rivista storica benedettina*, 10 (1915) 93-114, 245-250, 402-447.

Meade, R. J. "A Short Memoir of Bishops Aldhelme and Athelme or Adelme," *Proc. Somersetshire Archaeological and Natural History Soc.*, 20 (1874), 74-84.

Napier, A. S. [Report of the Philological Soc.], *Academy*, 45 (1894), 398-399.

Pfeilstücker, S. *Spätantikes und germanisches Kunstgut in d. frühangelsächsischen Kunst.* Berlin 1936.

Wildman, W. B. *Life of St. Ealdhelm.* London 1905.

DE METRIS

*Cogliani, V. *De septenario di Aldhelm.* Cagliari 1907.

Ehwald, R. "De aenigmatibus Aldhelmi et acrostichis," *Festschrift f. Albert von Bamberg.* Gotha 1905, 1-26.

Erhardt-Siebold, E. von. "Aldhelm in Possession of the Secrets of Sericulture," *Anglia*, 60 (1936), 384-389.

————. "An Archaeological Find in a Latin Riddle of the Anglo-Saxons," *Speculum*, 7 (1932), 252-255.

————. "The Hellebore in Anglo-Saxon Pharmacy," *Englische Studien*, 71 (1936), 161-170.

———— "Aldhelm's Chrismal," *Speculum*, 10 (1935), 276-280.

*Maleyn, A. "Rukopisnoe predanie zagodok Al'dgel'ma" ["The MSS of Aldhelm's Riddles"], *Zapiski istor. fil. faculteta imper. S. Pet. Universiteta* 1905.

Mazzoni, D. "Note Aldhelmiane," *Didaskaleion*, 2 (1914), 169-173.

O'Cavanagh, J. E. "St. Aldhelm: The Double Acrostic," *N&Q*, 3d Ser. 11 (1867), 249-250.

Pitman, J. H. *The Riddles of Aldhelm.* New Haven 1925.

Prehn, A. "Komposition und Quellen d. Rätsel d. Exeterbuches," *Neuphilologische Studien*, 3 (1883), 145-285.

*Silvestre, H. "Un petit extrait du *de metris* d'Aldhelm dans le ms Verdun 36 (s. XI)," *ALMA*, 34 (1964).

Wright, T. *The Anglo-Latin Satirical Poets and Epigrammatists of the Twelfth Century*. RS, 75.2.

Zupitza, J. "Eine Conjectur zu Aldhelm," *Romanische Forschungen*, 3 (1887), 280.

DE LAUDIBUS VIRGINITATIS

Cook, A. S. "Aldhelm and the Source of Beowulf 2523," *MLN*, 40 (1925), 137-142.

Langenhove, G. van. *De laudibus virginitatis . . . MS 1650 of the Royal Library in Brussels*. Bruges 1941.

Lowe, E. A. "Membra disiecta," *RB*, 39 (1927), 191-192.

*Prago, G. "La legenda di S. Ilarione a Epidauro in Adelmo scrittore anglosassone," *Archivo storico di Dalmazia*, 25 (1938), 83-91.

DE LAUDIBUS VIRGINUM

Cook, A. S. "Beowulf 1422," *MLN*, 39 (1924), 77-82.

Ehwald, R. *Aldhelms Gedicht de virginitate*. Gotha 1904.

LETTERS

Cook, A. S. "Aldhelm's 'Rude Infancy,'" *PQ*, 7 (1928), 115-119.

———. "Who was the Ehfrid of Aldhelm's Letter?" *Speculum*, 2 (1927), 363-373.

Lejay, P. "Le grammarien Virgile et les rythmes latins," *Rev. de philologie, de littérature et d'histoire anciennes*, N.S. 19 (1895), 45-64.

Müller, L. "Zu Aldhelmus," *Rheinisches Museum*, 22 (1867), 150-151.

Traube, L. "Perrona Scottorum," *Munich SB*, Philos.-Phil. Hist. Kl. (1900), 469-537.

———. "Virgilius Maro Grammaticus," *Hermes*, 24 (1889), 647-649.

Zimmer, H. "Keltische Beiträge I," *Zt. f. deutsches Alterthum*, 32 (1887), 196-334.

Doubtful and Spurious

Bradley, H. "On Some Poems Ascribed to Aldhelm," *EHR*, 15 (1900), 291-292.

Cook, A. S. "A Putative Charter to Aldhelm," *Studies in English Philology . . . in Honor of Frederick Klaeber*. Minneapolis 1929, 254-257.

Lehmann, P. "D. Grammatik aus Aldhelms Kreise," *HV*, 27 (1932), 758-771.

———. "Ein neuentdecktes Werk eines angelsächsischen Grammatikers vorkarolingischer Zeit," *HV*, 26 (1931), 738-756.

Strecker, K. "Aldhelms Gedichte in Tegernsee," *Archiv*, 143 (1922), 177-182.

Chapter Two: Bede

2.0. Editions

No editions prior to Giles (1843-1844) are mentioned, nor are translations into languages other than Modern English.

Anon. *An All-Hallowtide Sermon* [by Bede]. London 1911.

Anon. *The Epistle of the Ven. Bede to Bp. Egbert.* Oxford 1882.

Anon. *A Little Work Concerning the Holy Places which Bede Composed* (Palestine Pilgrims Text Ser. 10). London 1889.

Anon. *The Pan-Anglican Synod . . . or Ven. Bede's Account of the Christianity that Came from Rome.* London 1878.

*Anon. *St. Bede the Venerable, Ecclesiastical History of the English People.* London 1935.

Anon. *Ven. Bede, historia ecclesiastica liber tertius.* Warminster 1892.

Arngart, O. *The Leningrad Bede* (Early English MSS in Facsimile, 2). Copenhagen 1952.

Blair, P. H., and R. A. B. Mynors. *The Moore Bede* (Early English MSS in Facsimile, 9). Copenhagen 1959.

Colgrave, B. *Two Lives of St. Cuthbert.* Cambridge 1940. Cf. especially the review by M. L. W. Laistner, *AHR,* 46 (1941), 379-381.

Delehaye, H. *Martyrologium e codice Basilicae Vaticanae.* Brussels 1931. (Extr. from *AB,* 49 [1931], 51-97.)

Fraipont, J. *Bedae Venerabilis opera,* IV : *Opera rhythmica. CC,* 122 (1955). Cf. W. Bulst, "Bedae Opera Rhythmica?" *Zt. f. deutsches Altertum und deutsche Literatur,* 89 (1959), 83-91.

Geyer, P. *Itinera hierosolymitana saeculi IV-VIII* [incl. Bede *De locis sanctis*]. *CSEL,* XXXIX (1898).

Gidley, L. *Ecclesiastical History of the English Nation.* Oxford 1870.

Giles, J. A. *Anecdota Bedae, Lanfranci et aliorum.* London 1851.

————. *The Biographical Writings and Letters of the Ven. Bede.* London 1845.

————. *Opera quae supersunt omnia Venerabilis Bedae.* London 1843-1844, 12 vols. (*PL,* Vols. 90-95.)

————. *The Ven. Bede's Ecclesiastical History of England* (2d edn.). London 1892.

Hagen, H. *Lib. I. hist. gent. aediti a Bede.* Leiden 1897.

Halm, K. F. *Bedae venerabilis de schematibus et tropis liber. Rhetores latini minores.* Leipzig 1863.

Holder, A. *Baedae historia ecclesiastica* (new ed.). Freiburg/B. 1895.

Hurst, D. *Bedae Venerabilis opera.* II.2 : *In primam partem Samuhelis libri III; In Regum librum xxx quaestiones. CC,* 119 (1962).

[265]

Hurst, D. *Bedae Venerabilis opera,* ii.3: *In Lucae evangelium expositio; In Marci evangelium expositio. CC,* 120 (1960).

————. *Bedae Venerabilis opera,* iii: *Opera homiletica. CC,* 122 (1955).

Hussey, R. *Baedae historia ecclesiastica gentis anglorum.* Oxford 1846.

Jaager, W. "Bedas metrische Vita Sancti Cuthberti," *Palaestra,* 198 (1935; also published separately, Weimar 1935).

Jane, L. C. *The Ecclesiastical History of the English Nation* (repr.). London 1954.

Jones, C. W. *Bedae opera de temporibus.* Cambridge, Mass. 1943. Cf. esp. the reviews by H. Henel, *AHR,* 49 (1944), 694-696 and *JEGP,* 43 (1944), 411-416.

————. *Bedae pseudepigrapha. Scientific Writings Falsely Attributed to Bede.* Ithaca 1939.

Keil, H. *Bedae Venerabilis de arte metrica liber; de othographia liber. Grammatici latini* vii. Leipzig 1880.

King, J. E. *Baedae opera historica, with an English translation* (2d edn.). New York and London 1954.

Knowles, D. *Ecclesiastical History of the English Nation.* London 1954.

Knowles, E. H., and J. F. Welsh. *Ven. Baedae historica ecclesiastica* (2d edn.). London 1893.

Laistner, M. L. W. *Bedae Venerabilis expositio actuum apostolorum et retractatio.* Cambridge, Mass. 1939.

Liverani, F. *Spicilegium liberianum.* Florence 1863.

Maglagan, M. *Ecclesiastical History of the English Nation, Books 1-2.* Oxford 1949.

Marshall, E. *The Explanation of the Apocalypse by Ven. Beda.* London 1878.

Mayor, J. E. B., and J. R. Lumby. *Historia ecclesiastica gentis anglorum libri III, IV* (4th edn.). Cambridge 1892.

Meyer, W. "Bedae oratio ad deum," *Gött. Nachrichten,*

Phil.-Hist. Kl. (1912), 228-235. (Also published separately, Göttingen 1912.)

Moberly, G. H. *Ven. Baedae historia ecclesiastica, historia abbatum, epistola ad Ecgberctum.* Oxford, repr. 1881.

Mommsen, T. *Bedae chronica maiora, chronica minora. MGH*, Auct. ant. XIII.2, Berlin 1895.

Plummer, C. *Venerabilis Baedae historia ecclesiastica.* . . . Oxford 1946 (repr. 1896 edn.).

*Poussin, C. *Panégyriques de la Ste. Vierge et d. saints.* 1857.

Scudder, V. D. *The Ecclesiastical History of the English Nation.* London 1910.

Sellar, A. M. *Ecclesiastical History of England.* London 1912.

Sherley-Price, L. *Bede, A History of the English Church and People.* Baltimore 1955.

Stapleton, T. *The History of the Church of England.* London 1909; Oxford 1930.

Stevenson, J. *Historical Works* [of Bede]. London 1853.
———. *The Life of Cuthbert* [by Bede]. London 1887.

Tobler, T., and A. Molinier. *Itinera hierosolymitana.* Geneva 1879.

Wallis, C. S., and C. H. Gill. *Ven. Baedae historia ecclesiastica . . . liber III.* London 1909.

Welsh, J. F. *Ven. Baedae. Historia ecclesiastica gentis anglorum liber tertius.* London 1894.

Wilcock, P. *Lives of the First Five Abbots of Wearmouth and Jarrow.* Sunderland 1910.

Williams-Fisher, T. J. *Ven. Bedae historia ecclesiastica . . . liber III.* Oxford 1910.

Wilmart, A. *Precum libelli quattuor aevi Karolini I.* Rome 1940.

2.1. Life and General Works

Abbott, W. C. "An Uncanonized Saint: The Venerable Bede," *Conflicts with Oblivion.* New Haven 1924.

Allen, G. "The Ven. Bede," *Gentleman's Mag.*, N.S. 25 (1880), 84.

Anon. "Editors and Biographers of the Ven. Bede," *Dublin Rev.*, 36 (1854), 290.

Anon. "The Ven. Bede," *North American Rev.*, 92 (1861), 36.

Anon. "The Ven. Bede: Ascension Eve 735-1935," *TLS*, 34 (1935), 317-318.

*Anon. *Vita del Ven. Beda.* Asti 1889.

Le Bachelet, X. "Bède et l'eucharistie," *Etudes*, 118 (1909), 493-504.

————. "Le Vén. Bède témoin de la foi eucharistique dans l'église anglo-saxonne," *Report of the 19th Eucharistic Congress.* London 1909.

Beda Venerabilis: Bibliographie. Deutscher Gesamtkatalog. Sonderheft. (Berlin 1938). Identical with the Bede portion of the *Deutscher Gesamtkatalog* 14 (1939); lists editions and translations of Bede and pseudo-Bede in German libraries in 1939.

Beeson, C. H. "The Manuscripts of Bede," *CP*, 42 (1947), 73-87.

Bischoff, B. "Zur Kritik d. Heervagenschen Ausgabe von Bedas Werken," *SMGB*, 51 (1933), 171-176.

Bolton, W. F. "A Bede Bibliography, 1935-1960," *Traditio*, 18 (1962), 436-445.

Boutflower, D. S. "The Venerable Bede," *Sunderland Daily Post*, May 26, 1903.

Boyer, B. B. "Insular Contribution to Medieval Literary Tradition on the Continent," *CP*, 43 (1948), 31-39.

Brown, R. "An Inquiry into the Origin of the Name 'Sunderland'; and as to the Birth Place of the Ven. Bede," *Arch. Ael.*, 1st Ser. 4 (1855), 277-283.

Browne, G. F. *The Venerable Bede.* London 1919.

Carroll, M. T. A. *The Venerable Bede: His Spiritual Teachings.* Catholic University of America Studies in Medieval History, N.S. 9, Washington, D.C. 1946.

Chambers, R. W. "Bede," *PBA*, 22 (1936), 97-127 (repr. in *Man's Unconquerable Mind*, London 1939).

Librarian of Chetham. "A General Literary Index: Index of Authors: Venerable Bede," *N&Q*, 4th Ser. 9 (1872), 193, 529.

Colgrave, B. *The Venerable Bede and His Times.* Jarrow 1958.

Condamin, A. "L'inerrance biblique d'après S. Bède," *RSR*, 4 (1913), 73-75.

*Daniels, J. "Viering van het Eeuwfeest van Beda Venerabilis," *Studiën*, 126 (1936), 33-43.

Danzer, G. "Beda d. Ehrwürdige," *Benediktinische Monatschrift*, 17 (1935), 229-237.

Davis, R. "Bede's Early Reading," *Speculum*, 8 (1933), 179-195.

Dougherty, J. J. "A True Monk—the Ven. Bede," *Catholic World*, 34 (1882), 558.

Duncan-Jones, C. M. *The Candle of the North.* London 1924.

*Eliason, N. E. "The Age of Bede," *Lectures in the Humanities.* Chapel Hill 1960, 23-38.

Foggon, J. "The Ven. Bede," *Reliquary*, 22 (1882), 145-151.

*Franses, D. "Sanctus Beda Venerabilis," *Referaat van de vereeniging tot het bevorderen van de beoefening d. wetenschap onder de Katholieken in Nederland.* The Hague 1936.

Furlong, P. J. "On the Twelve Hundredth Anniversary of the Death of Bede," *Catholic Historical Rev.*, 22 (1936), 297-303.

Gasquet, F. A. *Saint Bede 673-735.* London 1901.

———. "The Story of St. Bede," *The Mission of St. Augustine.* London 1924. (Also published separately, Manchester 1900.)

Gehle, H. *Disputatio historico-theologica de Bedae Venera-*

bilis, presbyteri anglo-saxonis, vita et scriptis. Leiden 1838.

Gillett, H. M. *St. Bede the Venerable.* London 1935.

Goodier, A. "St. Bede the Venerable," *The Month,* 165 (1935), 205-215.

Grosjean, P. "Le 'De Excidio' chez Bède et chez Alcuin," *AB,* 75 (1957), 222-226.

Heilig, K. J. "Beda in Oesterreich," *ZDG,* 1 (1935), 286-298.

Hill, E. *The Venerable Bede.* London 1935.

*Hilpisch, H. "Beda und d. germanische Christentum," *Pastor bonus,* 46 (1935), 225-237.

Home, G. "Bede, Durham and Northumbria," *Geographical Mag.,* 1 (1935), 299-300.

Inguanez, M. "Il Ven. Beda nei codici e negli scrittori cassinesi medioevali," *Studia anselmiana,* 6 (1936), 41-50.

James, W. C. *The Birthplace of Bede.* London 1866.

John, E. "A Note on Bede's Use of Facultas," *RB,* 72 (1962), 350-355.

Keldany, H., *et al. Beda Book* (reprints of articles from *Beda Rev.*). London 1957. Includes: H. Keldany, "St. Bede our Patron"; T. Holland, "St. Bede the Theologian"; P. J. Morris, "St. Bede and the Sacred Scriptures"; D. Matthews, "The Ven. Bede as a Historian."

Laistner, M. L. W. "Bede as a Classical and a Patristic Scholar," *Trans. Royal Historical Soc.,* 16 (1933), 69-94.

———. "The Western Church and Astrology during the Early Middle Ages," *Harvard Theological Rev.,* 34 (1941), 251-275.

———, and H. H. King. *A Handlist of Bede Manuscripts.* Ithaca 1943. See esp. reviews by N. Ker, *MAe,* 13 (1944), 36-40; B. Smalley, *JTS,* 45 (1944), 228-231; V. de Montmollin, *Rev. du moyen âge latin,*

4 (1948), 395-396; H. Silvestre, *Scriptorium*, 6 (1952), 287-293; C. H. Beeson, *CP*, 43 (1948), 31-39.

*Lebhe, D. B. "Le xiie centenaire de S. Bède le Vénérable," *Rev. liturgique et monastique*, 20 (1935), 197.

Lehmann, P. "Ioannes Sichardus und d. von ihm benutzten Bibliotheken und HSS," *Quellen und Untersuchungen zur lateinischen Philologie d. Mittelalters* iv.1 (1911).

Levison, W. "Modern Editions of Bede," *Durham Univ. Jnl.*, N.S. 6 (1945), 78-85.

Longstaffe, W. H. D. "Unused Evidences Relating to SS. Cuthbert and Bede," *Arch. Ael.*, N.S. 13 (1889), 278-283.

Low, J. L. *The Ven. Bede and his Durham Editors.* Durham 1883.

Manitius, M. "Zu Aldhelm und Beda," *Vienna SB*, Phil.-Hist. Kl., 112 (1886), 535-634.

Manser, A. "Von Bedas früherer Verehrung auf deutschem Boden," *ZDG*, 1 (1935), 298-303.

Mathew, G. "St. Bede," *The English Way*, ed. M. Ward. London 1933.

Maycock, A. L. "Bede and Alcuin (735-1935)," *Hibbert Jnl.*, 33 (1935), 402-412.

Meagher, J. R. "St. Bede the Venerable," *Clergy Rev.*, 10 (1935), 1-9.

Meyvaert, P. "Bede and the *Libellus Synodicus* of Gregory the Great," *JTS*, N.S. 12 (1961), 298-302.

de Montault, B. "Le vén. Bède," *Rev. de l'art chrétien*, 4th Ser. 3 (1892), 105.

Nicholl, D. "St. Bede," *The Month*, 22 (1959), 253-266.

Orchard, B. "Bede the Venerable," *Downside Rev.*, 53 (1935), 344-368.

Patterson, J. "The Birthplace of the Ven. Bede," *Antiquities of Sunderland*, 12 (1911), 41-50.

Percy, T. G. "The Ven. Bede," *Expository Times*, 451 (1933-1934), 517-518.

Plaine, B. "Le vénérable Bède, docteur de l'église," *Rev. anglo-romaine*, 3 (1896), 49-96.

Plummer, A. *The Ven. Bede.* Newcastle upon Tyne 1884.

Raby, F. J. E. "Bede, 735-1935," *Laudate*, 13 (1935), 140-155.

Rawnsley, H. D. *The Ven. Bede, His Life and Work.* Sunderland 1904.

Rupicastrensis (pseud.) *et al.* "Ven. Bede," *N&Q*, 1st Ser. 10 (1854), 139-140, 229-230, 329-331, 494; 11 (1855), 132, 373; 12 (1855), 106-107, 292.

Salaverri, J. "S. Beda il venerabile e la sua fede nel primato di S. Pietro," *La Civiltà Cattolica*, 3 (1935), 337-349.

*Sanmiguel, G. "S. Beda el Venerable," *Monasticon*, 2 (1935), 57-64, 110-114.

*Sarabia, J. M. "La romanidad de S. Beda el Venerable," *Estudios ecclesiasticos*, 14 (1935), 51-74.

Schreiber, H. "Beda in buchgeschichtlicher Betrachtung," *Zentralblatt f. Bibliothekswesen*, 53 (1936), 625-652.

*———. "Beda und d. literarische Tradition," *St. Wiborada*, 3 (1936), 36-41.

———. "Beda-Überlieferung in Sachsen," *ZDG*, 1 (1935), 278-285.

———. "Beda Venerabilis und d. mittelalterliche Bildung," *SMGB*, 55 (1937), 1-14.

Schütt, M. "Ein Beda-Problem," *Anglia*, 72 (1954), 1-20.

Shrimpton, T. and G. *The Life of St. Bede, Priest.* Oxford 1854.

Silvestre, H. *Les manuscrits de Bède à la Bibliothèque Royale à Bruxelles.* Léopoldville 1959.

———. "A propos de quelques mss de Bède," *Scriptorium*, 17 (1963), 110-113.

Southern, R. W. "Bede, the Monk of Jarrow," *The Listener*, 71 (1964), 267-269.

[272]

Stranks, C. J. *The Venerable Bede.* London 1955.

Sutcliffe, E. F. "Some Footnotes to the Fathers," *Biblica,* 6 (1925), 205-210.

———. "The Venerable Bede's Knowledge of Hebrew," *Biblica,* 16 (1935), 300-306.

Thomas, G. P. "The Ven. Bede," *Expository Times,* 45 (1934), 517-518.

Thompson, A. H., ed. *Bede: His Life, Times and Writings.* Oxford 1935. Includes: C. F. Whiting, "The Life of the Venerable Bede"; E. W. Watson, "The Age of Bede"; A. H. Thompson, "Northumbrian Monasticism"; C. Peers, "Monkwearmouth and Jarrow"; W. Levison, "Bede as Historian" (repr. in *Aus Rheinischer und Fränkischer Frühzeit,* Düsseldorf 1948); C. Jenkins, "Bede as Exegete and Theologian"; B. Colgrave, "Bede's Miracle Stories"; M. L. W. Laistner, "The Library of the Venerable Bede" (repr. in *The Intellectual History of the Early Middle Ages,* Ithaca 1957).

Welzhofer, K. "Bedas Citate aus d. naturalis historia d. Plinius," *Abh. aus d. Gebiet d. klas. Altertums-Wissenschaft Wm. v. Christ zum 60 Geburtstag dargebracht.* Munich 1891, 25-41.

Werner, K. *Beda d. Ehrwürdige und seine Zeit.* (2d edn.) Vienna 1881.

Whitaker, T. D. *Loidis and Elmete; or, an Attempt to Illustrate the Districts Described in those Words by Bede.* n.p. 1816.

Whitelock, D. *After Bede.* Jarrow 1960.

Whiting, C. E. "Bede in After History," *Trans. Architectural and Archaeological Soc. of Durham and Northumberland,* 7 (1936), 178-199.

Willard, R. "The Venerable Bede: 735-1935," *American Church Monthly,* 37 (1935), 266-280.

Williams, S. B. *The Ven. Bede.* London 1892.

[273]

Winmill, J. M. "The Ven. Bede," *IER*, 75 (1951), 445-452.

Zimmer, H. "Zur Orthographie d. Namens Beda," *NA*, 16 (1891), 599-601.

2.2. Exegesis

Bardy, G. "La littérature patristique d. 'Quaestiones et responsiones' sur l'Ecriture Sainte," *Rev. biblique*, 42 (1933), 14-30.

Barré, H. "Marie et l'église, du Vénérable Bède à S. Albert le Grand," *Etudes Mariales*, 9 (1951), 59-143. (Also published separately, Paris 1952.)

Beumer, J. "D. Kirchenbild in d. Schriftkommentaren Bedas d. Ehrwürdigen," *Scholastik*, 28 (1953), 40-56.

Bischoff, B. "Wendepunkte in d. Geschichte d. lateinischen Exegese im Frühmittelalter," *Sacris erudiri*, 6 (1954), 189-281.

Capelle, B. "Le rôle théologique de Bède le Vénérable," *Studia anselmiana*, 6 (1936), 1-40.

Willmes, A. "Bedas Bibelauslegung," *Archiv f. Kulturgeschichte*, 44 (1962), 281-314.

COMMENTARY ON ACTS; RETRACTATION

Bolton, W. F. "An Aspect of Bede's Later Knowledge of Greek," *CR*, 77 (1963), 17-18.

Cook, A. S. "Bede and Gregory of Tours," *PQ*, 6 (1927), 315-316.

Craster, H. H. E. "The Laudian Acts," *Bodleian Quarterly Record*, 2 (1919), 288-290.

Jones, C. W. "Bede and Vegetius," *CR*, 46 (1932), 248-249.

Laistner, M. L. W. "The Latin Versions of *Acts* Known to the Venerable Bede," *Harvard Theological Rev.*, 30 (1937), 37-50.

———. "The Spanish Archetype of MS Harley 4980 (Bede's Exposition of Acts)," *JTS*, 37 (1936), 132-137.

MacDonald, G. "Bede and Vegetius," *CR*, 47 (1933), 124.

Motzo, B. R. "Beda e il codice Laudiano degli Atti," *Ricerche religiose*, 3 (1927), 453-456.

Ogilvy, J. D. A. "A Noteworthy Contribution to the Study of Bede," *Univ. of Colorado Studies in the Humanities*, 1 (1942), 261-264.

COMMENTARY ON THE APOCALYPSE

Kamlah, W. *Apokalypse und Geschichtstheologie*. Berlin 1935.

Sparks, H. F. D. "A Celtic Text of the Latin Apocalypse Preserved in Two Durham MSS of Bede's Commentary on the Apocalypse," *JTS*, N.S. 5 (1954), 227-231.

COMMENTARY ON THE CATHOLIC EPISTLES

Jenkins, C. "A Newly Discovered Reference to the 'Heavenly Witnesses' (I John v.7,8) in a MS of Bede," *JTS*, 43 (1942), 42-45.

Laistner, M. L. W. "An Addition to Bede in MS Balliol 177," *JTS*, 43 (1942), 184-187.

COLLECTANEUM ON THE PAULINE EPISTLES

Affeldt, W. "Verzeichnis d. Römerbriefkommentare d. lateinischen Kirche bis zu Nikolaus von Lyra," *Traditio*, 13 (1957), 369-406.

Charlier, C. "La compilation Augustinienne de Florus sur l'Apôtre," *RB*, 57 (1947), 132-186.

Fransen, I. "Les Commentaires de Bède et de Florus sur l'Apôtre et S. Césaire d'Arles," *RB*, 65 (1955), 262-266.

———. "Description de la collection de Bède le Vénérable sur l'Apôtre," *RB*, 71 (1961), 22-70.

BIBLIOGRAPHY

Wilmart, A. "La collection de Bède le Vénérable sur l'Apôtre," *RB*, 38 (1926), 17-53.

———. "Note sur les citations du Vén. Bède et sur celles de Florus," *Miscellanea agostiniana*, 2 (1931), 266-268, 292-294.

———. "Note sur Florus et Mannon à propos d'un travail récent," *RB*, 38 (1926), 214-216.

COMMENTARIES ON LUKE AND ON MARK

Laistner, M. L. W. "Source-marks in Bede MSS," *JTS*, 34 (1933), 350-354.

Schönbach, A. E. "Ueber einige Evangelienkommentare d. Mittelalters," *Vienna SB*, Phil.-Hist. Kl. 146 (1903), Abh. iv.

Sutcliffe, E. F. "Quotations in the Ven. Bede's Commentary on S. Mark," *Biblica*, 7 (1926), 428-439.

COMMENTARY ON PROVERBS

de Bruyne, D. "Note sur les mss et les éditions du commentaire de Bède sur les Proverbes," *JTS*, 28 (1926-1927), 182-184.

Denifle, H. "D. HSS d. Bibel-Correctorien d. 13 Jrhts.," *Archiv f. Literatur- und Kirchengeschichte d. Mittelalters*, 4 (1888), 471-601.

Druhan, D. "Note sur les mss et les éditions du commentaire de Bède sur les proverbes," *JTS*, 28 (1927), 182-184.

Hablitzel, J. "Bedas *Expositio in Proverbia Salomonis* und seine Quellen," *Biblische Zt.*, 24 (1939), 357-359.

*Obersteiner, J. "D. Erklärung von Proverbia xxxi, 10-31, durch Beda d. Ehrwürdigen und Bruno von Asti," *Theologisch-praktische Quartalschrift*, 102 (1954), 1-12.

Vaccari, A. "Le antiche vite di S. Girolamo," *Scritti di erudizione e di filologia*, 2 (1958), 31-51; Bede, pp. 36-38.

COMMENTARY ON SAMUEL

d'Alès, A. "Tertullien chez Bède?" *RSR*, 27 (1937), 620.

COMMENTARY ON THE SONG OF SONGS

Ohly, F. "Beda und d. Karolingerzeit," *Hohelied-Studien.* Wiesbaden 1958, 64-91.

Riedlinger, H. *D. Makellosigkeit d. Kirche in d. lateinischen Hoheliedkommentaren d. Mittelalters* (Beiträge zur Geschichte d. Philosophie und Theologie d. Mittelalters XXXVIII.3). Münster 1958, 71-88.

DE TABERNACULO

Krabben, P.v.D. "Beda als Bron van d. Gheesteliken Tabernakel," *Ons Geestelijk Erf*, 9 (1935), 382-387.

2.3. Hagiography

Loomis, C. G. "The Miracle Traditions of the Venerable Bede," *Speculum*, 21 (1946), 404-418.

MARTYROLOGY

Piper, F. *D. Kalendarien und Martyrologien d. angelsachsen.* . . . Berlin 1862.

Quentin, H. *Les martyrologes historiques du moyen âge.* Paris 1908.

METRICAL LIFE OF ST. CUTHBERT

Hornung, H. "Ein Fragment d. metrischen St. Cuthbert-Vita d. Beda im Nachlass d. Brüder Grimm," *Scriptorium*, 14 (1960), 344-346.

PROSE LIFE OF ST. CUTHBERT

Colgrave, B. "The New Bede MS," *Durham Univ. Jnl.*, 30 (1936), 1-5.

———. "The History of British Museum Additional MS 39943," *EHR*, 54 (1939), 673-676.

Colgrave, B. and I. Masson. "The *editio princeps* of Bede's
Prose Life of St. Cuthbert, and its Printer's xiith
century 'copy,'" *The Library*, 4th Ser. 19 (1938),
289-303.

DE LOCIS SANCTIS

Morin, G. "Le ms namurois du Liber de locis sanctis de
Bède," *RB*, 16 (1899), 210-211.

2.4. Chronology

Jones, C. W. "Polemius Silvius, Bede, and the Names of
the Months," *Speculum*, 9 (1934), 50-56.
———. "Two Easter Tables," *Speculum*, 13 (1938), 204-
205.
Wynn, J. B. "The Beginning of the Year in Bede and the
Anglo-Saxon Chronicle," *MAe*, 25 (1956), 71-79.

DE TEMPORUM RATIONE

B., A. E. "Ven. Bede's Mental Almanac," *N&Q*, 1st Ser.,
4 (1851), 201-203.
*Brandstetter, J. L. "D. Jahresepochen d. hl. Beda,"
*Kathol. Schweizerblätter f. Wissenschaft . . . und
Leben*, 11 (1869).
Cordoliani, A. "A propos du chapitre premier du *De
temporum ratione* de Bède," *Le moyen âge*, 54 (1948),
209-223.
———. "Notes sur le ms latin 7418 de la Bibliothèque
Nationale," *Bibliothèque de l'école d. chartes*, 103
(1942), 61-68.
Delisle, L. V. *Note sur un ms interpolé de la Chronique
de Bède conservé à Besançon*. Nogent-le-Rotrou 1895
(Extr. from *Bibliothèque de l'école d. chartes*, 56
[1895], 528-536, 758).
Dillon, M. "Vienna Glosses of Bede," *Celtica*, 3 (1955),
340-344.
Fordyce, C. J. *A Rhythmical Version of Bede's De ratione*

temporum (Repr. from *ALMA*, 3 [1927], 59-73, 129-141). Paris 1927.

Förster, M. "D. Weltzeitalter bei d. Angelsachsen," *D. neueren Sprachen*, 6 (1925, Bhft., Festgabe Karl Luick dargebracht), 183-203.

Jones, C. W. "A Note on Concepts of the Inferior Planets in the Early Middle Ages," *Isis*, 24 (1936), 397-399.

——. "The Victorian and Dionysiac Paschal Tables in the West," *Speculum*, 9 (1934), 408-421.

*Lejay, P. "Note sur un passage de Bède et sur un systeme de numération," *Compte rendu du Congrès scientifique Catholique*, 6 (1898), 129.

*Richardson, L. J. "Digital Reckoning among the Ancients," *American Mathematical Monthly*, 23 (1916), 7.

Tille, A. "Yule and Christmas: Their Place in the Germanic Year," *Trans. Glasgow Archaeological Soc.*, N.S. 3 (1899), 426-497.

*Wetzel, G. *D. Chroniken d. Baedae Venerabilis*. Halle 1878.

COMPUTUS

Cordoliani, A. "Un ms de comput intéressant," *Scriptorium*, 12 (1958), 247-253.

Jones, C. W. "The 'Lost' Sirmond MS of Bede's 'Computus,'" *EHR*, 52 (1937), 209-219.

2.5. Didactic Works

DE NATURA RERUM

*Bober, H. "An Illustrated Medieval School-Book of Bede's *De natura rerum*," *Jnl. of the Walters Art Gallery*, 19-20 (1956-1957), 64-97.

Jones, C. W. "MSS of Bede's *De natura rerum*," *Isis*, 27 (1937), 430-440.

Strunz, F. "Beda in d. Geschichte d. Naturbetrachtung und Naturforschung," *ZDG*, 1 (1935), 311-321.

Strunz, F. "Beda Venerabilis in d. Geschichte d. Natur-betrachtung," *Rivista di scienza,* 66 (1939), 57-70. Cf. *F. Strunz, "S. Beda el Venerable en la historia de la investigación de la naturaleza," *Investigación y progresso,* 12 (1939), 407-413.

Thum, B. "Beda Venerabilis in d. Geschichte d. Natur-wissenschaften," *Studia anselmiana,* 6 (1936), 51-71.

DE ARTE METRICA

Cook, A. S. "Bede and Homer," *Archiv,* 147 (1924), 93-94.

Gładysz, Bronislas. "Eléments classiques et post-classiques de l'oeuvre de Bède *de arte metrica,*" *Eos,* 34 (1933), 319-343.

Palmer, R. B. "Bede as Textbook Writer: A Study of his *De arte metrica,*" *Speculum,* 34 (1959), 573-584.

DE SCHEMATIBUS ET TROPIS

Elder, J. P. "Did Remigius of Auxerre Comment on Bede's *De schematibus et tropis?*" *Mediaeval Studies,* 9 (1947), 141-150.

2.6. Homilies

Lambot, C. "La tradition manuscrite anglo-saxonne d. sermons de S. Augustin," *RB,* 64 (1954), 3-8.

Leclercq, J. "Le IIIe livre d. homélies de Bède le Véné-rable," *Recherches de théologie ancienne et médiévale,* 14 (1947), 211-218.

Morin, G. "Le recueil primitif d. homélies de Bède sur l'évangile," *RB,* 9 (1892), 316-326.

Wilmart, A. "Un sermon de S. Augustin sur la prière cité par Bède," *RB,* 41 (1929), 5-14.

2.7. Verses

Lehmann, P. "D. Erstveröffentlichung von Bedas

Psalmen-Gedichten," *Zt. f. Kirchengeschichte,* 34 (1913), 89-92.

Schreiber, H. "Beda als Dichter," *ZDG,* 1 (1935), 326-327.

Whitbread, L. "Note on a Bede Fragment," *Scriptorium,* 12 (1958), 280-281.

———. "A Study of Bede's *Versus de die iudicii,*" *PQ,* 23 (1944), 193-221.

2.8. History

Anon. "The Father of English History," *CQR,* 43 (1896), 112-132.

*Betten, F. S. "St. Bede the Venerable," *Church Historians* (ed. P. Guilday). London 1926.

Boult, J. "The Credibility of the Ven. Bede," *Proc. Literary and Philosophical Soc. of Liverpool,* 32 (1878), 127-150.

Jones, C. W. "Bede as Early Medieval Historian," *Medievalia et humanistica,* 4 (1946), 26-36.

Redlich, P. V. "Beda und d. deutsche Geistesgeschichte," *ZDG,* 1 (1935), 273-277.

ECCLESIASTICAL HISTORY OF THE ENGLISH PEOPLE

Anderson, O. S. *Old English Material in the Leningrad MS of Bede's Ecclesiastical History.* Lund 1941.

*Anon. *Cardinal Manning and History. An Answer to the Cardinal's Appeal to the History of the Ven. Bede.* 1876.

Anon. "Ecclesiastical History of the Ven. Bede," *Princeton Rev.,* 42 (1870), 401.

Anon. *Interpolations in Bede's Ecclesiastical History.* Edinburgh 1883.

Anscombe, A. "The Date of the Council of Hertford," *Athenaeum* (September 22, 1900), 380.

———. "The Date of the First Settlement of Saxons in Britain," *ZCP,* 3 (1901), 492; 6 (1908), 339.

Anscombe, A. "The *Exordium* of the 'Annales Cambriae,'"
  Eriu, 3 (1907), 117.
Aurner, N. S. "Bede and Pausanias," *MLN*, 41 (1926),
  535-536.
Bénevot, M. "Towards Dating the Leningrad 'Bede,'"
  Scriptorium, 16 (1962), 365-369.
Blair, P. H. *Bede's Ecclesiastical History of the English
  Nation and its Importance Today.* Jarrow 1959.
———. "The *Moore Memoranda* on Northumbrian His-
  tory," *The Early Cultures of North-West Europe*
  (eds. C. Fox and B. Dickins). Cambridge 1950, 245-
  257.
Blasche, H. *Angelsachsen und Kelten im Urteil d. His-
  toria ecclesiastica gentis anglorum d. Beda.* Göt-
  tingen 1940.
Chadwick, N. K. "The Conversion of Northumbria: a
  Comparison of Sources"; "The Battle of Chester: a
  Study of Sources"; "Bede, St. Colmán and the Irish
  Abbey of Mayo"; *Celt and Saxon.* Cambridge 1963,
  chaps. 4, 5, 6.
Clausen, W. "Bede and the British Pearl," *Classical Jnl.*,
  42 (1947), 277-280.
Colgrave, B. "The Leningrad MS of Bede," *Times* (Janu-
  ary 7, 1953), 8.
*Cronholm, A. *Bedae historia ecclesiastica critice exami-
  nata.* Lund 1841.
Deanesly, M. "Roman Traditionalist Influence among the
  Anglo-Saxons," *EHR*, 58 (1943), 129-146.
Dempf, A. "Beda und d. Entstehung d. Artussage,"
  ZDG, 1 (1935), 304-310.
Dobiache-Rojdestvensky, O. "Un ms de Bède à Lénin-
  grad," *Speculum*, 3 (1928), 314-321.
Druhan, D. R. *The Syntax of Bede's Historia ecclesiastica.*
  Catholic University Studies in Medieval and Renais-
  sance Latin, 8. Washington, D.C. 1938.

[282]

BIBLIOGRAPHY

Gorton, C. V. *The Ven. Bede and Bishop Stubbs.* Oxford 1901.

H., J. C. "The Church History of the English Nation," *Ampleforth Jnl.*, 2 (1897), 257-270.

Haverfield, F. J. "Some Place-Names in Bede," *EHR*, 10 (1895), 710-711.

Jones, P. F. *A Concordance to the Historia ecclesiastica.* Cambridge, Mass. 1929.

Kirby, D. P. "Bede and Northumbrian Chronology," *EHR*, 78 (1963), 514-527.

———. "Problems of Early West Saxon History," *EHR*, 80 (1965), 10-29.

Klaeber, F. "Beowulfiana Minora," *Anglia*, 63 (1939), 400-425, esp. 403-404.

Knappert, L. (trans. A. Dirr). "Le christianisme et le paganisme dans l'histoire ecclésiastique de Bède le Vén.," *Rev. de l'histoire d. religions*, 34 (1896), 59-85, 145-173, 296-317 (Annales du Musée Guimet). Original in *Theolog. Tijdschr.*, 31 (1897), 171-209, 272-301.

Köhler, T. *D. altenglischen Namen in Baedas HE.* Berlin 1908.

Kühn-Steinhausen, H. "Bedas Kirchengeschichte in d. ältesten Münchner HSS," *ZDG*, 1 (1935), 325-326.

Lowe, E. A. "An Autograph of the Venerable Bede?" *RB*, 68 (1958), 200-202. Cf. the notice by T. J. Brown, *Book Collector*, 8 (1959), 180.

———. "A Key to Bede's Scriptorium," *Scriptorium*, 12 (1958), 182-190.

———. "A New MS Fragment of Bede's Historia ecclesiastica," *EHR*, 41 (1926), 244-246.

———. "The Script of the Farewell and Date Formulae in Early Papal Documents as Reflected in the Oldest MSS of Bede's *Historia ecclesiastica*," *RB,* 69 (1959), 22-31.

[283]

Malone, K. "The Meaning of Bede's *Iutae*," *Anglia Bei-blatt*, 51 (1940), 262-264.

Markus, R. A. "The Chronology of the Gregorian Mission to England. Bede's Narrative and Gregory's Correspondence," *JEH*, 14 (1963), 16-30.

Meyer, W. "D. Legende d. hl. Albanus d. Protomartyr Angliae in Texten vor Beda," *Gött. Abh.*, Phil.-Hist. Kl., N.F. 8.1 (1904), 3-81.

Meyvaert, P. *Bede and Gregory the Great*. Jarrow 1965.

Meyvaert, P. "The Bede 'signature' in the Leningrad Colophon," *RB*, 71 (1961), 274-286.

———. "Colophons dans d. mss de Bède," *RB*, 69 (1959), 100-101.

Misonne, D. " 'Famulus Christi': A propos d'un autographe de Bède le Vénérable," *RB*, 69 (1959), 97-99.

Mitchell, B. "Bede's *habere* = Old English magan?" *Neuphilologische Mitteilungen*, 66 (1965), 107-111.

Mohr, W. "D. geographische Beschreibung Englands in Bedas Kirchengeschichte," *ZDG*, 1 (1935), 322-324.

Mommsen, T. "D. Papstbriefe bei Beda," *NA*, 17 (1892), 387-396.

Morin, G. "Le Libellus Synodicus attribué par Bède à S. Grégoire le Grand," *RB*, 11 (1894), 193-208.

Mozley, J. H. "Bede, *Hist. Evang.*, bk. 5, ch. 2" (Notes de lecture, 86), *Latomus*, 19 (1960), 578.

Pepperdene, M. W. "Bede's Historia ecclesiastica," *Celtica*, 4 (1958), 253-262.

*Plummer, C. "Mémoire sur un ms de l'histoire ecclésiastique du peuple anglais de Bède, dit le Vénérable," *Annales de la Société Archéologique de Namur*, 19.

Poole, R. L. "The Chronology of Bede's *Historia ecclesiastica* and the Councils of 679-680," *JTS*, 20 (1919), 24-40.

Posner, E. "D. Register Gregors I," *NA*, 43 (1922), 245-315.

Potter, S. "The Winchester Bede," *Wessex*, 3 (1935), 39.

"The Prig," *The Ven. Bede Expurgated, Expounded and Exposed.* London 1886.

Ramsay, J. H. "Chronology of Baeda: Death of King Alfred," *Athenaeum* (November 3, 1900), 579.

Schapiro, M. "The Decoration of the Leningrad Manuscript of Bede," *Scriptorium*, 12 (1958), 191-207.

Schmidt, L. "Ravennatische Annalen bei Beda," *NA*, 9 (1884), 197-200.

*Schorer, M. T. "Alguns aspectos do monasticismo irlandês, através da *Historia ecclesiastica gentis anglorum* do Ven. Beda," *Revista de história*, 5 (1954), 273-301.

*Schuster, M. F. "Bede and the Sparrow Simile," *American Benedictine Rev.*, 8 (1957), 46-50.

Stengl, E. E. "Imperator und Imperium bei d. Angelsachsen," *Deutsches Archiv f. Erforschung d. Mittelalters*, 16 (1960), 15-72, esp. 17-28.

Stephan, J. "A Bede MS," *Times* (January 9, 1953), 7.

Ström, H. *Old English Personal Names in Bede's History.* Lund 1939.

*Thum, B. "S. Beda in historia ecclesiastica Angliae," *Comm. pro religiosis*, 17 (1936), 30-36.

Torreta, L. "Coscienza nazionale e ideale d'universalità nella *Historia ecclesiastica* del venerabile Beda," *Atti del vo congresso nazionale di studi romani*, 3 (1942), 9-20.

Visentin, P. "La posizione de S. Beda e del suo ambiente riguardo alla traslazione del corpo di S. Benedetto in Francia," *RB*, 67 (1957), 34-48.

Walker, H. E. "Bede and the Gewissae," *Cambridge Historical Jnl.*, 12 (1956), 174-186.

Wallace-Hadrill, J. M. *Bede's Europe.* Jarrow 1962.

Watson, J. *Interpolations in Bede's Ecclesiastical History.* Peebles 1883.

Wright, D. H. "The Date of the Leningrad Bede," *RB*, 71 (1961), 265-273.

2.10. Doubtful and Spurious Works

Albers, B. "Wann sind d. Beda-Egbert'schen Bussbücher verfasst worden, und wer ist ihr Verfasser?" *Archiv f. katholisches Kirchenrecht*, 81 (1901), 393-420.

Barré, H. "L'Homilaire carolingien de Mondsee," *RB*, 71 (1961), 71-107.

Bertola, E. "Il *De trinitate* dello pseudo Beda," *Rivista di filosofia neo-scolastica*, 48 (1956), 316-333.

Canter, H. V. "The Venerable Bede and the Colosseum," *Trans. and Proc. American Philological Assn.*, 61 (1930), 150-164.

Carpentier, E. *Acta Sanctorum*. October, Vol. VIII, 326.

Laistner, M. L. W. "The Mediaeval Organ and a Cassiodorus Glossary among the Spurious Works of Bede," *Speculum*, 5 (1930), 217-221.

———. "Was Bede the Author of a Penitential?" *Harvard Theological Rev.*, 31 (1938), 263-274 (repr. in *Intellectual History of the Early Middle Ages*, Ithaca 1957, 165-177).

Lehmann, P. "Wert und Echtheit einer Beda abgesprochenen Schrift," *Munich SB*, Phil.-Hist. Kl. (1919), Abt. 4.

Lentini, A. "Il sermone di S. Bertario su S. Scolastica," *Benedictina*, 1 (1947), 197- 232.

Manser, A. "Eine Rückerstattung an d. hl. Beda Venerabilis," *Benediktinische Monatsschrift*, 1 (1919), 434-437.

Morin, G. "Notes sur plusieurs écrits attribués à Bède le Vénérable," *RB*, 11 (1894), 289-295.

———. "Le pseudo-Bède sur les Psaumes, et l'*opus super Psalterium* de maître Manegold de Lautenbach," *RB*, 28 (1911), 331-340.

Pizzani, U. "Uno Pseudo-Trattato dello Pseudo-Beda," *Maia*, 9 (1957), 36-48.

Salmon, P. *Les 'Tituli Psalmorum' d. mss latins* (Collectanea Biblica latina XII; Rome 1959), "Série de Cassiodore, résumée par Bède," 149-186.

Schildenberger, J. "D. altlateinischen Texte d. Proverbien-Buches," *Texte und Arbeiten*, 1.32-33 (1941), 145-149.

Strecker, K. *MGH*, Poetae IV.2, 841-2, Berlin 1923.

Tupper, F., Jr. "Riddles of the Bede Tradition," *MP*, 2 (1905), 561-572.

Vaccari, A. "Scripsitne Beda commentarium in Job?" *Biblica*, 5 (1924), 369-373.

Weisweiler, H. "D. handschriftlichen Vorlagen zum Erst-druck von Pseudo-Beda, in Psalmorum librum exegesis," *Biblica*, 18 (1937), 197-204.

————. *D. Schrifttum d. Schule Anselms von Laon und Wilhelms von Champeaux in deutschen Bibliotheken* (Beiträge zur Geschichte d. Philosophie und Theologie d. Mittelalters XXXIII.1/2). Münster 1936, 54-64.

Wilmart, A. "Un témoin anglo-saxon du calendrier métrique d'York," *RB*, 46 (1934), 41-69.

CHAPTER THREE: The Age of Bede

3.1. Aethilwald

Bradley, H. "On Some Poems Ascribed to Aldhelm," *EHR*, 15 (1900), 291-292.

Brandl, A. "Zu d. angeblichen Schreiben d. altmercischen Königs Æthelwæld an Aldhelm," *Archiv*, 171 (1937), 70.

Collins, S. T. "Corruptions in Christian Latin Poetry," *JTS*, 50 (1949), 68-71.

Ehwald, R. *Aldhelmi opera. MGH*, Auct. ant. XV.2, Berlin 1919.

Meyer, W. "D. rythmischen Jamben d. Auspicius," *Gött. Nachrichten*, Phil.-Hist. Kl. (1906), 192-229.

Schulze, F. W. "Reimstrukturen im Offa-Preislied Aethilwalds und d. Entwicklung d. altenglischen Alliterationsverses," *Zt. f. deutsches Altertum und deutsche Literatur*, 92 (1963), 8-31.

3.2. *Vita antiquissima Sancti Gregorii*

Almond, L. "The Whitby Life of St. Gregory," *Downside Rev.*, 25 (1904), 15-29.

Bishop, E. [Review of Ewald, "D. älteste Biographie"], *Downside Rev.*, 5 (1886), 271-274.

Butler, E. C. [Chronicle of recent work], *JTS*, 7 (1906), 312-313.

Colgrave, B. "The Earliest Life of St. Gregory the Great," *Celt and Saxon* (ed. N. K. Chadwick). Cambridge 1963, 119-137.

Ewald, P. "D. älteste Biographie Gregors I," *Historische Aufsätze d. Andenken an Georg Waitz gewidmet*. Hannover 1886, 17-54.

Gasquet, F. A. *A Life of St. Gregory the Great*. London 1904.

Grisar, H. "D. Gregorbiographie d. Paulus Diakonus in ihrer ursprünglichen Gestalt, nach italienischen HSS," *Zt. f. katholische Theologie*, 11 (1887), 158-173.

Moretus, H. "Les deux anciennes vies de S. Grégoire le Grand," *AB*, 26 (1907), 66-72.

Seely, J. R. "Paul Ewald and Pope Gregory I," *EHR*, 3 (1888), 295-310.

Stuhlfath, W. *Gregor I. d. Grosse: sein Leben . . . nebst einer Untersuchung d. ältesten Viten*. Heidelberg 1913 (Heidelberger Abhandlungen mittleren und neueren Geschichte), XXXIX, 63-89.

Thurston, H. "The Oldest Life of Gregory," *Month*, 104 (1904), 337-353.

Wright, C. E. *The Cultivation of Saga in Anglo-Saxon England*. Edinburgh 1939, 43-48.

3.3. *Vita anonyma Sancti Cuthberti*

Battiscombe, C. F. *The Relics of St. Cuthbert*. Oxford 1956.

Colgrave, B. *Two Lives of St. Cuthbert*. Cambridge 1940.

Colgrave, B., and O. G. S. Crawford. "The Anonymous Life of St. Cuthbert," *Antiquity*, 8 (1934), 97-100.

Forbes-Leith, W. *The Life of St. Cuthbert*. Edinburgh 1888.

Low, J. L. "On the Authorities for the History of St. Cuthbert," *Arch. Ael.*, N.S. 11 (1886), 18-26.

3.4. Waldhere of London

H&S, III, 274-5.

3.5. Aelffled of Whitby
3.6 Berhtwald of Canterbury

Tangl, M. *D. Briefe d. hl. Bonifatius und Lullus. MGH, Ep. Sel.* 1, Berlin 1916.

3.7. Acca of Hexham

Cook, A. S. "The Old English *Andreas* and Bp. Acca of Hexham," *Trans. of the Connecticut Acad. of Arts and Sciences*, 26 (1925), 245-332.

Raine, J. *The Priory of Hexham. Surtees Soc.*, XLIV, XLVI (1864).

3.8. Ceolfrid of Jarrow
3.9. *Historia abbatum anonyma*

Bishop of Salisbury, *et al.* [Correspondence on Ceolfrid and the Codex Amiatinus], *Academy*, 31 (1887), 111-113, 130-131, 148-150, 165-167, 183-184, 309, 327, 414-415, 449.

Boutflower, D. S. *Life of Ceolfrid by an Unknown Author*. Sunderland 1912.

Lowe, E. A. "A Key to Bede's Scriptorium," *Scriptorium*, 12 (1958), 182-190.

Plummer, C. *Venerabilis Baedae historia ecclesiastica*. . . . Oxford 1946 (repr. 1896 edn.).

de Rossi, G. B. "La bibbia offerta da Ceolfrido abbate al sepolchro di S. Pietro," *Al sommo Pontefice Leone XIII omaggio giubilare della Bibl. Vat.* Rome 1888.

3.10. Eddius Stephanus
(see also 1.4)

Blair, P. H. "The Northumbrians and their Southern Frontier," *Arch. Ael.*, 4th Ser. 26 (1948), 98-126.

Colgrave, B. *Eddius Stephanus' Life of Bp. Wilfrid*. Cambridge 1927.

Levision, W. *MGH*, Scriptores rerum merovingicarum VI.163-263. Hanover and Leipzig 1913.

Moonen, H. *Eddius Stephanus, Het Leven van Sint Wilfrid*. Bois-le-Duc 1946.

Raine, J. *Historians of the Church of York* I, *RS* 71.1, 103.

Wells, B. W. "Eddi's Life of Wilfrid," *EHR*, 6 (1891), 535-550.

3.11. Tatwine of Canterbury

3.12. Hwaetberht of Jarrow

Bolton, W. F. "Tatwine's *De cruce Christi* and *The Dream of the Rood*," *Archiv*, 200 (1963), 344-346.

Buechler, F. "Coniectanea," *Rheinisches Museum*, 36 (1881), 329-342.

Ebert, A. "D. Räthselpoesie d. Angelsachsen, insb. d.
Aenigmata d. Tatwine und Eusebius," *Berichte über
d. Verhandlungen d. königl. Sächsischen Akad. d.
Wissenschaften,* Phil.-Hist. Kl. 29 (1877), 20-56.
Erhardt-Siebold, E. von. "History of the Bell in a Riddle's
Nutshell," *Englische Studien,* 69 (1934), 1-14.
Giles, J. *Anecdota Bedae, Lanfranci et aliorum.* London
1851.
Hahn, H. "D. Räthseldichter Tatwin und Eusebius,"
Forschungen z. deutschen Geschichte, 26 (1886), 601-
632.
Müller, L. "Sammelsurien," *Fleckeisens Jrb.,* 93 (1866),
555-568 esp. 566.
Wilmanns, A. "D. Katalog d. Lorscher Klosterbibliothek
aus d. 10. Jrht.," *Rheinisches Museum,* 23 (1868),
385-410.
Wright, T. *The Anglo-Latin Satirical Poets and Epigram-
matists of the Twelfth Century. RS,* 75.2, 525-534.

3.13. Felix

Birch, W. d. G. *Memorials of St. Guthlac of Croyland.*
Wisbech 1881.
Bolton, W. F. "The Background and Meaning of *Guthlac,*"
JEGP, 61 (1962), 595-603.
———. "The Croyland Quatrefoil and *Polychronicon,*"
Jnl. Warburg and Courtauld Insts., 21 (1958), 295-
296.
———. "The Latin Revisions of Felix's *Vita Sancti
Guthlaci,*" *Mediaeval Studies,* 21 (1959), 36-52.
Colgrave, B. *Felix's Life of St. Guthlac.* Cambridge 1956.
Forstmann, H. "Untersuchungen zur Guthlac-Legende,"
Bonner Beiträge zur Anglistik, 12 (1902), 1-40.
Kurtz, B. "From St. Antony to St. Guthlac," *Univ. of
California Pubs. in Modern Philology,* 12 (1926),
103-146.
Schütt, M. "Vom hl. Antonius zum hl. Guthlac," *Antike
und Abendland,* 5 (1956), 75-91.

ADDENDA

Page 229

Crawford, S. J. *Anglo-Saxon Influence on Western Christendom, 600-800.* Cambridge 1966.

Page 232

Wilson, P. A. "Romano-British and Welsh Christianity: Continuity or Discontinuity?" *Welsh History Rev.,* 3 (1966), 5-22, 103-120.

Page 233

* Borse, U. *D. Kolosserbrieftext d. Pelagius.* Bonn 1966.

Page 234

*Frede, H. J. "D. Paulustext d. Pelagius," *Sacris erudiri,* 16 (1965), 165-183.

Page 235

de Plinval, G. "Précisions sur l'authenticité d'un prologue de Pélage: *Primum quaeritur," Rev. d. études augustiniennes,* 12 (1966), 247-253.

Page 240

*Bieler, L. "D. Patrickslegende," *Anzeiger d. Oesterreichischen Akademie d. Wissenschaften,* Philos.-Hist. Kl. 102 (1965), 207-223.

Page 251

*Duft, J. "St. Columban in d. St. Galler HSS," *Zt. f. schweizerischen Kirchengeschichte,* 59 (1965), 285-296.

Page 252

*Leclercq, J. "L'univers religieux de S. Colomban et de Jonas de Bobbio," *Rev. d'ascétique et de mystique,* 42 (1966), 15-30.

Page 252

*Lomiento, G. "La bibbia nella compositio di S. Colombano," *Vetera christianorum,* 3 (1966), 25-43.

Page 252

*Müller, I. "Zum geistigen Einfluss d. kolumbanischen

Bewegung im mittleren Europa," *Zt. f. schweizerischen Kirchengeschichte,* 59 (1966), 265-284.

Page 252

*Quacquarelli, A. "La prosa d'arte di S. Colombano," *Vetera christianorum,* 3 (1966), 5-24.

Page 279

McKee, L. "A Fragment of Bede's *De temporum ratione* in Vat. Reg. Lat. 838," *Manuscripta,* 10 (1966), 43-44.

Page 281

Whitbread, L. "The Sources and Literary Qualities of Bede's Doomsday Verses," *Zt. f. deutsches Altertum und deutsche Literatur,* 95 (1966), 258-266.

Page 281

Campbell, J. "Bede," *Latin Historians* (ed. T. A. Dorey). London 1966, 159-190.

Page 283

Kirby, D. P. "Bede's Native Sources for the *HE,*" *Bulletin of the John Rylands Library,* 48 (1965-66), 341-371.

index

Abel, 33, 35

Abraham, 148

Acca of Hexham, 107, 109-10, 112, 114, 116-17, 119-20, 122, 168, 202-04, 210-11

Acheldemach, 132-33

acrostich, 82, 92, 215-16

Actus Silvestri, 196

Adam, 148, 150

Adamnanus, 131-32

adiaphoros, 81

Ado, 145

Adola of Pfalsel, 200

Aeddi, *see* Eddius Stephanus

Aelffled of Whitby, 192, 199-200

Aelfric of Eynsham, 80, 166

Aelfwald, King of East Anglia, 223

Aelli, King of Deira, 194

Aethelbald, King of Mercia, 186, 191, 224

Aethelberht, King of Kent, 51-52

Aethilred, King of Mercia, 171

Aethilwald, 100, 186-91

Agatho, Pope, 67-68

Agilberht, Bishop, 66

Agito ter consuli gemitus Britannorum, 34

Agricola, 5

Agroecius, 158

Aidan, 53, 196

Alban, 10-11

Albinus, 60, 183

Alcimus Avitus, 21, 138

Alcuin, 68, 77, 106, 125, 158, 168

Aldfrith, King of Northumbria, 67, 71, 77-79, 87, 169, 196, 199

Aldhelm, 48, 52, 60-61, 68-100, 138, 159, 169, 186-87, 189-91, 199-201, 216-17, 222, 224; *Carmina ecclesiastica,* 72-76, 97; *De laudibus virginum,* 73, 76-77, 87-93, 140; *De laudibus*

virginitatis, 87-92, 140, 224; Letters, 75, 93-100; *De metris,* 71, 76-87, 159, 224; *De octo vitiis principalibus,* 92; riddles, 79, 82-85, 216-17, 222

Aldwulf, King of East Anglia, 171

Alexander of Ashby, 224

Alfred, King of England, 99

Alhfrith, King of Deira, 66

alliteration, 31, 75, 97, 99, 139, 162, 198

Ambrose, 113, 158, 166, 196, 203

Ambrosiaster, 16

Anastasius, 134

Anatolius, 156-57

Andrew (Apostle), 202

Andrew (monk), 59

Anegray, 41

Annals of Ulster, 39

Antioch, 33

antiphrasis, 163

Apollinaris, 82

Apulicus, 12

Arator, 73, 81, 97, 108, 138, 161

Arculf, 132

Aristobulus, 9

Aristotle, 3, 16, 79

Arius, 12-13, 111

Arles, Council of, 10-11, 147

Armagh, 40

Arminium, Council of, 10

Ars anonyma bernensis, 218

Asper, 218

assonance, 47

asteismos, 163-65

Atfrith, Abbot, 98

Audax, 82, 161

Augustine of Canterbury, 10, 46, 49-59, 61-62, 142, 169, 175-76, 181, 194

Augustine of Hippo, 15, 19, 109, 113, 125, 138, 144, 155, 158, 166; *City of God,* 193; *De gratia Christi,* 16; homilies,

[295]